# Three Mothers

# Three Mothers

How the Mothers of
Martin Luther King,
Malcolm X and James Baldwin
Shaped a Nation

ANNA MALAIKA TUBBS

WILLIAM
COLLINS

William Collins
An imprint of HarperCollins*Publishers*
1 London Bridge Street
London SE1 9GF

WilliamCollinsBooks.com

HarperCollins*Publishers*
1st Floor, Watermarque Building, Ringsend Road
Dublin 4, Ireland

First published in Great Britain in 2021 by William Collins

First published in the United States as *The Three Mothers: How the Mothers of Martin Luther King, Malcolm X, and James Baldwin Shaped a Nation* by Flatiron Books in 2021

1

A catalogue record for this book is available from the British Library

ISBN 978-0-00-840532-8 (hardback)
ISBN 978-0-00-843105-1 (trade paperback)

Typeset in Fournier MT
Printed and bound by CPI Group (UK) Ltd, Croydon

MIX
Paper from
responsible sources
FSC
www.fsc.org    FSC™ C007454

This book is produced from independently certified FSC™ paper to ensure responsible forest management.

For more information visit: www.harpercollins.co.uk/green

*This is for all the mamas.*

*You deserve respect, dignity, and recognition.*

*I honor you.*

*I celebrate you.*

*I see you.*

# Contents

Introduction                                                          1

*Part I:* The Circumstances of Our Birth                             17

*Part II:* The Denial of Our Existence                               39

*Part III:* Our Men and Marriages                                    59

*Part IV:* The Birth of Our Children                                 81

*Part V:* Our Trials, Tribulations, and Tragedies                   105

*Part VI:* Loving Our Sons                                          127

*Part VII:* Losing Our Sons                                         149

*Part VIII:* The Circumstances of Our Death                         179

*Conclusion:* Our Lives Will Not Be Erased                          201


*Author's Note*                                                     223

*Acknowledgments*                                                   225

*Bibliography*                                                      229

*Index*                                                             253

# Introduction

Our mothers were the ashes and we were the
light. Our mothers were the embers and we were
the sparks. Our mothers were the flames and we
were the blaze.

—EDWIDGE DANTICAT

I can't breathe. I can't breathe. I can't breathe.
Mama, I love you. Tell the kids I love them. I'm
dead.

—GEORGE FLOYD

On February 14, 2019, my husband, Michael, and I were in Washington, D.C. We'd traveled there for the Frederick Douglass 200 Awards Gala, held in the Library of Congress. I remember feeling annoyed with myself that evening—in a rushed week filled with commitments, I'd packed an off-white dress to wear to the event. While there, I remembered that my monthly visitor was due and I excused myself to use the restroom several times throughout the night, paranoid I might find a red stain on the back of my dress. Each time, I breathed a sigh of relief and returned to my seat. Following the ceremony, I figured we would rest before our flight the next morning, but Michael had other plans. He surprised me with a dessert-and-wine reservation for Valentine's Day.

Our ride dropped us off to enjoy the rest of the night. I ordered a deconstructed peanut-butter-and-jelly cheesecake that I excitedly waited to try. When it arrived and I took my first few bites, I suddenly felt sick to my stomach. I paused and sat back in my chair to take a breath. Then it occurred to me that my period wasn't only due, it might actually be late. I was in my own world; I pulled out my phone to count my days again. The small possibility filled my mind with excitement—we'd recently decided to start trying for a baby. I was clearly distracted, and Michael asked what I was thinking about. I replied with a smile, "Let's go to CVS."

Long story shortened, that night, toward the last hours of Valentine's Day, following an event honoring those carrying Frederick

Douglass's work forward, I held a positive pregnancy test in my hands. My heart filled with an indescribable feeling and my eyes watered as I showed the result to my life partner. A human being was developing inside of me. I was going to be a mother. I was going to bring a life into this world. Joy quickly started to vacillate with worry, the weight of the world falling on my shoulders. I wondered if up until that moment I'd been taking enough care of myself and my little one. I worried that I didn't know enough about the steps I was supposed to take to make it through my pregnancy successfully. As if all the research I had done up until that point, as if all our conversations before deciding to try, had simply not been enough—a worry that so many feel. I was overjoyed, yes, but I was also instantly scared of losing my child. I prayed to God that we, my baby and I, would be protected.

I suppose this is an accurate and pithy description of motherhood, a lifelong wavering between utmost happiness and consuming worry. This might sound strange, but I was more grateful in that initial moment than I had ever been for the work that I do, especially for my Ph.D. I had just begun the second year of my doctoral studies at the University of Cambridge and was on my Leave to Work Away. This meant that the year was dedicated to my fieldwork and research, which happened to be on Black motherhood. I was grateful because my research, which led to this book, gave me examples of three incredible women and mothers who could guide me in the next stage of my life. In the journey of finding evidence of their lives, I was able to acknowledge the very real fears that come with motherhood, specifically Black motherhood, both during and after pregnancy, but I also found encouragement and a warm embrace to welcome me.

The three women I speak of are Alberta King, Berdis Baldwin, and Louise Little—women who have been almost entirely ignored throughout history. While this disregard of Black women's contributions is widespread and so extensive that it is unquantifiable, the women I honor here have been ignored differently: ignored even though it should have been easy throughout history to see them, to at least wonder about them, and to think about them; ignored in ways that are blatantly obvious when the fame of their sons is considered. They were the mothers of Martin Luther King, Jr., James Baldwin, and Malcolm X, respectively. While the sons have been credited with the success of Black resistance, the progression of Black thought, and the survival of the Black community, the three mothers who birthed and reared them have been erased. This book fights that erasure.

Through the lives of the three mothers—Alberta, Berdis, and Louise—I honor Black motherhood as a whole and celebrate knowledge passed from generation to generation through the bodies and teachings of Black women. While we are all influenced by our mothers in one way or another, it is especially clear in these three instances just how influential each mother's life experiences and teachings were on her son's views and actions. Because of who Alberta, Berdis, and Louise were, Martin, James, and Malcolm were able to become the great leaders we all revere. Because of who Alberta, Berdis, and Louise were, the world was changed forever and it is time they receive their due credit.

In the book *All the Women Are White, All the Blacks Are Men, But Some of Us Are Brave: Black Women's Studies*, editors Akasha (Gloria T.) Hull, Patricia Bell Scott, and Barbara Smith make a case for the significance of studying Black women in order to raise our collective consciousness. They highlight the crucial role an understanding of Black women's lives can play in *saving* Black women's lives. They write, "Merely to use the term 'Black women's studies' is an act charged with political significance. At the very least, the combining of these words to name a discipline means taking the stance that Black women exist—and exist positively. . . ." My work is largely inspired by the guidelines found in *But Some of Us Are Brave* and specifically addresses the stance that "Black women exist—and exist positively."

We must affirm Black women—a group that has historically been dehumanized—in humanizing ways. "Positively" does not mean that we should focus only on the positive facts about Black women's lives; instead we must take in the whole picture, one that includes diverse perspectives, an acknowledgment of oppressive forces as well as an understanding of the ways in which Black women have survived such circumstances. Erasure, misrecognition, and historical amnesia have certainly contributed to the formation of our identity as Black women, but our fight against such forces with our affirmation and recognition of ourselves and each other has been much more telling. Through these practices we've created new possibilities that defy the limits placed upon us.

*Writing about Black motherhood* while becoming one gave me a much deeper perspective than I had before. As my own life and body transformed, it became even more important to me to tell Alberta's, Berdis's, and Louise's stories before they became mothers. Their lives did not begin with motherhood; on the contrary, long before their sons were even thoughts in their minds, each woman had her own passions, dreams, and identity. Each woman was already living an incredible life that her children would one day follow. Their identities as young Black girls in Georgia, Grenada, and Maryland influenced the ways in which they would approach motherhood. Their exposure to racist and sexist violence from the moment they were born would inform the lessons they taught their children. Their intellect and creativity led to fostering such qualities in their homes. The relationships they witnessed in their parents and grandparents would inspire their own approaches to marriage and child-rearing. Highlighting their roles as mothers does not erase their identities as independent women. Instead, these identities informed their ability to raise independent children who would go on to inspire the world for years to come.

These women's lives create a rich portrait of the nuances of Black motherhood. Yes, all three were mothers of sons who became internationally known, and their stories share many similarities, but by no means can their identities be reduced into one. Each woman carried different values, faiths, talents, and traumas. I hope their rich differences will open our eyes to the many influences and manifestations of Black motherhood in the United States and beyond.

The narratives of these three women have fueled and empowered me, but this work has been extremely difficult at times. Black motherhood in the United States is inextricable from a history of violence against Black people. American gynecology was built by torturing Black women and experimenting on their bodies to test procedures. J. Marion Sims, known as the father of American gynecology, developed his techniques by slicing open the vaginal tissues of enslaved women as they were held down by force. He refused to provide them with anesthesia. François Marie Prevost, who is credited with introducing C-sections in the United States, perfected his procedure by cutting into the abdomens of laboring women who were slaves. These women were treated like animals and their pain was ignored.

There is a paradoxical relationship between the dehumanization we Black women and our children face and our ability to resist it. Beyond the normal worries all mothers encounter as they progress through pregnancy and get closer to their labors, we Black mothers are aware that we are risking our lives. Black women in the United States are more likely to die while pregnant and while giving birth than other mothers. Beyond the normal fear that all mothers feel when the gut-wrenching thought of losing their child creeps its way into their minds, we Black mothers experience a heightened level of worry. We are aware of how differently our children are seen and treated in society, and our fears are confirmed by articles and news stories reporting the violence that Black children experience constantly, whether at parties, in school, or at their local parks. This fear continues as our children become adults who are in danger even as they sleep in their beds, sit in their own apartments, when they call for help, or when they go on a run.

Louise, Berdis, and Alberta were well aware of the dangers they and their children would be met with as Black people in the United States, and they all strove to equip their children not only to face the world but to change it. With the knowledge that they themselves were seen as "less than" and their children would be, too, the three mothers collected tools to thrive with the hopes of teaching their children how to do the same. They found ways to give life and to humanize themselves, their children, and, in turn, our entire community. As history tells us, all of their sons did indeed make a difference in this world, but they did so at a cost. In all three cases, the mothers' worst fears became reality: each woman was alive to bury her son. It is an absolute injustice that far too many Black mothers today can say the same thing.

In the face of such tragedy, each mother persisted in her journey to leave this world a better place than when she entered it. Yet their lives continued largely to be ignored. When Malcolm X was assassinated, when Martin Luther King, Jr., was killed shortly after, and even when James Baldwin died from stomach cancer years later, their works were rightly celebrated, but virtually no one stopped to wonder about the grief their mothers were facing. Even more painful to me is the fact that their fathers *were* mentioned, while their mothers were largely erased.

I chose to focus on mothers of sons. Black men were certainly not the only leaders of the civil rights movement; mothers of revolutionary daughters have also been forgotten. I simply chose three figures who are often put in conversation together and who demonstrate the distressingly strong erasure of identity in the mother/son relationship. Coincidentally, I gave birth to a boy, my incredible little boy, and I have already faced others' attempts to erase my influence on his identity. Phrases like "He's strong, just like his father!" or "He's already following in his dad's footsteps" when he reaches a milestone cause more harm than people think. By choosing three mothers of sons, I do not want to erase daughters or other children. I am instead making the point that no matter our gender, everything starts with our birthing parent.

In telling the stories of these three mothers, I hope to join others who have responded to *Brave*'s call for "Black women to carry out autonomously defined investigations of self in a society which through racial, sexual, and class oppression systematically denies our existence. . . ." It is crucial to understand the layers of oppression Black women face, while remembering that solely studying oppression keeps us from honoring "the ways in which we have created and maintained our own intellectual traditions as Black women." I pay close attention to this balance and bear witness to the many challenges Berdis, Alberta, and Louise faced while acknowledging their ability to survive, thrive, and build in spite of them.

Louise, Berdis, and Alberta were all born within six years of each other, and their famous sons were all born within five years of each other, which presents beautiful intersections in their lives. Because they were all born around the same time and gave birth to their famous sons around the same time, and two of them passed away around the same time, I reflect on Black womanhood in the early 1900s, Black motherhood in the 1920s, and their influence on the civil rights movement of the 1960s. The first of the three mothers was born in the late 1890s, and the last of the three passed in the late 1990s. Their lives give us three incredible perspectives on an entire century of American history. By seeing the United States develop through the lives of Berdis, Alberta, and Louise, you will be left with a richer understanding of each world war, the Great Depression, the Great Migration, the Harlem Renaissance, race riots, police brutality, welfare debates, the effects of policies proposed by each president they lived to witness, and much more.

But their stories go beyond a new understanding of American history, especially the civil rights movement of the 1960s. An ode to these three women is an ode to Black womanhood—perhaps Black women of today will also be able to find themselves in the life stories of Berdis, Alberta, and/or Louise, as I have.

When I first started this work, it quickly became apparent that without knowledge of the stories of these three women, the world was missing an enormous piece of our understanding of Black resistance in the United States. The fascinating facts I have been able to uncover provide incredible new depth for our appreciation of Black American history, but this research is about far more. The women's lives offer invaluable new knowledge about the context of the past, how the storyteller influences the story, and how reevaluations guide our contemporary understanding of individuals, communities, and society. This kind of writing becomes even more needed and holds even more power when thinking about groups who have historically been erased and misrepresented, groups who have been kept from telling our side, groups who suffer the repercussions of such exclusion to this day, and groups who continue to resist all of this.

In my desire to better understand the circumstances of the lives of Louise, Berdis, and Alberta, I have called upon the work of Black feminists in the fields of sociology, history, and political science and others outside the academy. Interwoven with their life stories and historical context, you will also find an engagement with Black feminist analysis relating specifically to dehumanization, resistance, and motherhood. Black women have been, and continue to be, treated as less than human, so it's crucial to break down the terms I will be using to discuss this going forward.

Dehumanization takes various forms. People are treated as less than human when their basic rights are not granted/respected, when their agency is taken away, when they are objectified through language and actions, when violence is used against them, and when they are expected to remain silent despite these circumstances. All three mothers experienced this throughout their lives. Audre Lorde—one of the most renowned poets, essayists, and activists in history—writes about the reason dehumanization happens in the introduction to her essay "Age, Race, Class, and Sex: Women Redefining Difference":

Much of Western European history conditions us to see
human differences in simplistic opposition to each other:
dominate/subordinate, good/bad, up/down, superior/
inferior. In a society where the good is defined in terms
of profit rather than in terms of human need, there must
always be some group of people who, through system-
atized oppression, can be made to feel surplus, to occupy
the place of the dehumanized inferior. . . . Institutionalized rejection of difference is an absolute necessity in a
profit economy which needs outsiders as surplus people.

Lorde shows that dehumanization is a component of any society
that views capital as more important than humanity and as something
that affects and implicates all members of such a society. However,
each member is inherently treated differently depending on levels of
disadvantage.

As you read about Alberta, Berdis, and Louise, keep Lorde's words
in mind. In order to understand their beliefs and their actions, we
must know the extent to which their humanity was denied. This denial
stemmed from times of slavery and continued in both obvious and dis-
creet forms from their birth until the day each died. In the same essay,
Lorde continues, "Unless one lives and loves in the trenches it is difficult to remember that the war against dehumanization is ceaseless. But
Black women and our children know the fabric of our lives is stitched
with violence and with hatred, that there is no rest." At each stage of
the three mothers' lives, we witness their knowledge of this unfortunate
truth and their need to resist.

By "resist," I am talking about the ways in which Berdis, Louise,
and Alberta pushed against dehumanization, refusing to acquiesce to
the notion of their supposed inferiority. Resistance, like dehumanization, takes place in many forms; I see it as any action taken to assert

Black humanity. Martin Luther King, Jr., James Baldwin, and Malcolm X are known for their resistance, and in this book you will see how the three women's teachings, through both words and actions, translated directly into their sons' writings, speeches, and protests. These men became symbols of resistance by following their mothers' leads.

Even after death, Berdis, Louise, and Alberta continue to face a denial of their humanity when they are either erased or misrecognized. Up until this book, portrayals of the three mothers have been mostly limited or completely inaccurate. The three women have been hidden not only behind their sons but also behind their husbands. And in the rare moments when the mothers are mentioned, they are often presented as footnotes that are out of context. This in and of itself is wrong, and it contributes to the inhumane treatment of Black women as a whole. I do not blame the sons or the husbands for such erasure, I blame a society that devalues women and mothers, especially women and mothers of color. In *Eloquent Rage: A Black Feminist Discovers Her Superpower*, Brittney Cooper, associate professor in the Department of Africana Studies/Women's and Gender Studies at Rutgers University, writes, "Recognition is a human need, and there is something fundamentally violent about a world that denies Black women recognition on a regular basis." This book acts as a site of resistance to the dehumanization Berdis, Louise, and Alberta continue to face posthumously and to the dehumanization Black women and mothers face all over our country today.

In her book *Sister Citizen: Shame, Stereotypes, and Black Women in America*, Melissa V. Harris-Perry talks about Black women living in a "crooked room," referencing a cognitive psychology experiment where participants were placed in a crooked chair in a crooked room and asked to straighten themselves vertically. Surprisingly, individuals who were tilted as much as thirty-five degrees reported that they were sitting completely straight so long as they were aligned with other objects and images in the room that were at the same angle. Harris-Perry uses the symbol to discuss the circumstance Black women find themselves in. The other objects and images in the room that try to keep Black women from standing tall speak to the many strategies in place to dehumanize Black women by erasing and misrepresenting them. Harris-Perry writes: "When they confront race and gender stereotypes, black women are standing in a crooked room, and they have to figure out which way is up. Bombarded with warped images of their humanity, . . . [Black women can find it] hard to stand up straight in a crooked room."

In this book, I write about the circumstances contributing to the crooked rooms that Berdis, Louise, and Alberta inhabited and how the rooms developed and changed throughout their lives. More important, I think of the ways each woman found to get out of the crooked chair she was forced to live on and continue to stand with her head held high. I also think of the ways they started to change the room to fit their own view of themselves, their children, and their community. Reading this book, knowing the names Alberta King, Berdis Baldwin, and Louise Little, and sharing what you learn with others are all acts that help to straighten the room for Black women today.

I have pieced these stories together from several different sources. I read and watched many of the works of Martin Luther King, Jr., Malcolm X, and James Baldwin—books, speeches, letters, interviews—and pulled out the places where they mentioned their mothers or where a character was based on their moms. I also spoke to scholars who studied the sons and read the books they and others had written. If any family members had written or spoken about their experiences, I read those books and transcripts as well. I spent hours scanning letters and documents from the New York Public Library's Schomburg Center for Research in Black Culture, the National Museum of African American History and Culture, the Martin Luther King, Jr., Research and Education Institute at Stanford University, and the King Center in Atlanta. While the three mothers have mostly been ignored by scholars, in

Louise's case, I was extremely fortunate to have examples of extensive research from the late novelist Jan Carew, as well as a recent study from Professor Erik S. McDuffie of the University of Illinois at Urbana-Champaign. With their work on Louise as inspiration, I reached out and spoke to family members of the three women who were willing to speak with me. I have also spoken to local historians and gained access to birth and death certificates with their help. I've used what I could find in census data, although this information was limited.

All of these women could have several books written about their lives, just as their sons have, so I don't claim to have captured everything here. But I am proud of how much I've been able to find. It's also true that with any biographical work it can be difficult to know what is and is not factual, especially when you write about people society has not deemed "important." One source claims that Louise was born in 1894 and another shows she was born in 1897; a family member says that Berdis was born in 1903, but her own mother's death certificate reads 1902 and Berdis's name never appears on any census; a scholar can claim that Alberta was quiet, while a friend of the family describes her as lively. All this to say it's impossible to know what is "true" if you weren't the one who lived it, and there are many layers to the truth, depending on your perspective. This book, like all history, is composed of many sources that might contradict one another in small ways, but it still holds truth about the significance and influence of each of these mothers and speaks to their legacy.

When I began writing this book, I wondered what it would be like if I could sit down with Berdis, Louise, and Alberta. I wondered what they were like before they became mothers, what their dreams were, what they cared about, whom they were friends with. I wondered what I would look for if I could follow them for a few days, if I could learn what inspired them and what scared them. I thought to myself, If I could sit down with these three mothers, what would I ask them? I realized I would want to know how they pushed themselves to keep going even when various factors tried to stop them in their tracks: how Louise held on to her courage even when her husband was killed; how Berdis stood up to her husband even when he was abusive; how Alberta saw hope even after her sons died. I would want to know what advice they would give us after witnessing some of the most transformative moments in American history and after seeing progress come and go. In the absence of being able to speak with them directly, I am consoled by my ability to study them, write about them, and share their stories. It is time that the world knows their names.

In Alice Walker's book and essay of the same name, *In Search of Our Mothers' Gardens*, she writes:

> Our mothers and grandmothers, some of them: moving to music not yet written. And they waited. They waited for a day when the unknown thing that was in them would be made known; but guessed somehow in their darkness, that on the day of their revelation they would be long dead. . . . But this is not the end of the story, for all the young women—our mothers and grandmothers, *ourselves*—have not perished in the wilderness. And if we ask ourselves why, and search for and find the answer, we will know beyond all efforts to erase it from our minds, just exactly who, and of what, we black American women are.

With Walker's words in mind, I hope to bring more Black women's stories out of the darkness and into the light, to find the clues laid out for me by women who possessed their own dreams and talents, to revisit our current accounts and reread them with Black women's lives at the forefront, and to better know who, and of what, we Black women are. By paying tribute to Louise, Alberta, and Berdis, by recognizing who they were, I believe I have a better understanding of who we as Black women are today. I hope you will feel the same way.

## Part I

# The Circumstances of Our Birth

I had reasoned this out in my mind; there was one of two things I had a right to, liberty, or death; if I could not have one, I would have the other; for no man should take me alive; I should fight for my liberty as long as my strength lasted, and when the time came for me to go, the Lord would let them take me.

—HARRIET TUBMAN

[Negro women] are the greatest menace possible to the moral life of any community where they live. And they are evidently the chief instruments of the degradation of the men of their own race. When a man's mother, wife and daughters are all immoral women, there is no room in his fallen nature for the aspirations of honor and virtue. . . . I cannot imagine such a creation as a virtuous black woman.

—AN ANONYMOUS WHITE WOMAN

When multiple forces are working to deny life, to take away rights, to coerce people into submission, hope persists, the fight does not weaken, and life continues to be birthed. Through individual agendas that battle oppression and in the uniting of efforts, Black women have found a way, even when seemingly impossible, to give life. This sentiment sets the scene for the arrival of our three girls: girls who would grow up to become their own givers of life; Black girls who were born in a time of social upheaval, particularly in the United States, and also a time of Black women's continued battle for their community.

We do not begin in the United States, however. Instead, we launch in a majestic place where a ridge of mountains runs north and south; where the reds, yellows, and greens of the flora and agriculture are surrounded by the blues of the Caribbean Sea. Here, you find a culture that stems from a mix of West Indian, West African, and Caribbean traditions that were forever changed by British and French colonization. Originally inhabited by the Arawaks, who were displaced by the Carib Indians, who were then colonized by the French and later the British, the area is now populated primarily (82 percent) by people of West African ancestry who are descendants of slaves. This island of volcanic origin is filled with rain forests, waterfalls, beaches, rum, nutmeg, calypso, reggae, and soca. We begin on the island of Grenada, where Louise Langdon Norton was born.

In order to understand Louise, in order to know how the color of her skin influenced her thinking, in order to comprehend why her grandparents were so important in her life and, as a result, in Malcolm X's life, we cannot begin with her birth. Louise would become a warrior and a symbol of resistance because the struggle for freedom pulsed through her genes. The blood of her ancestors carried with it messages of liberation, while the land that held her whispered tales of revolutions it had witnessed over the years. The water all around her held the bodies of fighters who came before her, and she was proud to continue the legacy of her country, her people, and her family.

To this day, one of the defining features of Grenadians is their resistance, specifically to white supremacy. In 1650, more than two hundred years before Louise was born, dozens of French soldiers were sent to the island to capture and colonize the Caribs. Striking at night and beginning a bloody slaughter on May 30, the French sought to take control of Carib land and life. Instead of surrendering, at least forty people chose to jump several hundred feet to their deaths from a hill overlooking the Caribbean Sea. The story of these Caribs is known in Grenada's history as a symbol of resistance to European domination, and the hill from which they leapt is known as Leapers Hill. Through history like this, Louise would learn of the bravery of Carib people. She would learn that sacrificing one's life in the name of freedom was more admirable than living in captivity.

A century later, in 1795, Grenada witnessed more radical resistance to colonization, this time in the form of Fedon's Rebellion. Led by Julien Fedon, a man inspired by the Haitian Revolution, an estimated fourteen thousand enslaved Africans joined forces with freed Africans to revolt against British rule. The rebels burned houses and dragged British settlers into the streets where they would be executed. This rebellion engulfed Grenada for more than a year until sixteen regiments were deployed on the island to regain British rule. The revolt was halted by the British force, but Fedon was never captured. Though his whereabouts were unknown, his revolutionary spirit was there to stay, and the rebellion contributed to Grenada's eventual independence. From hearing stories like Fedon's, Louise knew to never simply accept defeat. She found champions of rebellions and revolutions. She knew fighting against injustice called for serious measures.

In the first years of the twentieth century, the population of Grenada was approximately sixty-three thousand. Two of these residents were Louise's grandparents, "Liberated Africans" by the names of Jupiter and Mary Jane Langdon who brought six children into the world. To be a "Liberated African" meant that of an estimated four million Africans brought as slaves to the Americas, Atlantic Ocean and Indian Ocean islands, Arabia, and India, you were part of the 6 percent who had been emancipated by a judicial network made up of international courts and local authorities. In the nineteenth century, British and U.S. governments passed laws to diminish and ultimately ban maritime human trafficking. This by no means signaled the end of slavery; instead it furthered the already detestable sexual exploitation of slaves. With fewer slaves being captured overseas, more slaves would need to be produced on land to meet labor demands. However, some did find freedom as a result. With this kind of legislation in place, authorities seized any ships that were suspected of violating maritime rules, and when slaves were found, their fate was decided. A small percentage of these slaves were actually freed.

Jupiter and Mary Jane were captured in Nigeria and then released by the Royal Navy. With them, they brought their own stories of resistance against colonial rule. They shared these with their children and grandchildren. Not only was Louise raised on stories of the Carib Indians and revolutionaries like Fedon, she was also well aware of her West African roots.

One of the most famous stories of resistance to colonial rule in West Africa is that of a queen mother by the name of Yaa Asantewaa, who eventually became the commander in chief of the Ashanti people in Ghana. Yaa Asantewaa fought in the War of the Golden Stool in the late nineteenth century. After the British had successfully dethroned and exiled other Ashanti leaders, Yaa Asantewaa refused to give up. She stated that if the men of the kingdom would not defend their people, the women would rise to the challenge. She reinvigorated her people to fight, and although she was captured during the rebellion, she too has become known in history as a symbol of unwavering resistance to European rule.

After being enslaved and subsequently emancipated, Jupiter and Mary Jane found themselves in the small village of La Digue in Grenada. Despite being "liberated," they were not spared the pains of colonization and racism. They still lived in a world where their rights were constantly violated and where they tried to teach their children how to resist. As their children grew older, Jupiter and Mary Jane continued to lead the household with strength and love no matter what came their way.

In the late nineteenth century, their daughter Edith gave birth to a child. This child stood out from the rest of her family members. Because of her skin, which was nearly white, and her hair, which was long and straight, it was rumored that she was the product of rape. While the exact details of her conception have been lost in history, this tragic possibility was unfortunately a common one.

The effects of slavery, one being the constant control of Black women's bodies through sexual violence, was universal far after emancipation; countless Black women and girls were raped while perpetrators faced only minor consequences, if any. This injustice took place in colonies all over the world long before Edith's time. As Pamela Scully states in her article "Rape, Race, and Colonial Culture," "Colonialism created conditions that authorized the pervasive rape of black women by white men." The colonized were seen as less civilized and less worthy of protection. Women of color were viewed as more promiscuous than their white counterparts, and therefore violence against them was justified. Scully begins by telling the story of Anna Simpson, a woman who was raped on April 2, 1850, near Cape Town. Her perpetrator, David Booyson, was originally found guilty and sentenced to death. However, when it was discovered that Anna was a colored woman instead of a "respectable woman," Booyson's death sentence was replaced with temporary hard labor.

The lack of appropriate punishment for the perpetrators of sexual violence against women of color also continued to take place long after Edith's time. One of the most famous examples is that of Recy Taylor in Alabama. On the night of September 3, 1944, Recy, a twenty-four-year-old at the time, was walking home from church when she was abducted and raped by six white men. Even though one of the men *admitted* guilt, none of the six was indicted.

Countless women have experienced this atrocity, and most of their stories will never be known, but the historian Danielle McGuire used her book *At the Dark End of the Street: Black Women, Rape, and Resistance* to pay tribute to as many women as she could. The book details forty separate cases similar to Anna's, Recy's, and possibly Edith's. One of the dozens of stories she shares is that of Betty Jean Owens, a young Black woman who was raped by four white men in Tallahassee, Florida, in 1959. The terror began when the four men made a pact to "go out and get a nigger girl" and have an "all night party." Armed with shotguns and switchblades, they searched for victims near a local park. They hijacked a car and ordered two female Florida A&M University students to get out. One of the girls escaped, but the other, Betty Jean Owens, was raped seven times.

In 1897, Edith gave birth to her first and only baby, a girl named Louise. Jupiter and Mary Jane helped to raise her. Her skin was so light, she could easily pass as white, and Louise hated this about herself. From the very beginning, she faced a choice that many mixed-race people faced before her and that she would continue to face for the rest of her life: whether, even in times of danger, to declare her African descent and claim her Blackness—and if so, how to do so. She would find strategies in her family, in her education, in the stories she was raised on.

The Langdon family was dealt a devastating blow when Louise's grandfather and father figure, a carpenter and farmer who did everything he could to provide for his family, passed away in 1901, leaving Mary Jane to raise six children and a grandchild on her own. The lessons Jupiter passed on to Louise during her first years of life were essential, but even more influential was the radical feminist energy in her household. Louise was empowered by the strength of her mother, grandmother, and aunts as she stepped into her own womanhood. Her humble yet powerful upbringing would equip her to face the many battles that awaited her.

*Our next story begins* in a city more than two thousand miles away from Grenada. This city, once a southern colony, possessed one of the largest slave populations in the United States. By 1870, its Black population constituted 46 percent of the city's 21,700 residents. It is home to the Eastern Continental Divide, which separates water between the Gulf of Mexico and the Atlantic Ocean. This city is known for its diverse music, southern hospitality, rich history of Black educational institutions, and status as the birthplace of the civil rights movement in America. However, this city is also in the state where the second-largest number of lynchings took place between 1877 and 1950. Burned to the ground during the Civil War, it rose like a phoenix from the ashes, symbolizing its resilience against destruction.

We continue our journey in Atlanta, Georgia, where Alberta Christine Williams was born on September 13, 1903. In order to understand the foundation of Alberta's unwavering faith in the Lord, in order to know why Martin Luther King, Jr., even became a reverend, in order to identify the relationship between the Black church and a movement based in nonviolence, we begin with the family Alberta was born into.

One of the primary places of restoration for Black communities, where they could come together to cope with their heartache and celebrate each other, where they created their own nation within a nation, where they affirmed their humanity and fostered political power, was, and continues to be, the church. In Atlanta sits one of the most famous churches in the world, Ebenezer Baptist. Founded in 1886, Ebenezer Baptist has become a symbol of hope and resistance to oppression.

In 1894, a reverend by the name of Adam Daniel Williams became the head pastor at Ebenezer. He was a visionary who believed the church had a responsibility to fight racial injustice and empower its members through services that could meet all their basic needs. At the time, there were only seventeen members of the church. In 1899 he married Jennie Celeste, who became the president of the Women's Missionary Society at Ebenezer. Jennie Celeste was well educated and insightful. She matched her husband's heart and drive, and under their leadership the congregation grew continuously over the years. They promoted Black businesses, they urged their members to own property, and they spoke up for adequate public housing for African Americans, all in the face of Jim Crow.

We know the Jim Crow story well. In 1896, *Plessy v. Ferguson* upheld the constitutionality of racial segregation. Laws forbade Black people from dining in the same restaurants as their white counterparts without a partition in place. Black people were forced to enter and leave such restaurants from a different entrance; they were not to be seen socializing with a white person in public and could certainly not form romantic relationships with them. Schools were separated. People of color were not even allowed to give testimony or evidence against a white person. People of color were forced to live in the most underserved parts of their respective cities. In short, such laws forcefully limited where Black people could eat, where they could sit, where they could live, where they could use the restroom. Not a single part of a Black person's life was left untouched by the false claims of "separate but equal."

We know that if these dictates were ever defied, or if it was simply said that they were, the rule breaker would face the ultimate price. Between 1890 and 1917, two to three Black southerners were murdered each week. This era marked the highest number of lynchings and rapes of Black people across the United States as well as the beginning of mass incarceration of Black people through its various forms. Constantly looking for ways to keep Black people in slavery, white supremacists enforced a world where Black people could be locked away in prison, forced to work without pay to settle arbitrary debts, or put to death without any justification.

This can be seen through the horrific story of Mary Turner, born in 1899, whose life was cut short in 1918. While she is not one of the three women at the center of this book, her life illustrates the painful possibilities Black women born at the turn of the twentieth century faced. Mary and her husband, Hazel, had two children and were expecting their third when the owner of the plantation where they worked was killed. A manhunt began to find the killer, and more than a dozen Black men were lynched in the process while others were put behind bars. Mary tried to defend her husband. Although she was only nineteen and pregnant, she stood up for his innocence, demanding he be released from jail. This demonstration in the face of ruthless oppression was met with rage from the white residents of the city. For speaking up, she was tied by her ankles, strung upside down, set on fire, and cut open. Her unborn baby fell from her body and was crushed. Mary was then shot hundreds of times.

Black women were not safe. Black men were not safe. Black children were not safe. Violence against all Black people was justified by the law.

In the midst of all this, Jennie and Adam brought life into the world. Only one of their children survived past childhood, and her name was Alberta. She was born only four years after Mary Turner and only two hundred miles north of where Mary and her baby were brutally murdered.

Alberta was deeply loved by her parents, who gave her all of their attention and encouraged her faith as well as her education. She was born into a family of love, faith, vision, and means. She had access to resources, education, and the support of a budding congregation. From her parents, Alberta learned that everyone was equal in the eyes of God and that we all had a role to play in achieving such equality on earth. From the moment she was born, Alberta would be told that faith would guide and empower her to speak up for what she believed in. The small, happy, and influential family would buy a two-story Queen Anne–style home on Auburn Avenue, putting them only a short walking distance from Ebenezer Baptist.

In line with both the segregation laws of the South and teachings like those of Reverend and First Lady Williams, the early 1900s saw the beginnings of what is now known as the Sweet Auburn Historic District in Atlanta. Ebenezer Baptist Church was part of the Sweet Auburn community, once referred to as "the richest Negro street in the world." In addition to congregations, Black residents established a wide range of successful businesses and social organizations. It was even home to the second-largest Black insurance company in the United States. So important to Black history is Sweet Auburn that it was designated a national historic landmark in 1976.

Thinking of the young Williams family, I feel a sense of peace and joy as I imagine them moving into their home, as I think of the lessons Jennie Celeste and Adam Daniel passed to their daughter, as I envision Alberta holding her parents' hands as they walked to their church and back. However, being a Black family in the early 1900s was always accompanied by the possibility of unrest and interruption, and in 1906, when Alberta was only three years old, Black residents experienced one of the darkest moments in Atlanta's history.

Tensions rose during that year's governor's race, where candidates inflamed and capitalized on racist ideologies, stating that if they were elected, they would put Blacks, especially "uppity" ones, back "in their place." Fabricating stories painting Black people as criminals aiming to hurt innocent whites, newspapers continued to fan the flames with headlines like NEGRO DIVES AND CLUBS ARE THE CAUSE OF FREQUENT ASSAULTS and HALF-CLAD NEGRO TRIES TO BREAK INTO HOUSE. All of this came as backlash against the budding of a Black upper class.

On September 22, white men and boys formed mobs and began a rampage through Black neighborhoods. They destroyed Black-owned business buildings, broke home windows, wounded countless Black people, and beat dozens to death. There were reports of policemen participating in the mobs. After two days of havoc, the governor *finally* instructed authorities to control the violence. Yet the end to the riot came too late. The Black community in Atlanta was left devastated, as lives were forever changed and the economy they had worked so hard to build was almost completely destroyed. The riot also left the city as one of the most stratified and segregated in the United States.

However, devastation is not the end of the story. The Black community as a whole has never been influenced solely by the actions done to it but instead continued to grow in its incredible fight to persevere despite such actions. The Black citizens of Atlanta would come together to find a way to not only survive but go on to inspire the rest of the nation and the world for years to come. Atlanta later gained the nickname "Black Mecca of the South" because of its importance in the civil rights movement, being home to the largest consortium of historically Black colleges, its number of Black-owned restaurants and businesses, its immense Black political power, as well as the number of famous artists and activists who have called Atlanta their home.

Black women are the ultimate practitioners of this ability to turn tragedy into opportunity, face fear and persecution with faith and un-matched perseverance, and create something out of nothing, because it has been required of us. As the community organizer and editor Bethany M. Allen writes in her essay "My Girl," "I wish that I had a formula that I could have shared in response to the recurring 'How do you do it?' query. . . . I called upon the age-old tradition of the black everywoman, doing everything simply because *I had to*." Black women have faced a de-nial of their worth based on both their race and their gender. But despite the constant misrecognition and persecution of Black women, we have continued to resist because we see it as the only option.

As Melissa Harris-Perry puts it in *Sister Citizen*, "Sisters are more than the sum of their relative disadvantages: they are active agents who craft meaning out of their circumstances and do so in complicated and diverse ways." Harris-Perry reminds us that we must never focus on Black women solely as a type of conquered victim but instead acknowl-edge the circumstances that have oppressed them, while simultaneously highlighting the ways in which they have reclaimed their agency despite these circumstances and made meaning of their lives in their own ways.

The year that *Plessy v. Ferguson* was upheld is the same year that the National Association of Colored Women was formed at the First Annual Convention of the National Federation of Afro-American Women in Washington, D.C. The oldest African American secular organization still in existence today, the NACW was founded by Ida B. Wells-Barnett, Harriet Tubman, Frances E. W. Harper, Mary Church Terrell, and others who risked their lives daily to liberate as many people as they possibly could. While there were several atrocities that led to the NACW's creation, the final straw came in a letter written by John W. Jacks, the president of the Missouri Press Association. In it he stated:

> The Negroes in this country are wholly devoid of mo-rality. They know nothing of it except as they learn by

being caught for flagrant violations of law and punished
therefor [*sic*] . . . They consider it no disgrace but rather
an honor to be sent to prison and to wear striped clothes.
The women are prostitutes and all are natural liars and
thieves. . . . Out of the 200 in this vicinity it is doubtful
if there are a dozen virtuous women of that number who
are not daily thieving from the white people.

Jacks claims that Black people simply chose to spend their lives
caged. Like many others, he specifically attacks Black women, using the
infamous jezebel trope, and blames them for the sexual victimization
they were forced to endure. To top it all off, he states that Black people
are the robbers rather than the dispossessed.

Fed up with others taking control of their narrative in this way,
Black women, who had long devoted their lives to the uplift of their
people, united their efforts. Josephine St. Pierre Ruffin, another NACW
founder and the editor of the first national newspaper published by and
for African American women, summarized their mission at that initial
conference when she declared:

The reasons why we should confer are so apparent. . . .
We need to talk over not only those things which are of
vital importance to us as women, but also the things that
are of special interest to us as colored women, the training of our children, openings for our boys and girls, how
they can be prepared for occupations and occupations
may be found or opened to them, what we especially
can do in the moral education of the race with which we
are identified, our mental elevations and physical development, the home training it is necessary to prepare
them to meet [the] peculiar conditions in which they find
themselves.

Sadly, there is some agreement here with the sentiment that Black people were lacking in morality and needed to be taught differently, an example of what we would now call "respectability politics." Still, these Black women bound together, refusing to give up control over their bodies, minds, and reputations.

The NACW was made up of prominent women whose motto was "Lifting as We Climb." Their views on the role of Black women were similar to the expectations Alberta would have been taught as a young Black girl in a well-educated family. She would have been all too aware of the need to always be polished and well-spoken in order to combat demeaning representations of her people and to earn the respect she deserved. Alberta would also see the uplift of others as a crucial part of her role as a Black woman. She would follow in her parents' footsteps, continuing the legacy of combining faith with discipline and becoming a role model for many others along the way.

*Our final introduction takes* us farther up the East Coast of the United States. Some refer to this state as "America in Miniature" or "Little America" because in it you can find almost any kind of terrain, including mountains, farmland, and beaches. As a result of its location adjacent to the Chesapeake Bay, this state is known for its seafood and leads the nation in the production of blue crabs and soft clams. More important, this state is the birthplace of some of the most notable African Americans in history: Frederick Douglass, Frances E. W. Harper, and Thurgood Marshall all form part of a long list of Black leaders who were born in the state of Maryland.

Maryland is also the birth state of another woman who changed the course of our nation but one whose name you likely haven't heard before. Emma Berdis Jones was born on Deal Island, Maryland, in 1903. In order to know why she refused to let pain define her, in order to understand why she turned to writing and poetry to express herself, in order to see how James Baldwin eventually found his own voice, we must know the people and the place that gave Emma Berdis life.

Deal Island, once Deil's Island, once Devil's Island, is rumored to have gained its name when it became a hideout for pirates in the 1600s. A small, isolated island with a total area of 5.4 square miles and a population of 578 in 2000, Deal was never a place of ample opportunity. Although details on the history of the island are scarce, one known fact is that residents have always been dependent on the water to make their living. Most people who live there made, and continue to make, their living as sailors, watermen, or shipbuilders. Not only does the water provide the most possibilities for the population of Deal Island, it also poses its greatest risk. The island is vulnerable to flooding, erosion, storms, and rising water levels that leave its most disadvantaged residents almost defenseless against natural disasters.

It is here, on this tiny island, that a young couple by the names of Leah Esther and Alfred Jones built their life together. Alfred made money as a waterman, continuing a legacy of Black people who turned the water into a possibility for self-determination and dignity. Although water symbolizes the horrors of the transatlantic slave trade for African Americans, for Black watermen and sailors, it also represented opportunity. According to Harold Anderson, the author of "Black Men, Blue Waters: African Americans on the Chesapeake," during the antebellum era "Black sailors traveled to distant places and encountered other cultures, bringing knowledge back to their slave counterparts who usually spent their lives in one small region. . . . As early as 1796, the federal government issued Seamen's Protection Certificates which defined these black merchant mariners as 'citizens'—America's first black citizens."

These free Black people were known as "Black Jacks." Even Frederick Douglass escaped to freedom by wearing a Black Jack's uniform, which was sewn by his wife, Anna Murray Douglass. Anna not only created his disguise, but she also financed his escape.

Black Jacks carried messages of freedom with them wherever they went. They are one of the primary reasons slaves in Deal Island were still aware of what happened all over their state and their country despite their small size and relative isolation. One story that the Black residents of Deal Island heard rumors of was that of a woman originally named Araminta Ross, who later became known as the Moses of her people.

It is estimated that Araminta was born into slavery in Dorchester County, Maryland, less than one hundred miles away from Deal Island in 1820. Raised under the harrowing conditions of the antebellum South, she was subject to horror and abuse. While Araminta was considered too young to work during her first few years, she spent much of her time with her grandmother, who was considered too old to perform harder tasks. I like to imagine that the time she spent with her grandmother, a West African woman, influenced her awe-inspiring journey. Perhaps her grandmother taught her about West African queen mothers; perhaps she shared her own stories of resistance.

Their time together ended quickly, however, as slaves were usually put to work by the age of six. Araminta's tasks varied from checking muskrat traps to weaving and laboring as a house slave, but regardless of the particular work she was assigned, she was relegated to the indignities of her overseers. One particular horror led to a chronic, life-altering head injury when she was hit with a heavy metal weight as a mere teenager. By 1849, Araminta changed her name to Harriet, after her mother, and escaped to freedom using the Underground Railroad. She did not stay in the North for long before becoming a conductor herself and returning to free more slaves, including some of her own family members. She transformed the marshy Chesapeake Bay into a path to freedom for upwards of three hundred slaves. Harriet Tubman didn't pass away until 1913.

While I do not know exactly how Leah Esther and Alfred arrived on Deal Island—perhaps their family members were Black Jacks, perhaps they were also descendants of slaves—I do know that they were able to find a home there, making their living from the water. They also raised four children there, and in 1903, Leah Esther was pregnant with their fifth child, their second daughter. Emma Berdis Jones was born on Christmas Day. A joyous moment, the birth of a precious new baby, was paired with the worst of tragedies when Leah Esther passed away from hemorrhaging. She was sick with pulmonary fibrosis for months before she died. Alfred had lost his wife, and his five children had lost their mother. Through the devastation, the family held on to each other and their faith tightly. Berdis's father and siblings showered her in love.

Emma, called Berdis by her family, spent her early years out on the water with her father. Despite the seeming lack of opportunity for upward mobility on the island, its isolation, along with its small population and a shared reliance on the water, allowed residents to bond across race differences at times. Men and women on boats, making a living for their families, had to rely on one another in some sense. This modest upbringing, paired with witnessing people working together despite contrasting identities, informed Berdis even after she left the island. She was a girl who suffered one of the worst possible losses from an early age, but her family did not allow her to sit in her pain. They showed her that love and happiness were always possible to achieve no matter what you'd gone through, no matter how little you might have. Berdis would need to rely on her unwavering hope and ability to always find the light even in the darkest moments time and time again throughout her life.

*The quote that appears* at the beginning of this chapter comes from an article written by an anonymous woman from the South titled "Experiences of the Race Problem," published in the *Independent* in 1904. While she does not reveal her name, she does tell the reader that she is a white woman whose views on life have been influenced by her father's experiences, first in the Civil War and then upon his return. She writes about the disappointment her father faced when he came back and realized that his "Negroes and land had vanished." As a result of his dismay, he joined the Ku Klux Klan in order to "discipline" freed Black people. He acquired land again and benefited from restrictions placed on Black people that forced them to work on plantations. The writer speaks about her father as a kind of hero, romanticizing life on the plantation, and launches from her introduction of him into a rant of what she sees as the "race problem."

She writes, "The 'educated negro' is an artificial production, which does not fit in with our natural order." She blames Black men for white women's fear as well as white men's "bloodthirstiness," and as we see in the quote, she blames Black women for all of the above. She states, "Negro women evidence more nearly the popular idea of total depravity than the men do" and "the color of a negro woman's skin is generally taken (and quite correctly) as a guarantee of her immorality." She says all of this after telling the reader a story about playing with the Black girls on her plantation when she was a little girl herself. The writer thinks of herself as a kind and compassionate white woman but argues that her superiority over them was something she was always naturally aware of.

While it would be comforting to say that her article was shocking, that her stance was outdated, or that her opinions were unique, these statements would all be untrue. Disturbingly, this was the norm in 1904—an accepted stance to hold on Black women and girls. This was the world that Louise, Alberta, and Berdis were born into. This was the world they would have to face, even though they were hundreds and thousands of miles apart, even though their lives began in different contexts, and even though they would be raised in completely different circumstances. If this southern white woman were to ever meet them, she would see Louise, Alberta, and Berdis as immoral, unnatural, and depraved Black girls in need of disciplining.

Such anger as a result of Black progress also took form in propaganda aimed at further justifying any and all heinous attacks on African Americans. One startling example comes in 1900, when a book titled *"The Negro a Beast,"* or *"In the Image of God"* argues that Black people were more akin to apes than to human beings, that they were the "tempters of Eve"—and ironically, although they were the victims more often than not, that "mulatto brutes" were rapists and murderers who needed to be killed. The author, Charles Carroll, spent fifteen years of his life compiling "evidence" for his book, which was received with great praise from his audience. This publication was just one of the many ways in which African Americans were deemed less than human. In other words, it justified the need for white humans to be separated from "nonhumans" and confirmed the basic tenets of white supremacy while masquerading as a well-researched, scientific, and "biblical truth." In a climate of hatred and violence, Black Americans found themselves back in antebellum society despite promises of change and liberation.

When it came to location, job opportunities, and educational attainment, things had remained largely the same for Black people. Gains made during Reconstruction were mostly reversed by the beginning of the twentieth century. According to the census of 1900, 90 percent of African Americans still lived in the South and 75 percent of African American homes were in rural areas. Only one-fifth of African Americans owned their homes. Fifty percent of African American men and 35 percent of African American women worked as farm laborers, most likely on plantations. The rest worked in unskilled labor or service jobs. Most African American children were unable to attend school, and if they did, the conditions of their schools were abysmal compared with those of their white counterparts. Conditions were probably even worse than the census could capture, and it didn't appear as though things would get better anytime soon.

In 1901, Theodore Roosevelt was sworn in as the twenty-sixth president of the United States, and he brought with him the belief that the white race must continue to prosper over all others. While he was progressive in some ways, he also believed in the importance of "race purity," simply another argument for separate but equal. In his Lincoln Day speech of 1905, he said, "Full recognition of the fundamental fact that all men should stand on an equal footing as regards civil privileges in no way interferes with recognition of the further fact that all reflecting men of both races are united in feeling that race purity must be maintained." While this stance is not a surprising one for a U.S. president at the time to hold, Roosevelt's additional commentary on the role women played in maintaining their race adds to the climate our three girls were born into. In 1906, he delivered a speech titled "On American Motherhood," where he said:

> There are many good people who are denied the supreme blessing of children. . . . But the man or woman who deliberately foregoes these blessings, whether from viciousness, coldness, shallow-heartedness, self-indulgence, or mere failure to appreciate aright the difference between the all-important and the unimportant—why, such a creature merits contempt as hearty as any visited upon the soldier who runs away in battle. . . . For a race that practised such doctrine—that is, a race that practised race suicide—would thereby conclusively show that it was unfit to exist, and that it had better give place to people who had not forgotten the primary laws of their being.

Through these words and the rest of his speech, Roosevelt speaks to the declining birth rates among white women and urges them to keep up with the birth rate of minorities so as to avoid "race suicide." In 1800, the birth rate among whites is estimated to have been 55 births for every 1,000 white women. In 1900, the rate lowered to 30. Although data are not available for Black women in 1800, it is estimated that in 1850 the birth rate among them was 43.3 for every 1,000 Black women and 44.4 in 1900. These facts caused extreme worry for many white supremacists who feared what might happen if minorities, especially those they had enslaved for hundreds of years, were ever to become the majority.

Yet it is not here, in the face of this ignorance and hatred, that the three mothers' lives are planted. Instead, they are rooted in the lessons of their foremothers. They are nourished by Edith, Jennie Celeste, and Leah Esther, as well as *their* mothers. They are sustained by accounts of resistance dating back hundreds of years. Their lives are built on faith and stories that evolve and resonate across water and land. Our story begins with the declaration that although there are countless forces acting against their lives, Louise, Alberta, and Berdis have still breathed their first breaths. They have arrived.

## Part II

# The Denial of Our Existence

One of the things that has to be faced is the process of waiting to change the system, how much we have got to do to find out who we are, where we have come from and where we are going.

—ELLA BAKER

The enfranchisement of women would insure immediate and durable white supremacy, honestly attained; for, upon unquestionable authority, it is stated that in every Southern State but one, there are more educated women than all the illiterate voters, white and black, native and foreign, combined. As you probably know, of all the women in the South who can read and write, ten out of every eleven are white. When it comes to the proportion of property between the races, that of the white outweighs that of the black immeasurably. The South is slow to grasp the great fact that the enfranchisement of women would settle the race question in politics.

—BELLE KEARNEY

The same year that Harriet Tubman passed away, Woodrow Wilson took office as the twenty-eighth president of the United States. Under his administration, the country witnessed unprecedented segregation in public offices, interracial marriage became a felony, and attacks on Black people's very existence only grew. So too did the Black revolutionary spirit, however. A time period of increasing threats was also a time period defined by evolution.

The next decade of Berdis's, Alberta's, and Louise's lives saw unprecedented change in the United States; in every corner people could feel the growing volume of calls for Black freedom. Some leaders encouraged Black people to remain in the South and claim the cities that they and generations of their families had built with their own bodies. Others encouraged them to seek prosperity by leaving and starting over somewhere else, where they might live on equal terms with their white counterparts. And yet others advocated for the complete independence of Black people from white America and spoke in favor of Pan-Africanism and a return to the motherland.

Momentum and a glint of transformation loomed on the horizon. Much would change in this ten-year period as a result of World War I, the Great Migration, and the expansion of Black nationalism. Because of their locations, Louise, Berdis, and Alberta were affected differently by each of these landmark moments in history.

Grenada was the headquarters of the British Windward Islands from 1885 to 1958, making anything that affected the United Kingdom a concern for Grenadian people. Louise's fellow islanders would find themselves questioning the level of involvement they should have in the war. Like Black citizens in the United States, British colonies debated whether they should participate at all. Some called it a "white man's war" while others pledged their support for the United Kingdom, hoping it would create opportunities for advancement at home.

While the story of Caribbean troops has been largely ignored and virtually erased, it is estimated that around sixteen thousand Caribbean people voluntarily enlisted in World War I. They, like Black American troops, were seen as less valuable than their white counterparts. They were discriminated against and put in charge of some of the most dangerous work within range of German artillery. Many Caribbean troops suffered frostbite and pneumonia when they were given worse accommodations and resources as compared with white troops.

I do not know if any members of Louise's family enlisted, but based on the beliefs she was raised with, I would guess that they stood on the side of those who were not willing to risk their lives for their colonizer's gain. Before he passed, Jupiter, Louise's grandfather, was determined to be free from the grasp of whites. He was a skilled carpenter who was able to provide his family with more comfort than the average Black Grenadian. Over time he even acquired land in La Digue, where he built a home that would house generations of his family. He and Mary Jane taught their children the importance of landownership and trained them to raise their own food through gardening and hunting. Even after Jupiter's passing at the age of seventy-five, Louise's family enjoyed a degree of autonomy that most Blacks did not have access to. They saw their independence from the white man as key to their freedom.

Louise grew up in the warm embrace of a tight-knit extended family that did whatever they could to maintain their autonomy. She was mostly raised following the guidance of her female relatives. Her grandmother Mary Jane was a domestic worker who was known for being extremely resourceful, able to stretch the little that she was given to take care of her family as a single woman. Louise's aunt Gertrude was a skilled seamstress who used her gift to make her own money. I wish we could know more about these women and the memories they shared with Louise, as I am sure there are traces of them in Louise's children as well, but such precious moments have been lost in history. In regard to this loss, the Caribbean novelist Jan Carew wrote the following in 1998:

> Louise's extended family are now scattered across three continents. The stories of her growing up in rural Grenada are, therefore, fragmented and dispersed across the Caribbean and in Latin America, Great Britain, Canada, and the United States. All of those who knew her as a child growing up in La Digue, however, are now dead, and memory plays strange tricks when it is filtered from one generation to the next.

We may not know the specifics, but it is fair to say, based on the little we do have, that Louise learned to be resilient from her mother, learned to be creative and clever from her grandmother, and learned a trade as well as the value of self-determination from her aunt. Through all these lessons, she was taught to challenge the status quo. She also learned that the more you could do on your own the better. If you could build your own house, sew your own clothes, plant and hunt your own food, you could live a liberated life.

The fierce female energy in her home was paired with access to education at the local Anglican school. Her teachers believed in the maxim "Spare the rod and spoil the child," and they were strict with students, pushing Louise to be strict with herself as well. They also believed in the importance of poetry and would have students recite verses routinely. Louise developed a deep love of words. She tried to learn as many as she possibly could. If she encountered a word she didn't yet know, she would look it up and commit it to memory. Having grown up in a place as diverse and multilingual as La Digue, Louise learned to master not only English but French and patois as well. According to her granddaughter Ilyasah Shabazz, Louise spoke five languages.

Her family reminded her of her worth and ability to sustain herself, her schooling developed her understanding of the world and gave her more tools for survival, her island hinted at the expansive diversity of the world, and everything pushed her to want more for herself than what colonial Grenada could ever give her. She was a multilingual, cosmopolitan scholar who was aware of her excellence. She was unafraid to face the challenges that came with being a young woman of color.

During this time, many Grenadians sought better opportunities for themselves than what they could hope for at home. Following the crash of the sugarcane economy, Grenadians migrated to neighboring countries, and some even made their way to Canada and the United States, seeking better pay. Migration to the United States and Canada paled in comparison with migration to Central America and Cuba. Between 1899 and 1932, 108,000 people from all over the Caribbean are recorded to have entered the United States. And it is estimated that from 1900 to 1960, Canada accepted 21,500 immigrants from Caribbean countries. Yet upwards of 240,000 laborers from Jamaica and Barbados alone are recorded to have entered Panama between 1881 and 1915. If you were a Caribbean immigrant to the United States or Canada during this period, you would find less support and camaraderie in the experience than immigrants who moved to places that were closer. Regardless of where they went, Grenadians sought more opportunities for upward mobility, better pay, relief from hurricanes, and separation from British colonialism.

In 1913, Louise's uncle Edgerton Langdon was one of the few who emigrated from Grenada to Montreal, Canada. In 1916, he traveled to New York, where his friends took him to hear a man by the name of

Marcus Garvey speak. The message he heard that day changed his life, and when he traveled back to Montreal, he began to spread the word about Garveyism.

Garvey was a Pan-Africanist born in Jamaica in 1887. He would go on to become one of the most influential political leaders, journalists, and orators in world history. He was born into poverty as one of eleven children in his family and only one of two of the eleven who survived into adulthood. His family was poor, and Garvey was forced to leave school at the young age of fourteen to work as an apprentice in a printshop, where he became involved in the labor union for tradesmen. He eventually went on to study law and philosophy. Following the completion of his degree, he founded the Universal Negro Improvement Association, first in Jamaica and then in the United States in 1916. The UNIA advocated for racial unity, financial independence from whites, and the formation of independent Black nations in Africa. Despite religious differences, there are many ties between the UNIA and a group that would be founded years later, known to the world as the Nation of Islam.

Following in his footsteps, Louise accepted her uncle's invitation to join him in Montreal. She left Grenada in June 1917, traveling alone by steamship, never to be seen in La Digue again. Imagine being a young Black woman, an immigrant, traveling to North America in the early 1900s, all alone. Brave, excited, and ready for the next stage in her life, she landed in Saint John, New Brunswick, Canada, on June 26. Louise joined her uncle, not only in Montreal but also in his quest to spread the message of Black liberation. In Garveyism, Louise found echoes of the lessons she was brought up on. She found a home away from home where she could channel her anger against white supremacy, where she could use her writing to advance the cause of her people, where she could join others in the fight for Black independence.

Garvey encountered criticism from other civil rights leaders who called him an impostor who went against the best interests of Black advancement. In particular, he was often in opposition to leaders of an organization founded five years before the UNIA called the National Association for the Advancement of Colored People. As its name suggests, the NAACP was created to advance the interests of citizens of color and promote their equal civil rights. Its founders were exhausted by the indignities Black people were still subject to and brought their efforts together to organize mass movement and change. By 1919, the NAACP had upwards of ninety thousand members and more than three hundred branches across the United States. To this day, it is the nation's largest and most widely recognized civil rights organization.

Garvey criticized the NAACP in return, saying that they advocated solely for assimilation into white society. He argued that because whites did not see Blacks as equals, Black people should advocate for their own independence rather than join the causes of white America, including involvement in the war. One of Garvey's most famous quotations reads, "The first dying that is to be done by the black man in the future will be done to make himself free. And then when we are finished, if we have any charity to bestow, we may die for the white man. But as for me, I think I have stopped dying for him."

Among the disagreements that emerged between different Black movements and leaders concerning the best approach to achieving Black freedom, perhaps the most apparent during this decade concerned participation in World War I. Garvey spoke against the involvement of Black people in the war, while others saw World War I as an event with revolutionary implications for the future of Black people. These implications included possibilities for social, political, and economic growth as a result of enlisting. Many Black people saw the war as a chance to gain respect and full citizenship. They saw it as a moment to declare their patriotism by serving, believing that their civil rights would be waiting upon their return. Many were afraid that if they did not serve their country in the war, they would be declaring that they were disloyal to the United States, which might result in the loss of even more of their rights. Upwards of 350,000 African American men fought in World War I.

World War I was the first time in U.S. history that the army and navy nurse corps were activated and the first time in which women officially and openly served. However, Black women who tried to participate faced obstacle after obstacle. Fewer than a dozen Black women were allowed to cross the ocean as volunteer nurses. Still, Black women continued to serve the country as volunteers at home through organizations such the YMCA. Like their white counterparts, Black women covered jobs in the absence of their men. Temporarily, Black women were able to shift from domestic jobs to work in factories and offices. As the poet, essayist, and activist Alice Dunbar Nelson described it, "The women worked as ammunition testers, switchboard operators, stock takers. They went into every kind of factory devoted to the production of war materials, from the most dangerous posts in munition plants to the delicate sewing in aeroplane factories"—contributions that have often gone unnoticed.

It wasn't clear yet if the end of World War I would bring relief to African Americans, but horror certainly pursued Black people while the battle continued. They were constantly harassed and blamed for any hardship white families faced.

On September 9, 1912, an eighteen-year-old white woman by the name of Mae Crow was found beaten, bloody, and breathless in the Appalachian foothills north of Atlanta, Georgia. The mystery surrounding her murder remains unsolved to this day, but, unsurprisingly, Black families in Forsyth paid the price of Mae's bloodshed. On September 10, the county sheriff arrested two young Black men and one Black boy by the names of Rob Edwards, Oscar Daniel, and Ernest Knox, ages twenty-four, eighteen, and sixteen, respectively. While Ernest and Oscar were "formally" tried and sentenced to hang, death found Rob more quickly. White farmers stormed the county jail and dragged him from his cell while he pleaded for mercy. The streets filled with spectators as Rob's limp young body was hoisted upon a telephone pole. The audience's roars grew progressively louder while they took turns shooting the already mutilated corpse. The next morning, his body was left on display in front of the courthouse.

This was not enough for the bloodthirsty mobs. Weeks later, on the night of Mae's funeral, white men of Forsyth set out on horseback toward the Black cabins that dotted the woodlands. They gave Black residents two options: pack and leave the county before the following night or stay and die like Rob Edwards. Threatened with rifles, torches, and dynamite, an estimated eleven hundred Black people evacuated Forsyth County, leaving behind their homes, schools, and businesses. Forsyth would remain "all white" for decades to come and would stand as a clear reminder of the deadly vulnerability Black people lived with, where their survival rested on the whims of their white fellow citizens. Without any evidence, they would be blamed for any misfortune suffered by whites.

*Less than sixty miles* away from Forsyth County, the Williams family fought their own battles against racism. Alberta was raised by two devoted and distinguished parents, rooted in their religious faith and committed to the fulfillment of human rights for all. She was raised with beliefs that the human spirit would prevail over oppression, that love and fellowship would conquer hate and violence. Alberta's parents taught her to be an activist.

A young Alberta watched as her parents organized strategy meetings, as they addressed their congregation, as they stood up to injustice. Even while their daughter was very young, Reverend and First Lady Williams taught by example. Reverend Williams was one of the founders of the Atlanta chapter of the NAACP. The couple also led a successful drive for the first Black high school in Atlanta as well as a boycott of

*The Georgian*, a publication that did everything in its power to disparage African American residents. When Reverend and First Lady Williams noticed that many of the ads in the paper were from stores that Black people patronized, they and other church leaders stood in front of their members and encouraged them to boycott such businesses.

In the midst of racial violence, Alberta was raised with examples of resistance in the name of humanity and love. As a natural result of her parents leading Ebenezer Baptist, Alberta also became an active member and most of her life was tied to the happenings of the church. Although she was an only child, she grew up around several children in the congregation as well as youths the reverend and his wife took in when they had nowhere else to go. Through Ebenezer, Alberta also developed her love of music, and she brought back the church's choir, one that would become famous over the years. She was an extremely talented musician who learned to play several instruments, including the piano and the organ. As soon as visitors entered the Williams home, they would see a piano to the left of the front door that Alberta played for hours each day.

Beyond being an incredible instrumentalist and singer who would continue to develop her craft, Alberta, like Louise, was a brilliant student. She attended public institutions in her elementary and middle school years, before following in her mother's footsteps and attending Spelman Seminary. She was a young woman who paired her love of music and reading with an extensive knowledge of art and a passion to become a teacher. She put words together with ease and spoke confidently; her intelligence could not be ignored. Alberta went on to enroll in Hampton Normal and Industrial Institute, where she obtained her teaching certificate. Her parents cared deeply about her education and wholeheartedly supported their daughter's journey toward her career. Alberta wanted to share her privileges with as many others as she could, and she believed teaching was the best way for her to do so.

Keeping Black people from advancing by restricting their ability to become educated has long been a strategy of oppression. During times of slavery well through the 1800s, it was against the law to teach Black people to read and write. Once the law allowed it, Black people who pursued education were still met with attacks, intimidation, withholding of resources, shortened school years, and more. It was an act of resistance every time a Black family was able to prioritize education, but it was not an easy feat. According to the National Center for Education Statistics, in 1910, 5 percent of whites over the age of fourteen were unable to read or write at the most fundamental levels, as compared with 30 percent of Blacks. In 1920, the numbers changed to 4 percent of whites and 23 percent of Blacks.

Poorer Black residents across Georgia, especially those outside of Atlanta, sought the kinds of opportunities Alberta had access to. As the hub of transportation innovations, Atlanta was established as a center of commerce and finance. The city offered more chances for education and employment than many of its neighboring towns. By 1900, Blacks made up 40 percent of the city's total population, and over the years to come, more Black people from rural areas across Georgia found upward mobility in Atlanta.

Yet more resources for survival did nothing to shield residents from racial terror. In this decade, between 1910 and 1920, even while Black troops enlisted in World War I, helping to make Georgia home to more war-training camps than any other state, Black people in Atlanta faced the rebirth of the Ku Klux Klan. Inspired by the wildly successful film *The Birth of a Nation*, the KKK celebrated its second founding at Stone Mountain, less than a mile away from Ebenezer Baptist and Alberta's home, in 1915, and Atlanta became known to whites as the Imperial City of the Invisible Empire. As Black Americans slowly gained more liberties and found small successes, white supremacists became more enraged. The KKK recruited more members during this time period than ever before. It's estimated that their numbers grew to upwards of four million men and women who not only despised African Americans but were intent on controlling Jews, Catholics, and immigrants.

All across Georgia, Blacks were seeking refuge from the terror the KKK and Jim Crow inflicted. In Sandersville, Georgia, a young man by the name of Elijah Robert Poole was born in 1897. The son of a Baptist preacher and a sharecropper, he was forced to quit school after third grade so he could support his family by working in sawmills and brickyards. He was only a few years older than Alberta, and before the age of twenty he had already witnessed the lynching of three Black men. Exhausted by the hatred, he stated, "I've seen enough of the white man's brutality to last me 26,000 years." Elijah Robert Poole, who would later change his name to Elijah Muhammad, left his rural town, not for Atlanta but for the state of Michigan. He joined millions of other Black people who made up what's now known as the Great Migration.

The Great Migration was one of the largest internal migrations in history. Between 1915 and 1960, around five million southern Black residents moved north to cities including Chicago, Philadelphia, and New York. Others moved westward to Los Angeles, Oakland, and Seattle. It is estimated that during World War I, 450,000 Black southerners moved. This mass movement of people emerged as a result of continued racial violence and oppression as African Americans saw little change in their lives fifty years after the signing of the Emancipation Proclamation. It also came as a result of a growing activist movement that showed Black Americans options beyond inevitably becoming victims of southern laws that vilified and repressed them simply for living. Black southerners hoped for greater prosperity in the North, and Black families each faced the decision of whether to stay or to go; to fight for their rights where they already were or to believe that things could be different somewhere else. Many chose to take a chance on the latter.

Beyond the potential the North and the West offered for freedom from southern racism, World War I also created a demand for more workers across the United States as European immigration slowed significantly during these years. Countless Black families made whatever sacrifice was necessary to buy themselves railroad tickets, taking a chance by filling a vacancy and starting over somewhere new. Through doing so, they changed the North, the South, and the entire nation forever. At the turn of the century, nine in ten African Americans lived in the southern states of Georgia, Mississippi, and Alabama primarily. By 1970, on the other hand, New York, Illinois, and California housed the most African American residents.

The Williams family was not one of the thousands that left the South for something better in the North. They believed in standing their ground and defending their humanity right where they were. This decision was further informed by the privileges they were able to enjoy as an educated Black family supported by a large congregation they worked immensely hard to build over the years. The Williams family was rooted in Atlanta, but they were not satisfied with the conditions of the caste system they found themselves in. Instead, in staying, they made a commitment to change Atlanta with hopes of progressing the case for Black freedom across the United States.

*African American residents of* Maryland were affected by racial terror, World War I, and the Great Migration much like their kin in Georgia were. While racist attacks are more often associated with the Deep South in many minds, Black residents of Maryland were by no means spared the mistreatments of the Jim Crow era. At least forty-four of the hundreds of lynchings that took place during this time period were recorded in Maryland.

Approximately sixty-two thousand Marylanders enlisted in World War I, and roughly eleven thousand of them were Black. Black

Marylanders, especially those living in rural areas, also sought more opportunity for economic freedom and relief from racial injustice. Continuing the legacy of Black liberation fighters from the state, the beginning of the "New Negro Movement" found its way into Maryland, specifically in more urban areas, and the Baltimore branch of the NAACP was established in 1914.

In Deal Island, just a steamboat ride away from Baltimore, the Jones family also enjoyed a degree of economic autonomy that was not common for Black families at the time. Despite coming from humble means, Berdis's parents acquired one-half acre of their own land in 1884. All three families, the Langdons, the Williamses, and the Joneses, saw land ownership as an essential part of their agency and battle to gain dignity in their country.

Alfred Jones married Leah Esther on September 24, 1880. Before Berdis was born, Leah Esther had given birth to nine children, four of whom were still living: Isaak (born 1883), Joel (born 1888), Beulah (born 1890), and Alfred (born 1896). After losing Leah Esther, Alfred married his second wife, Mary, in 1906. During this period, it was not uncommon for children from previous marriages to move in with other family members when their fathers remarried. Berdis moved in with her older sister, Beulah, the only mother she ever knew. Beulah and her husband, Samuel, raised Berdis and Alfred Jr. In 1911, Alfred Sr. and Mary sold their property before moving away from Deal Island for good.

At the time, virtually all Black residents of Deal Island were educated at the John Wesley Methodist Episcopal Church, located in the middle of Deal Island's Black neighborhood. John Wesley M.E. Church has since been deemed a historic site by the Maryland Historical Trust because of its importance as the "Colored Church and School." Berdis likely worshipped and attended school in the Gothic Revival building that is described as "standing in sharp contrast to the low-lying marshy ground surrounding the site." Berdis was known to have a brilliant mind, and in these early years of her life she developed a love of writing and of poetry. She sometimes performed her pieces in front of her family members. This love for words and her education expanded her mind and allowed her to imagine what existed beyond what she could readily see.

It was a form of resistance for Black children to dream in this way, to see themselves past what was shown to them by a world intent on controlling their every move. Beyond what Berdis saw in her immediate surroundings, she and other Black children were also exposed to media representations that aimed to disparage them. Black children were represented in books and on television as pickaninnies: typically dark Black caricatures with bulging eyes, unkempt hair, and big mouths. They were shown on postcards running away from alligators toward watermelon or chicken. The presentation and popularization of the pickaninny served to objectify Black children as worthless and Black parents as inept. Pickaninnies were often portrayed crawling on the ground next to animals to suggest their lack of affiliation with humans. In the face of such dehumanization, Black families taught their children to love themselves. The families of Berdis, Alberta, and Louise encouraged them to believe in their dreams and future possibilities. They resisted by giving them a foundation of love and encouraging their minds by sacrificing whatever they needed to for each of the three to receive an education.

Just like her place of schooling, Berdis found herself standing in contrast with her surroundings and such racist representations. Similar to Louise, she formed a desire for more in life beyond what her island could offer her. Similar to Alberta, she was taught to believe in God and was therefore strengthened by her conviction. She found herself looking north, full of hope for better circumstances and more opportunity. Just a few years after Louise, she too made her move, taking a leap of faith on her ambition and joining thousands of others in the Great

Migration. Her first stop would take her to a cousin in Philadelphia before she ended up in New York City.

*Soldiers returned from World* War I at the end of 1918, women's newly acquired jobs were quickly taken away from them, and Black veterans were met with increased violence rather than the relief they were promised upon enlisting. After facing rigid segregation during the war and surviving the daily assaults of their fellow soldiers, they returned to find that conditions had become worse. Having fought for the ideals of their country and having displayed their commitment to the United States, Black soldiers came home with a sense of pride and accomplishment, knowing they had earned at least the most basic recognition. Instead, they were greeted with fear of their sense of fulfillment.

Their military experience made them more of a threat. Their pride was seen as something in need of control. Once again, irrational white supremacist fears turned into extreme forms of brutality. According to the Equal Justice Initiative, "No one was more at risk of experiencing violence and targeted racial terror than black veterans who had proven their valor and courage as soldiers. . . . Thousands of black veterans were assaulted, threatened, abused, or lynched following military service."

Violence targeted at Black veterans and their families led to one of the bloodiest summers for Black Americans, known in history as the Red Summer. Approximately twenty-five race riots broke out across the United States. In different cities, white rioters attacked Black men, women, and children, targeted Black organizational meetings, and destroyed Black homes and Black businesses. Hundreds of Black people were killed and thousands were injured in the onslaughts.

*The Chicago Defender* ran an article on August 2, 1919, titled "Ghastly Deeds of Rioters Told." The article begins with the subhead

"Defender Reporter Faces Death in Attempt to Get Facts of Mob Violence; Hospitals Are Filled with Maimed Men and Women" and goes on to describe several unimaginable instances of racial violence:

> In all parts of the city, white mobs dragged from surface cars, black passengers wholly ignorant of any trouble, and set upon them. An unidentified young woman and a 3 months old baby were found dead on the street at the intersection of 17th street and Wentworth avenue. She had attempted to board a car there when the mob seized her, beat her, slashed her body into ribbons and beat the baby's brains out against a telegraph pole. Not satisfied with this, one rioter severed her breasts, and a white youngster bore it aloft on a pole, triumphantly, while the crowd hooted gleefully. All the time, this was happening, several policemen were in the crowd, but did not make any attempt to make rescue until too late.

I choose this haunting and sickening tragedy because it sheds light on the terror Black women faced, terror that is often erased in our telling of history. Black men are frequently spoken about as the only victims of racial violence and police brutality, but we must also remember the women who lost their lives. It is estimated that around two hundred women were lynched between 1880 and 1930, and countless numbers of Black women and girls were victims of rape. *All* Black people were left unprotected, their bodies mutilated and justice for their lives denied.

Such horrible acts were further justified in the minds of those who carried them out because of representations that denied Black humanity. Berdis, Louise, and Alberta grew from children to teenagers to young women at a time when *The Birth of a Nation* characterized Black men as scoundrels intent on brutalizing white women; when the pickaninny equated Black children with animals; and, during the Jim Crow years, when the most popular image of the Black woman was the mammy. This devoted domestic servant did not possess her own desires; she would do anything to please her white family. If Black women acted in resistance to this image, if they spoke up for themselves, if they did not stay "in their place," if they cared more for their own children than white ones, they would be punished.

The mammy was docile, and happily so. Perhaps the most popular example of the mammy character came in the form of Aunt Jemima, characterized as loyal, plump, and ignorant of her own needs. The Quaker Oats Company used Aunt Jemima as the face of its pancake mix and sold more than 120 million boxes in 1910. It was nothing short of strategic to promote the image of an obedient servant during a time when whites felt themselves losing control of Black citizens.

It has recently come to light that the woman who was originally photographed as Aunt Jemima was in actuality named Nancy Green, and her real story is one of advocacy, bravery, creativity, and resilience. Green was born into slavery and went on to become a philanthropist and ministry leader who traveled the country and eventually cofounded one of the oldest Black Baptist churches in Chicago— Olivet Baptist Church. The nuance of her story was buried under the controlling image Quaker Oats needed her to portray.

Alberta, Berdis, and Louise contradicted such limiting representations on a daily basis. They were Black girls who learned to read and write above an average level, who were able to form passions for the arts of writing, poetry, and music, who dreamed of better futures for themselves and their community, and who acted upon such dreams. Even with different levels of access to resources, their families provided what they could as their daughters entered adulthood. Nothing about their existence can be seen as ordinary when the context of the time and space they inhabited is understood. Although as Black girls and women they faced obstacles at every turn of their lives, they found ways to thrive and succeed.

While the world around them tried to deny their humanity and their existence, Louise, Alberta, and Berdis found ways to create their own realities through their growing talents and skills. Among other dreams, Alberta wanted to teach, Louise wanted to write, and Berdis wanted to perform her prose. Perhaps they were all passionate about different forms of art because of the opportunity it offered them for creation; the opportunity to picture and build more beyond what was presented to them. Their passions would accompany them in every stage in their lives, even when their paths would take them in unexpected directions and their contributions to their families and to the world would become obscured. It is important that we remember this stage in their lives, their teenage and young adult years, where they formed their individual dreams and beamed at the possibilities that awaited them.

## Part III

# Our Men and Marriages

The complex of color . . . every colored man
feels it sooner or later. It gets in the way of his
dreams, of his education, of his marriage, of the
rearing of his children.

—JESSIE REDMON FAUSET

Why should the African prove more just and
generous than his Saxon compeers? If the two
millions of Southern black women are not to
be secured in their rights of person, property,
wages, and children, their emancipation is but
another form of slavery. In fact, it is better to
be the slave of an educated white man, than of a
degraded, ignorant black one.

—ELIZABETH CADY STANTON

In 1848, a group of abolitionist activists gathered in Seneca Falls to discuss women's rights. Black and white leaders came together to join their efforts and focus on the importance of advancing the cause of all women, specifically through a discussion of their right to vote. But by the time women's suffrage passed on August 26, 1920, white suffragists had separated themselves from Black leadership by choosing to uphold white supremacy and exclude Black women from their movement. Through decades of battles for women's rights stemming from the nineteenth century, alliances between white and Black women fissured. Many white women tried desperately to gain access to the same opportunities that were available to their male counterparts by aligning themselves with whiteness rather than with their fellow women.

The Nineteenth Amendment says that "the right of citizens of the United States to vote shall not be denied or abridged by the United States or by any State on account of sex." Although these words *technically* guaranteed the right to vote to all women, Black women were excluded through various levels of disenfranchisement and intimidation. Black women who attempted to vote would face obstacles like being forced to wait in line for up to twelve hours, to pay additional and arbitrary taxes, to take tests that were designed for them to fail. They also faced threats of bodily harm and of fabricated charges that could result in jail time.

White women sought their right to vote as a symbol of parity with their husbands, brothers, and sons. Black women sought their right to vote as a means of empowering their communities and escaping reigns of terror.

For many who sought relief from their hardships, the North offered potential for change. Southern Blacks arrived in places like Philadelphia and New York City, bright eyed and inspired as the WHITE ONLY signs began to disappear. They imagined, if only for a moment, opportunity abounding. Yet they found themselves facing Jim Crow in different forms, perhaps more subtle and implicit but still palpable. They were still treated as less than, still excluded not only from voting but also from certain restaurants, hotels, whole neighborhoods. Many were confined to labor and domestic jobs even if they had training to work in higher positions. The excitement of starting over, paired with the disappointment of realizing that things were more similar to the South than they were different, defined the experience of migrants like Berdis.

Berdis traveled on her own, leaving her sister's home and her small island, heading first to Philadelphia and then to New York City in the early 1920s. She was a petite young woman who spoke with an extremely soft voice; Maya Angelou would say she had to bow to nearly half of her height just to kiss Berdis on the forehead. This small, gentle young woman embarked on one of the scariest and most exciting adventures of a lifetime.

As Berdis and other migrants continued to make their way north, New York City became a mecca of Black culture, a space where Black identity was being reconstructed and reclaimed. When Berdis arrived, she found herself right in the center of the burgeoning Harlem Renaissance.

The Harlem Renaissance of the 1920s was a social and artistic explosion of Black strides in literature, music, stage performance, art, and more. Intellectuals and performers alike came together and experimented with their ideas and experiences of Black identity. More stories about Black life emerged than ever before, allowing for a celebration of the diversity of Black people. Participants in the Harlem Renaissance used their work to defy the stereotypical, demeaning images of Blackness that others continued to spread. The Harlem Renaissance came as a result of, and influenced, the development of Black self-determination, race pride, political activism, and new levels of militancy against white supremacy.

I like to picture Berdis, a writer and poet herself, reveling in the creative energy all around her despite money being extremely scarce. Perhaps between her shifts working as a cleaning woman and laundress she also found time to take in the excitement of the city; perhaps she pictured herself performing onstage one day.

Although the Nineteenth Amendment excluded Black women and ignored their contributions to the women's suffrage movement, Black women, especially those who contributed to the Harlem Renaissance, continued to find ways to express themselves, to gain control of their narratives, and to fight for their rights. Even though they were given less attention than their male equivalents, they greatly influenced the movement and continued to redefine what it meant to be Black women and Black people. They challenged tropes like the jezebel and the mammy and claimed ownership over their bodies and minds.

There was Zora Neale Hurston, the anthropologist, folklorist, and writer who celebrated Black women's stories and broke away from stereotypical portrayals of them; Josephine Baker, who used her controversial dances to claim her sexuality and used her performances to proudly proclaim the dignity and worth of the Black female body; Bessie Smith, who became a world-renowned blues and jazz singer, promoting messages of Black women's independence from men; and many more. Black women of the Harlem Renaissance told stories of Black women's everyday experiences, including the struggles they faced and conquered. They highlighted the need to tell Black women's stories from their own perspectives, and they laid the groundwork for the others coming after them by unapologetically breaking glass ceilings and stating that they had important opinions and countless talents to share. Through their art, they too gave life.

It is here, among this excitement, that Berdis met her first lover. While we have lost his name in history, as well as the basic details behind their relationship, we know that in 1924 Berdis gave birth to a child out of wedlock, a son who was the spitting image of his mother. He had her petite build, her big and inviting eyes, her friendly and welcoming smile. He brought her joy in the midst of tumultuousness. Some rumors say that his biological father suffered from drug addiction and/or that he passed away, but regardless of what actually happened, we know that Berdis was left to raise her son on her own.

By the mid-1920s, she struggled to make ends meet as a single mother without any kind of support system around her. She worked night shifts cleaning an office building, and although she did not enjoy the work, it allowed her to take care of her son during the day. She was able to save the little bit of money she made rather than spending it on childcare.

It was in the thick of this kind of desperate living that she met a preacher, laborer, and fellow migrant by the name of David Baldwin. David had arrived in New York after leaving Lone Pine, Louisiana, in the early 1920s. In its history of race relations, Louisiana differed slightly from the rest of the South in the nineteenth century as a result of a sizable free population of French-speaking Creoles of color; but by the 1900s, the regime of Jim Crow reigned supreme. In 1896, 130,334 Black people were registered to vote across the state of Louisiana, yet in 1904, only 1,342 could pass the newly imposed restrictions.

David was just one generation removed from slavery. His experiences were shaped by the overt racism and dangers he faced as a Black boy and man in the South. He witnessed the worst Jim Crow had to offer: he experienced the tragedies of racial violence and lived with the daily fear and torment. In seeking relief from these, he sought God. He saw the white man as the devil, and he became a preacher in the

Pentecostal tradition, hoping that in his sermons he could reveal the truth behind white supremacy. He wanted others to know what he knew, that although whites did not see him as a man, God did. And that God would punish white people for their sins.

Berdis, the kind, gentle, open-minded young woman from the small town of Deal Island who was facing the extreme financial struggles of being a young Black single mother, was introduced to David, the preacher who was afflicted by the pains caused by racism. Before meeting Berdis, David had already had at least two children, one of whom had died in prison and another who barely spoke to his father. I'm not sure who introduced them in real life, but in *Go Tell It on the Mountain*, James Baldwin's first and semiautobiographical novel, Gabriel (based on David) and Elizabeth (based on Berdis) are introduced by Florence (Gabriel's sister and Elizabeth's friend).

The fictionalized dialogue reads:

> Then Florence introduced them, saying: "Elizabeth, this here's my brother I been telling you so much about. He's a preacher, honey—so we got to be mighty careful what we talk about when *he's* around."
>
> Then he said, with a smile less barbed and ambiguous than his sister's remark: "Ain't no need to be afraid of me, sister. I ain't nothing but a poor, weak vessel in the hands of the Lord."
>
> "You *see*!" said Florence, grimly. She took John from his mother's arms. "And this here's little Johnny," she said, "shake hands with the preacher, Johnny." . . .
>
> "He a mighty fine boy," said Gabriel. "With them big eyes he ought to see everything *in* the Bible."

David and Berdis met each other during a trying time in both their lives. Perhaps in each other they saw the possibility to begin again. In

David, Berdis could find security and more stability, relief from raising her son on her own. In Berdis, David could find some peace, a partner to share his load with, a woman he could start a new family with. Their meeting brought potential, just like their move up north. However, the same mixed feelings loomed. Would this be an experience filled with the new opportunity it promised, or would it come on the wings of disillusionment and despair?

David Baldwin proved to be a husband who did his best to provide for his wife and his growing family but was constrained by the lack of opportunities and fair treatment for Black men. He was prevented from doing what he felt he must do as a man; provide a stable life for his family. He was riddled with despair and blamed white supremacy for not giving him a fair chance to fulfill his duty. While David did not leave Berdis and the kids they brought into this world together as he had done with his previous family, his inability to control his circumstances beyond the discrimination he faced drove him mad. His righteous anger was apparent in his sermons and felt deeply in his mistreatment of his wife and children.

Berdis maintained her sense of calm and her loving view of humanity but was often stifled by her husband's anger and his growing paranoia that everyone was out to get him. He was the victim of his circumstances, one who eventually could no longer see hope in his condition. The air grew heavier and heavier between them as their family grew.

In 1929, the Harlem Renaissance began to slow, and it ended soon after as a result of the stock market crash. Throughout the 1920s, the stock market was seen as a place where anybody could become rich. Virtually everyone invested in the stocks, and very few people saw this as a risky business. Even those who could not afford it took out loans to invest in the market. Prices continued to rise as more people invested, and the stock market boomed in 1928. Even with small dips like the reduced production of steel, the decrease in home construction, and the waning of car sales, people continued to have faith in their stocks. Many even invested their entire life savings. However, the market reached its peak before dropping and eventually plummeting in 1929. People panicked and started selling their stocks rapidly, in turn lowering the prices and leading to its collapse. This crash, paired with other factors of the decade, signaled the beginning of the Great Depression. Companies were ruined, families lost their savings, and people of color were hit the hardest, as they were often the last hired and first fired.

The crash also led to the end of the Harlem Renaissance. Performance venues went out of business as everyone suffered from economic turmoil, and artists were forced to find other ways to make ends meet. This era came to a close but left an unerasable mark on the portrayal and treatment of Black people, not only in the United States but across the world. One of its most impactful accomplishments was its celebration of Black pleasure and Black love—writers focused on Black relationships and Black families, singers and performers shared stories of finding love and dealing with marriage, and intellectuals discussed the role of Black unions in their continued strides toward Black liberation.

*In Alberta's love story,* we find a union that many dream of having. At the beginning of the second decade of the century, Alberta continued to grow in her passion for music and her pursuit of a career in education. She was a young woman who was concerned primarily with the future of the children in her community, who focused on her schooling, her family, and her church, leaving no room for any distractions. Her community members knew her to be a young woman who gave freely and unselfishly of her talents, her time, and her energy. She was gracious and scholarly, and she had a captivating smile. Alberta's light continued to shine and she thrived, pushing herself closer to her dreams while loving and supporting those around her. During this time, she continued her education at Spelman Seminary as a boarding student, returning home only on Sundays to attend her parents' church. She would also obtain her bachelor's degree at Morris Brown College.

During one of her visits home, she sat reading a book on her porch one evening when a young man approached her. She took a few moments before looking up. She glanced at him for several seconds and then smiled that captivating smile. She recognized him: he was one of her classmate's brothers, a young preacher by the name of Michael King. She greeted him. He was nervous, mumbling something that didn't make much sense, in awe of her and her eloquence. Trying to calm him, she asked about his work. He replied with his more rural speech: "Well, I'se preachin' in two places . . . ain't been here but a short while . . . we from down the country, an' we got a buncha brothers an' sisters." She stared at him. Then she smiled again, easing both of their nerves.

What Alberta didn't know was that this was not just a chance meeting. Michael had walked past her house every evening, trying to find his opportunity to speak with her. He'd seen her the previous summer when she'd returned home after breaking her ankle, and he'd fallen in love. His friends had made fun of him for wanting to date Alberta Williams, the well-educated and talented daughter of the Ebenezer Baptist Church, when he was just a green country boy. At the time of their meeting, Alberta was already a college student and he was continuing his middle school and high school education at Bryant Preparatory. During this time, the only way to study beyond eighth grade if you were Black was to pay for schooling, and Michael did not come from means like Alberta. His reading and writing skills were so poor, he was considered illiterate.

He had been born to two sharecroppers in Stockbridge, Georgia, in 1899. It was nearly impossible to make money sharecropping because Black people were constantly cheated from their earnings. When they approached the landowner at the end of the year to claim their profits, they were made to pay for using the land and the tools, keeping them in a perpetual state of virtually unpaid labor. As a result of the many in-dignities they were subject to, Michael's father turned to drinking. His mother, on the other hand, held on to her faith, never losing sight of the Lord. Michael grew up admiring his mother's strength, and church also became his way to avoid descending into bitterness. He became a licensed preacher at the age of eighteen.

Michael's years in Stockbridge were filled with racial terror. He himself had been beaten by a white man when Michael insisted on com-pleting a task for his mother instead of dropping everything to serve the white man. He'd also witnessed a lynching on his way home as a young boy. A Black man whom Michael did not know was also on his way home after collecting his pay from work when he was stopped by a group of white men. The white men harassed the Black man, trying to take his money. When he insisted that he needed that money for his children, they beat him mercilessly with a tree branch. They dragged him past a young Michael and hung him from a tree with one of their belts. They then proceeded to walk off laughing while Michael looked on in horror. These moments, among others, made leaving Stockbridge a necessity for Michael.

He found his way to the big city of Atlanta, following in his sister's footsteps, where she encouraged him to continue his schooling. At Bry-ant Preparatory he was introduced to activism. The principal of the school helped Michael to see that things *can* and *must* change; he specifi-cally taught Michael about the need for Black people to register to vote. Michael became a burgeoning young activist, his eyes opening to the power he had to transform what only *seemed* like a rigidly fixed world.

In the summer of 1920, a year after he'd first seen Alberta and months after they'd first spoken, Michael set out to begin their court-ship. He dropped his sister off at the Williams house and took the chance to speak to Alberta again. To his pleasure, she hadn't forgotten him. She complimented his car, and he asked if she might want to take a ride together sometime.

"But I don't know you, Reverend King," she answered.

"No better'n I know you," he replied. "Difference is that I'm interested in findin' out more about you 'cause you seem to me such a fine person, very gracious and all."

Their courtship lasted for six years before they were married.

Alberta's parents were concerned about Michael distracting her from her education. Marriage for their daughter would not be prioritized over her career. Her father told Michael that there were "no spare rooms in the house for broken hearts." At the time, there was also a law that kept married women from teaching. This "marriage bar," which called for the termination of a woman's employment after she married and even extended to some widowed women with children, lacked any logic; it was in place simply to restrict middle-class, educated women, and it was not fully terminated until 1964 with the passing of the Civil Rights Act.

Alberta's parents would not let their daughter give up on her dreams that easily. They made sure to test the young couple's commitment to each other before voicing their support. Insisting that they needed some time apart to cool things down, they sent Alberta to Virginia to pursue her teaching certificate. For a year and a half, the young couple communicated only through letters.

Yet they were unwavering in their love for each other. Upon Alberta's return, Michael swept her up in his arms, saying, "My bunch of goodness is back with me again!" He shortened "bunch of goodness" to "Bunch" and made this his official nickname for Alberta. It wasn't long before the couple announced their engagement, and they were married on Thanksgiving Day in 1926.

While they were engaged, Alberta insisted that Michael complete his education. She would say, "You're not an educated man, King, not yet. You've got work to do and you've got to get started." She even tutored him through his schooling. Alberta was not allowed to teach in schools anymore, but she used her schooling to teach her husband, her church, and her own children. She chose her marriage over an official career, a marriage filled with mutual support for each other.

This kind of love defined their many years together. Michael was fiery and quicker to anger, but Alberta gracefully balanced him out with her calmness and maturity. They moved in with Alberta's parents and followed in her parents' footsteps as the eventual leaders of the Ebenezer Baptist Church. The young couple built on the church's legacy of pairing faith with social justice and activism.

*Not all Black love* stories are allowed to flourish as peacefully as Alberta and Michael's was. Black unions have been targeted and disrupted as a strategy to uphold white supremacy. Black marriage in the United States has been intertwined with and inevitably influenced by the effects of slavery, racism, and white supremacist violence. Any efforts to build cohesive Black family units have faced the immense challenges of their respective time periods. The lack of environmental support for Black marriages and families has made them both fragile and precious.

During the earliest times of slavery, African families were separated from one another as soon as they were captured and put in groups with those who spoke different languages in order to keep them from communicating with one another. Once they arrived in the United States, many slaves were forbidden by law to marry, while others were forced to pair up in order for them to breed more children. In fact, many plantation owners gave rewards to slaves who birthed the most offspring.

Those who chose to marry even when their unions were not legally recognized constantly feared the forced separation of their families. Slaves could be sold off at any point, especially if they were young and in their prime years, whether they had a family or not. This fear allowed plantation owners to use Black love as a means of control; they could threaten to separate couples at any point for whatever reason and used this to invoke worse atrocities.

Slaves were constantly victimized sexually, making it so that their unions and vows to one another were consistently ignored. A slave could be told to impregnate another slave by force, they could be called to the master's house at any moment, they often gave birth to the master's children, and no slave could form a marriage under any semblance of peace. Still, they found ways to love each other and tried their best to protect their families.

After the Civil War, the option to marry legally became a priority for Black couples and a crucial aspect of their freedom. By 1880, 80 percent of African American families included a husband and a wife. Additionally, records show that Black women married at younger ages than their white counterparts. This was due in large part to the fact that Black women were not given many options outside of a heteronormative marriage. It was nearly impossible for a woman to take on independent agricultural work, for instance, because white men didn't believe in doing business directly with women. It was also the case that many Black people valued marriage as part of their Christian faith and their desire to protect their family units. Yet Black families continued to be separated by plantations, and they continued to face disenfranchisement, exploitation, and violence.

In later years, Black marriages were challenged by economic instability, high rates of unemployment, and poor health outcomes, all obstacles that erode relationships. They were subject to lynchings, rapes, race riots, and many forms of mass incarceration. The factors that led to the Great Migration also led to the separation of Black couples from their extended family members and their support systems.

The marriages of Berdis, Alberta, and Louise were inevitably influenced by these larger factors. Black marriage has been vulnerable to immeasurable stresses throughout the entirety of American colonial history. It is for these reasons that Black love and marriage are so revered and celebrated in the Black community. It goes without saying that Black couples, especially in the nineteenth and twentieth centuries, came up against seemingly unending obstacles, but if they survived these, they became a symbol of Black resistance. These unions evidenced that nothing was more powerful than Black couples' love for each other, that through this love the possibilities were endless.

*Out of all the* places Louise, a slender, light-skinned, five-foot-eight woman, would live throughout her life, Montreal proved to be the most peaceful outside of her home village. She arrived there during the summer of 1917, and it did not take long for her to find her community, although a small one, away from home. Canada is not exempt from historic racism and the enduring effects of slavery, but in many ways, Canadian cities served as a symbol of freedom for Black Americans in the late nineteenth and early twentieth centuries. Black Canadians also faced racism and many of the same restrictions as their American peers, yet Canada was viewed as an escape from the fierce indignities of the United States, more specifically the South. Many African Americans were not trying to make it only to northern American cities; they wanted to go as far north on the continent as they possibly could, all the way to Canada.

Louise built relationships with Black Americans, Black Canadians, and fellow Caribbeans who were also finding their way and further discovered and developed her activism by becoming an influential member of the Universal Negro Improvement Association. As a well-educated, multilingual, confident person who carried herself with her head held high, she was able to write for the *Negro World*, "a paper devoted solely to the interests of the Negro race," founded by Marcus Garvey. As a branch reporter, she became an indispensable member of her local UNIA branch.

It was in her community, mixed with other activists, that she met Earl Little, a young man just a few years her senior. At one of the chapter's organizing meetings, Louise laid eyes on a six-foot-four muscular man with dark skin. In other words, he was tall, dark, and handsome. Despite their obvious physical differences, it was the similarities between them that Louise noticed first. She knew that he too was proud of his African heritage, that he too cared about social justice, and that he had also come to Montreal in search of something better for himself. He was confident, he was self-sufficient, and he was willing to stand up to the white man. Earl was unafraid, but he had grown this sense of conviction for reasons that differed slightly from Louise's. She had been empowered, among other factors, through her family's independence and her education, one that Earl viewed as illustrious.

Earl Little had come to Montreal from his hometown of Reynolds, Georgia. Reynolds was a dangerous and violent place for Black people, and many were forced to seek refuge elsewhere. Growing up, Earl, the son of a farmhand, had seen violence firsthand, just like the young Elijah Poole. In Earl's case, four of his six brothers died as a result of violence, at least three of them at the hands of white men, and at least one was lynched. This violence fueled his desire to fight not only for his rights but for the rights of all Black people. The violence also fueled his immense anger and inability to control his actions at times.

Earl struggled with this lack of control in his previous relationship. By the time he fell in love with Louise, he had already married and left another woman in Reynolds. They had three children together. But after tiring of constantly hearing from his in-laws about his mistreatment of his first wife, compounded by the exhaustion of facing racist violence daily, he walked away from his tumultuous marriage and left his first family behind. Earl had drive and a desire to do more with his life, yet his temper was only further fed by racial injustice.

Earl was educated at no more than a third- or fourth-grade level, but he had an entrepreneurial and creative spirit. Like Jupiter, he had trained as a carpenter to make ends meet. He was a Baptist preacher and dreamed of one day opening his own small business. He left Reynolds first for Philadelphia, then for New York City, and then for Montreal, searching for meaning. When he met another dreamer, someone who also stood against white supremacy and saw herself beyond the confines of her space and time, he could not help falling in love.

Louise and Earl married on May 10, 1919. Together, they dedicated their lives not only to each other but also to the "dangerous cause of freeing the souls of Black folk" through Garveyism, as Jan Carew described it. This decision would dictate every part of the rest of their lives. They were committed to spreading Garvey's message of the African empire and Black self-reliance, even when at times Garvey appeared to be inconsistent and questionable.

Garvey's initial manifesto described his aims: "to establish a Universal confraternity among the race; to promote the spirit of the race, pride and love . . . [and] to assist in civilizing the backward tribes of Africa." He often used pageantry, exaggerated titles, and colorful uniforms to evoke additional excitement. Leaders in the movement were called "Knights of the Nile," "Knights of the Distinguished Service Order of Ethiopia," and "Dukes of Niger and of Uganda." He even crowned himself the provisional president of Africa. It didn't seem to matter that he did not have ownership over any territory on the African continent. These embellishments, among other factors, caused many to critique Garveyism for selling a "hopelessly utopian back-to-Africa movement."

Despite this, Garveyism offered many Black people hope for the future and a sense of pride, two things that both Louise and Earl cherished. Garveyism advocated for Black independence from whites through economic independence and self-reliance. Louise grew up with a version of these same lessons stemming from her grandparents, and Earl practiced them through his carpentry, seeing more ways of expanding them through entrepreneurship.

The two young activists started their mission of spreading the word of Garveyism in the United States by first settling in

Philadelphia—perhaps unknowingly crossing paths with Berdis. They lived there for only two years before moving to Omaha, Nebraska, in 1921 and continuing their journey as field organizers. Conditions were difficult for the young couple throughout the decade; as their family grew with children, their already limited resources dwindled.

In addition to their involvement in the Black freedom movement, they both raised their children and held other jobs. Louise found work as a seamstress and a domestic worker, while Earl took on jobs as a carpenter and made a little bit of money from his routine preaching. Pooling their resources, they were able to purchase a home and rely on planting vegetables and hunting for food.

Despite the difficulty of making ends meet, they were pushed to continue their Garveyist work every time they were reminded of the ills of white supremacy. Earl was an active speaker and organizer for the movement, and Louise took on the role of branch secretary. In all the cities they lived in, they were haunted by white supremacist groups such as the KKK and the Black Legion. Threats and violence followed the two young, vocal, proud activists and parents everywhere. In Omaha, they were called "uppity niggers" for owning land, for wanting to open a business, and for trying to corrupt the "good" Black people who followed the rules.

Organizing around the country forced Earl to be away from home often, leaving Louise and their children vulnerable to KKK intimidation. After several years in Omaha, the Little family moved to Wisconsin, followed by Indiana and then Michigan.

The violence Louise and Earl faced had perhaps inevitable adverse effects on their marriage. Constantly running away from threats, constantly having to start over, and constantly worrying about their survival took a toll on the ambitious couple. The tragedy is that in many ways they just wanted the same things as any other young couple of their time period. They wanted to build a life together, to own their land without issue, to provide for themselves, to teach their children self-sufficiency and pride. They thought about opening a store, and they wanted to share this feeling of agency with their diasporic community. Yet at every turn they were stopped, intimidated, and threatened, their property was destroyed or seized, their human worth and dignity were ignored. Unfortunately, they too had a tumultuous marriage. Earl's anger and despair clashed with Louise's unbreakable confidence and tenacity.

*It's interesting to see* how the quotes at the beginning of this chapter play out in the lives of David Baldwin, Michael King, and Earl Little. The first, by the Harlem Renaissance poet Jessie Redmon Fauset, offers a pithy summary of a Black man's experience in the 1920s. The creation of race dictated every single part of a Black man's life. One's ambition, schooling, and relationships were all pursued with simultaneous reactions to violent racism. The second, by Elizabeth Cady Stanton, argues that Black men were disgraceful, ignorant, and unworthy of the same dignity as their white counterparts. Stanton degrades Black men in order to further push her agenda of securing white women the right to vote.

From the moment David, Michael, and Earl were born, each faced the challenges of being seen and treated as less than, as unworthy of respect. Learning how the world viewed them threatened even their own view of themselves. The racism they faced influenced every decision they made in their lives. Their reaction to white supremacist violence dictated the kinds of men they would become, as well as the kinds of husbands and fathers they could be.

In these three men, we witness several similarities. All three were born with little means and all three were born in the Deep South. They each witnessed racial violence firsthand early on in their lives. None of them were granted opportunities to pursue their education as their wives were. They all sought something more for themselves. They had dreams for better circumstances than the ones they'd been dealt as poor southern Black men. They all tried to turn to God for salvation and as a means to make a living as preachers. They all had a hard time controlling their anger. And all three left their hometowns seeking to take control of their own lives.

Yet they also differed in several ways, and these differences would dictate the kinds of husbands and fathers they would be. These differences were influenced by their own birth families, the women they married, and the families they married into. It is impossible to know how Michael would have approached his marriage had he not had the support of the Williams family to get him through his education, to give the young couple a place to live, to make it possible for him to become head pastor of the church the family had spent years building up. Perhaps we cannot commend him for his loving nature and his peaceful marriage while castigating the actions of Earl and David. Earl and David were not able to continue their education, they had to work several jobs to try to make ends meet, and they were far away from their support systems, just like their wives.

This is not to say that the abuse and violence they brought to their families were in any way justified; it is simply that the circumstances of these three men teach us the effects of class, education, access to social capital, and familial support—things the Kings had but that the Littles and Baldwins were denied during their years together. We learn that at least in these three cases, in order for a Black couple to thrive and be able to provide for their family in peace, multiple factors need to be present, in particular an extensive support system. We have to ask ourselves as modern readers what Earl's and David's options were. They could not seek relief anywhere—they were denied more money from a better job, a safe space to voice their feelings to a therapist, protection from law enforcement, and opportunity by continuing their education. They were caught in a hopeless situation.

Through the husbands, we learn even more about the characters of the three mothers. We witness Alberta's understanding of the need for education to enable her family to thrive; she does not take this privilege for granted, and she pushes Michael to complete his own. We also learn of Alberta's reimagining of her own dreams in order to start her family. We see Berdis's ability to provide for herself and do whatever it takes to move forward. Unlike her husband, she is able to keep her calm and loving demeanor despite the seemingly unending hardships they faced. We observe Louise's constant ability to adapt to all the changing circumstances around her as she moves from place to place. We witness her ability to stand bravely in the face of racial injustice, to use her gifts to support the larger cause of liberating Black people. Their interactions with their husbands and reactions to their circumstances speak to the extraordinary women they were.

*Despite the exclusion of* Black women from the Nineteenth Amendment, on November 2, 1920, more than eight million American women voted across the United States for the first time, helping to elect Warren G. Harding in a landslide. Although Harding's presidency lasted only two years before he passed away from a heart attack, he was a wildly popular president during his time. He surprisingly delivered one of the most progressive speeches concerning race relations in the twentieth century, a speech that shook the nation.

Following his election, he traveled to Birmingham, Alabama, where he spoke to a crowd of southern whites and Blacks who were separated by a chain. He used his speech to address, among other things, the "race problem." He spoke of what would later be called the Great Migration, he highlighted the South's industrial dependence on Black labor, and he acknowledged Black men who had served in the war and pointed out their patriotism. His audience members were stunned, yet he continued. Although he did not advocate for integration, he voiced that Blacks and whites deserved a chance to "enjoy full citizenship."

Harding's presidency did not last long, and following his passing, scandal after scandal emerged about his personal affairs, but his speech meant something to both white and Black spectators. He angered white southerners who stood silently and criticized him openly following his visit. Yet his words offered a hint of progress, an acknowledgment of Black people's accomplishments in their struggle for freedom.

Black people continued their valiant fight: they demanded their rights while practicing revolutionary love.

## Part IV

## The Birth of Our Children

Raising Black children—female and male—in the mouth of a racist, sexist, suicidal dragon is perilous and chancy. If they cannot love and resist at the same time, they will probably not survive. And in order to survive they must let go. This is what mothers teach—love, survival— that is, self-definition and letting go.

—AUDRE LORDE

On its negative side it shows us that we are paying for and even submitting to the dictates of an ever-increasing, unceasingly spawning class of human beings who never should have been born at all.

—MARGARET SANGER

Like Black marriage, Black parenthood—specifically Black motherhood—is both awe-inspiring and extremely vulnerable. When a Black woman is able to choose when she will bring children into the world of her own accord, it is a revolutionary act in the context of American history. When she is able to raise her children or choose to prioritize her children over obligations outside her home, it is in many ways an incredible feat. This is especially the case in times of desperation on a national level. When the country is suffering from the effects of war, economic loss, health crises, or social upheaval, the most disadvantaged groups experience the most misfortune. They are the first to lose jobs, the first to be forgotten, and the first to be unable to feed their young.

The three mothers brought their children into the world during such a time in American history, when resources were scarce and racism was rampant. It was also a time when Black voices continued to rise and demand the rights they deserved.

Black pride movements surged. Based on the conditions they were facing, conditions that seemed only to grow worse rather than better, Black organizers called for change through political activism, boycotts, and protests. In the 1920s, groups such as the NAACP and NACW focused on challenging segregation in schools and pushing forward their anti-lynching campaigns, Negro History Week was celebrated for the first time, and Marcus Garvey reached the height of his power with more than seven hundred UNIA branches in thirty-eight states.

Louise and Earl continued spreading the message of Garveyism across the United States. And as their involvement in the movement for Black lives grew, so did their family. Their first child, Wilfred, was born in Philadelphia in 1920, and his siblings would later say that he was highly favored by his mother. Louise adored her eldest son. Having the most experience witnessing his parents' ability to stand against injustice in the many places they lived over the years, Wilfred would gain a deeper understanding of their incredible resilience.

The young couple's lives were dictated simultaneously by their pursuit of a home where they could actively resist white supremacy and their need to leave when the threats and violence they faced became too dangerous for them to endure. They joined communities of Black folks who were known for their unapologetic and bold responses to white groups, because in them the Littles could further progress their Garveyite mission.

Louise and Earl moved to Omaha, Nebraska, after a violent race riot broke out in 1919 when thousands of white mob members burned down the county courthouse and lynched a Black man. The Black community in Omaha refused to sit idly by in the face of this injustice, and many responded by fighting back with their own guns. This active resistance forced Garvey and the Littles to take note of what was happening in Omaha, and the Littles were sent there to aid in the liberation struggle. They were already being threatened by the Ku Klux Klan in Philadelphia, so they moved to Omaha in 1921.

Here, like everywhere else, they faced threats from white supremacist groups who feared the influence the couple had on the "good negroes" of the community. In the midst of verbal and physical violence, Louise and Earl brought three more children into the world. Their first daughter, Hilda, was born in 1921. Their second son and third child, Philbert, was born in 1923. Shortly after, they found themselves expecting their fourth.

One evening before putting the children to bed, Louise heard men galloping on horses toward the house. They were yelling, and when she looked through the window she could see the shotguns and rifles they brandished. Earl was away from home, traveling for work. A pregnant Louise had stayed back with the children.

Wilfred, Hilda, and Philbert watched as their mother, seemingly unafraid, opened the front door and stepped outside. She stood tall, she did not tell her kids to hide, she did not turn to run. The white men demanded to speak with her husband. They hurled insults. They warned her about what they would do if she and her husband continued to disrupt the town. Louise held her head up high and bravely told the white riders that she was alone with her three small children.

Louise knew what these white men were capable of. She knew the possibility of violence she faced at their hands. But maybe in that moment she thought of all the atrocities Black mothers had faced before her; all the times white men had degraded a Black mother while her children watched; all the heartbreak white men had caused mothers of color from the moment they'd colonized native lands. Maybe she stood tall for all of those mothers as well. Maybe she called upon them for courage and strength.

Since their arrival as slaves in America, Black women have been subject to the many abuses of white supremacy, seen most clearly in their relationship to motherhood. Slavery relied on reproduction and marked Black women and their procreation as commodities to control. Giving birth was not a Black woman's choice; it had very little to do with her will and everything to do with fulfilling a white man's economic needs. Slavery relied on Black procreation, and white slave masters did everything in their power to increase production of their most valuable resource. Black procreation was determined by the needs of plantation owners. This reality rendered slaves extremely vulnerable to sexual violence. The rape of Black women equaled financial gains, and since the law defined them as objects, Black women had no rights over their own bodies or those of their offspring. Children born to slaves were slaves, regardless of how they were conceived.

Becoming a mother did not change a slave woman's primary task of being a physical laborer for her masters, and so long as she was not killed by the abuse she endured at their hands, they were free to do whatever they wanted to her. Black mothers were not revered or respected; they were simply vessels through which new property would arrive. They barely received any time to rest during or after pregnancy, and they were still subject to beatings, even while they were pregnant.

Louise knew this history, and she knew that neither the presence of her children nor the fact that she was pregnant would protect her; but she was determined to stay strong. She was determined to never cower, especially when white men were watching. Like the Caribs on Leapers Hill, she would rather die than bow down to her oppressor.

After addressing the men, she returned inside and shut the door. Undeterred, the men surrounded the house as they shattered windows and yelled more threats. Louise placed her hand on her pregnant belly and comforted her other children in the midst of the chaos. The men eventually left. And though damage was done to the property, Louise and her children were safe, at least for that night. This moment was ingrained in her children's minds. They were proud of their mother, and they were learning what she wanted them to do in the face of injustice—stand tall.

When Earl returned, he was enraged to hear of the attack, but considering the impending arrival of their child, he resisted retaliating. Instead, he thought it would be best for the family to relocate once the baby was born. Louise gave birth to her fourth child and third son at home on May 19, 1925. The house, located at 3448 Pinkney Street, has since been demolished. Louise and Earl named their son Malcolm. Even though he was still in her womb when she faced the mob, he too was influenced by his mother's radical courage, something the world would see years down the line.

The young family moved once again, this time to Milwaukee, Wisconsin. In Milwaukee, the Littles found a budding Black community. In 1923, the Black population was estimated to be around five thousand, and this number increased by 50 percent by the end of the decade. Black workers were paid slightly more in Milwaukee. They also had a robust entrepreneurial spirit and a tangible sense of racial awareness and solidarity. Here, Louise brought another son into the world, Reginald. Reginald was unfortunately plagued with a hernia and required more care than the other children as he cried for hours on end. This worried his parents and stretched their energy even more, but the Little family pushed forward.

Their next move would take them to Lansing, Michigan, where another son, Wesley, was born in 1928 and another daughter, Yvonne, was born a year later. In 1929, Louise and Earl were able to purchase a small farmhouse on the outskirts of town. However, they did not realize that the deed for the house contained a racial exclusion clause that voided the sale if the owners were Black. These kinds of clauses were common across the United States and were used to exclude Black families from neighborhoods and economic advancement. Their white neighbors filed to evict the couple and their children from their home. Louise and Earl sought the help of a lawyer, who filed an appeal; and as they waited on the due process of the law, the family experienced yet another painful tragedy, one that happened when Yvonne was only a few weeks old.

One night as Louise, Earl, and their little ones slept, they were suddenly awakened by a boom that brought fire and smoke billowing into their home. They sprang out of bed, Louise and Earl yelling as they tried to round up their children, terrified one would get caught inside. The children, confused and scared, were running into each other and the walls, stumbling as they tried to follow their parents' directions. Thankfully, they all made it out of the burning house alive, but their property and their possessions were destroyed. A group of white men had doused the back of the house in gasoline before setting it on fire. These men didn't possess an ounce of sympathy for the children, including a newborn, who were asleep in the home. They wouldn't have cared if any of them had lost their lives or their parents that night. They would have celebrated.

Rattled, yet determined to get back on their feet, the Little family slowly recovered. Earl, a skilled carpenter, built a house with his own hands in a new area of town where they were able to acquire a cheap piece of land.

The Littles' unbelievable ability to bounce back, to be unafraid, to continue in their bold proclamation of the value of Black lives, framed the many lessons Earl and Louise taught in their household. They were proud of their militancy, proud of their roots, proud of their self-sufficiency, and they never failed to share this pride with their children.

Louise named some of her children after her relatives in Grenada, instilling her culture in them and reminding them of their extensive family ties across the world. She would have them recite the alphabet in French; she would make them read the *Negro World*, the UNIA's paper that she herself had written for, and *The West Indian*, written by the Grenadian advocate Theophilus Albert Marryshow. Louise and Earl nurtured their family with Garveyite principles of self-determination, self-reliance, discipline, and organization. The Littles were aware of current affairs and knowledgeable about global issues.

The children were also taught how to raise and grow their own food, they were even allotted their own patch of garden. Malcolm particularly loved growing peas. It made him proud to have them on the table after watching over them for weeks as they bloomed. He would spend days crawling on his hands and knees tending to his garden. He'd pick out any worms and bugs, burying them in the soil. Then he'd lay by his peas, looking up at the sky, watching the clouds pass, and think about his dreams. Here he found tranquility.

Louise and Earl's teachings showed their children the meaning of hard work, persistence, agency, and unbreakable resolve. Wilfred, Hilda, Philbert, Malcolm, Reginald, Wesley, and Yvonne would all grow up to believe in their worth as members of the African diaspora; they would be given the skills necessary to survive on their own and would later go on, in their own ways, to continue the fight their parents passed down to them.

One of the main things Garvey and his followers were known for were their parades. Hundreds of thousands of UNIA members would take to the streets in Afrocentric outfits, marching proudly, holding signs, playing trumpets and drums, as part of their annual conference. The largest of these parades took place in Harlem in August 1924. Garvey wore a military uniform with a feathered helmet as he led his members through the streets of New York City. On their way to Liberty Hall, they passed by Harlem Hospital on Lenox Avenue.

*A day later, on* August 2, Berdis sat in that same hospital as she held her baby boy for the first time. The Black maternity ward of this segregated hospital was overcrowded and understaffed, but that would not keep Berdis from her joy. On that warm and humid Saturday, James Arthur Jones, called Jimmy or Jamie by his family, came into the world screaming. Immediately, he became the apple of Berdis's eye. The two shared an unparalleled bond with one another. During James's first two years of life, they had only each other to count on, only each other to hold through the good and bad times.

Berdis struggled to make ends meet, but she eventually landed a live-in job as a domestic worker for a rich family, where she was able to provide some stability for herself and her son. In 1927, when Jimmy was a little over two years old, Berdis met and married a man, several years older than her, who seemed to genuinely love her and her son. He wanted to take care of them, to provide for them, and to build a family with them.

One of Jimmy's earliest memories was of being held by his mother and seeing his stepfather smiling at him. Looking over his mother's shoulder, Jimmy beamed as he sensed David's pride. This moment would unfortunately stand as an anomaly, something Jimmy would never experience again. As he grew up, Jimmy began to feel that his stepfather despised him. Jimmy had a hard time finding ways to please his stepfather and deal with his stepfather's anger as David's circumstances and mental state worsened.

During the Great Depression, unemployment rates rose to 25 percent in the United States. The unemployment rate among African Americans at the time reached 50 percent by 1932. Businesses were forced to reduce wages and lay off workers. Sharecroppers were evicted, families defaulted on loans, and hundreds of thousands of Americans found themselves homeless. Black people were forced to continue working the most menial jobs for even less pay than before. These effects were felt especially strongly by Black southerners who had migrated north and were now being turned away in favor of European immigrants. They could not find a break from such a bleak economic situation and lived in conditions that were sometimes worse than what they'd left behind in the South.

David was not in a position to provide sufficiently for his family, and they lived in rough conditions. As Jimmy described it, poverty and decay surrounded them—"cold slush . . . cooling piss . . . weary sweat . . . rusted dried blood"—accompanied by the presence of drug dealers and broken dreams on every street corner. In her book *The Warmth of Other Suns: The Epic Story of America's Great Migration*, Isabel Wilkerson echoes Jimmy's description when she writes about the housing conditions Black migrants were forced to endure in the North: "[Animals] roamed alleyways that reeked of rotting vermin. Front doors hung on single hinges. The sun peeked through cracks in outer walls. Many rooms sat airless and windowless, packed with so many people that some roomers had to sleep in shifts, all of which made a mockery of city codes devised to protect against these very things."

Wilkerson explains that Black tenants were also charged more than white tenants even for rooms in the poorest condition. In Harlem, "some half a million colored people were crammed into a sliver of upper Manhattan that was about fifty blocks long and only seven or eight blocks wide. A 1924 study by the National Urban League confirmed what colored tenants already knew: that colored renters paid from forty to sixty percent higher rents than white tenants for the same class of apartment."

Such inequity led to David's worsening despair and bitterness. He became meaner, it seemed, as the years went by. Jimmy's memory turned from feeling love and pride from his father to feeling scorn and mockery. His father made fun of his looks, specifically commenting on his big eyes, and called Jimmy the ugliest child he had ever seen. Jimmy took this as an insult not only to himself but to his mother, from whom he'd inherited his strong traits directly. Jimmy started to see himself and his mother as ugly, and he questioned his own worth.

One day, a young Jimmy pulled Berdis to the window when he noticed a drunk woman stumbling outside. He pointed at her excitedly and exclaimed, "She's uglier than you, Mama! She's uglier than me!" Berdis was not hurt by this. She could see that Jimmy desperately needed a reminder of his own beauty, that he needed to know how much he was loved. She tirelessly countered David's comments by holding her son and reminding him of his dignity.

As conditions grew worse for all Black Americans across the country with the approach of World War II, the Baldwin family expanded. Between 1927 and 1943, Berdis and David brought eight more children into the world: George, Barbara, Wilmer, David, Gloria, Ruth, Elizabeth, and Paula Maria. More children meant more joy, but it also meant much more strain on the budget. The family became accustomed to visits from white welfare workers and bill collectors. Each week they would pick up their package of food from Home Relief that consisted heavily of corned beef. Berdis would try to be creative with preparing it—she would "fry it, boil it, bake it, mix it with potatoes or corn bread or rice," as Jimmy would later describe—but the Baldwins grew tired of their limited options.

The pressure of it all weighed heavily on the entire family, and David could not contain his anger. Jimmy would later describe his stepfather, saying, "When he took one of his children on his knee to play, the child always became fretful and began to cry; when he tried to help one of us with our homework the absolutely unabating tension which emanated from him caused our minds and our tongues to become paralyzed, so that he, scarcely knowing why, flew into a rage and the child, not knowing why, was punished."

David became so bitter about the situation he faced as a Black man and his inability to break away from such stifling circumstances that he became less sought after as a preacher. His messages were filled with hatred, not hope. Eventually, he was also laid off from his job. There didn't appear to be a way out of the downward spiral. His wife and children did not know it at the time, but he was dealing with a mental illness that even he could not understand. He was growing more depressed and paranoid by the minute, and he began pacing the floor in his pajamas at all hours of the day, mumbling Bible verses. He often grew violent with his children, especially his stepson, fighting with them until Berdis pushed them apart.

Berdis fought a constant game of tug-of-war. The complete hopelessness and unhappiness the Baldwin children witnessed in their father was lightened only by Berdis's love and faith. If David was consumed by the crippling effects of racism, then Berdis was the cure for such a destructive disease. Berdis was her children's protector, the voice that reminded them of the importance of family unity despite whatever was happening around them. Her children have since described her as the embodiment of love. Jimmy would later describe his mother's smile, saying it was a "smile which she reached for every day that she faced her children (this smile she gave to no one else), reached for, and found, and gave . . . the smile counselled patience."

When Jimmy was a teenager, Berdis said to him, "I don't know what will happen to you in life. I do know that you have brothers and sisters. You must treat everyone the way I hope others will treat you when you are away from me, the way you hope others will treat your brothers and sisters when you are far from them." Berdis reminded her children of the need to care for one another, to love one another, and to do the same for others outside of their home.

Although David grew more intolerable over the years, Berdis and her relationship with her children grew stronger. Jimmy continued to be his mother's right-hand man. As she gave birth to her other children, Jimmy stepped in to support her in raising them. He helped to bathe them, to change their clothes, to walk them to school. He even named his youngest sister Paula Maria, who was born when he was nineteen. In the face of David's all-consuming illness, the Baldwins were still able to foster and share an incredibly deep love. David wanted all of his children to follow in his footsteps and join the ministry, consistently reminding them of their need to seek redemption in the Lord. Berdis, on the other hand, encouraged her children to follow their passions— many of them had inherited her artistic talents.

The Baldwin children found their way out of the cycle that trapped their father by focusing on their education. Jimmy was quickly noticed by his teachers as a young student with a brilliant mind, and he found mentors in school who desired to help him grow his skills, especially in writing. When he was around nine or ten, he wrote a play that was then directed by a young white schoolteacher. She could see that his talent was unique and that it needed encouragement, so she gave him books to read and asked if she could take him to see some plays.

David forbade the family from going to the theater because he saw it as sinful, and he did not trust that this white woman had Jimmy's best interests at heart. But Berdis stepped in and reminded David of the importance of Jimmy's education, even though she risked being on the other end of her husband's temper. She would not let anything get in the way of her children's futures. Against David's will, Jimmy was able to leave and see his first play, followed by many more. The teacher spent time with the Baldwins over the years and helped them through some of their tougher financial times. Her dedication, paired with Berdis's support and intervention between Jimmy and David, allowed Jimmy to follow his and his mother's shared dream of becoming a writer.

*Berdis and Louise both* gave birth to large families during a time when this was frowned upon for Black mothers, especially poor Black mothers. After the Civil War, it was no longer directly beneficial to whites for Black people to procreate. Black conception was no longer seen as a means of white economic gain. For this reason, Black women's bodies were regulated in new ways. Strategy after strategy attempted to curb Black birth rates. Some whites feared that Black people would someday outnumber them and take control of the country. Other arguments stemmed from fears of Black people taking jobs and resources from their white counterparts. And all arguments relied on racist and antiquated beliefs that Black people were less than human and did not deserve equal treatment in the country they had built. Plans to eradicate Black lives grew in numbers and variations over the years and always worsened during times of national economic insecurity like the Great Depression.

One attempt to curb African American birth rates came in the development of birth control and growth in American women's "reproductive freedom." While the advent of birth control has guaranteed several rights for women, allowing them to choose when they will or will not become mothers, giving them agency over their bodies and reproductive decisions, it also came on the wings of ugly eugenicist agendas. Building on President Franklin D. Roosevelt's "American Motherhood" speech, those originally in opposition to birth control could not see the need for white women to keep themselves from having children. But they could see the benefit of curtailing the birth of groups they found to be undesirable.

With debates around birth control increasing and desires to stop Black births growing, a new trope concerning Black women would enter the conversation later in the century. The "welfare queen" was a derogatory term used to imply that some women had children simply to receive the benefits of welfare. Images aimed at criticizing Black mothers, rather than the societal conditions that held them down, grew in popularity over the century.

Black and poor women were also targeted by forced sterilization. Thousands of women of color across the United States were sterilized against their will throughout the twentieth century. In fact, it is said that Nazis in Germany based their own forced sterilization laws on those practiced in the United States. In her book *Killing the Black Body: Race, Reproduction, and the Meaning of Liberty*, Dorothy Roberts writes that "between 1929 and 1941, more than 2,000 eugenic sterilizations were performed each year in the United States. It has been estimated that a total of over 70,000 persons were involuntarily sterilized under these [American] statutes." Black and poor women, like Berdis and Louise, were often coerced into signing papers they did not understand that "authorized" sterilization, after they'd come to a hospital for another reason, including to give birth. While the U.S. government was able to dedicate immense amounts of money and time to curbing Black women's reproduction, they never managed to match these efforts when it came to providing Black families with adequate care to make it through the hardest times.

*Already overcharged, underpaid, underprotected,* and underresourced, Black communities and families suffered worse blows during this time. Their ability to survive through such obstacles would once again be a testament to their extraordinary strength, creativity, and persistence. In fact, the Great Depression only furthered the efforts of Black organizers. And during times of such great need, Black churches were essential. Faith leaders widened their community outreach and increased social services to their members, banding closer together to collect clothing, food, and money for one another. Many Black churches like Ebenezer Baptist also found housing for their members.

Alberta and Michael would inherit Ebenezer Baptist during the Great Depression and would have to rally their members and fundraise money to keep their doors open and their services available. But before they embarked on their journey as the new leaders of the church, Alberta and Michael began their journey as parents. A year after their wedding, while Alberta focused on teaching music and Michael continued to work on completing his studies, the couple found themselves expecting their first child.

On September 11, 1927, Alberta gave birth to a daughter in an upstairs bedroom of their two-story home. Willie Christine King arrived earlier than expected, even before her parents had the chance to buy her crib, and for the first few days they laid her in a drawer. Their daughter brought the young couple immediate joy, yet her first few weeks of life were filled with crisis and anxiety. She cried at the top of her lungs, shaking violently through the days and nights; she had a high fever that refused to come down, and no one could find any remedy for her distress. Alberta was incredibly weakened by the birth, and her baby's illness only worsened her ability to recover. With all the worry, Michael found himself pacing outside at night in front of the patio where he'd first introduced himself to Alberta, praying to God for peace and guidance.

One night, after several weeks of this distress, Willie Christine's crying ceased suddenly. Alberta and Michael ran to the room to see their daughter sleeping peacefully at last. They would never know what caused the painful symptoms, but Michael went on to say that he believed Willie Christine's difficult entry into the world strengthened her soul for the pain her family would endure in her adult years. Before then, the small family would enjoy happiness too grand for words to describe. The Kings seemed to be natural parents, and they found the utmost joy in their daughter.

Sixteen months following Willie Christine's arrival, the couple welcomed their second child into the world. On a cold Tuesday morning in the middle of January, Alberta was at home with her husband and daughter, as well as her parents and other family members who were visiting from out of town, when her contractions began. The women, including Alberta's midwife, escorted Alberta to the room upstairs and closed the door while Michael was left to pace and wait outside. Worried about his wife, he stayed close to the door, listening to Alberta move through her labor. Before he knew it, he heard his son's first cries right around noon. He jumped up and touched the ceiling in excitement.

He wouldn't be let into the room until the women had cleaned everything up—childbirth wasn't seen as something for men to be involved in—so he waited anxiously as he heard their movements and laughter. When Michael was finally allowed to enter, he saw Alberta sitting up in bed with their baby, Michael Jr., snuggled next to her. In awe, he moved closer to join them. The newborn was already strong and observant as he held his parents' fingers and took in the little he could see of his new world.

Although she'd been weakened by this birth as well, Alberta wanted a large family and insisted on having a third baby. In July 1930, the couple's second son and last child, Alfred Daniel, given the same initials as Alberta's father, was born. The children brought Alberta and Michael more fulfillment than either had ever experienced before, and their family became their top priority.

All of their children were forming unique personalities and paths early on. Christine, the eldest and only girl, was quiet and polite, so gentle and well behaved that she was often teased by her younger brothers. She took after her mother and dreamed of becoming an educator someday. Michael Jr., their middle boy, was always a sensitive child who preferred to negotiate and compromise over losing his temper. He took after his father's growing talent for orating and had his mother's love of music and singing. He was also a prankster. Sometimes he would hide in the bushes outside his house, place Alberta's fox furs on sticks, and poke them out to scare people passing by. Their youngest, Alfred Daniel, was the rebel of the three. He was rougher around the edges, fiery like his father but also determined to steer in his own direction, away from what his father wanted him to do.

The Kings raised their children as Alberta had been raised. The couple embedded love and respect in all of their teachings. The children spent their early years in Alberta's childhood home and attended Ebenezer Baptist. Michael Sr. and Alberta balanced each other: Michael angered more easily and was more strict with the children; Alberta was strict, too, but gentler in her approach; calm and collected.

The family operated on the rules of a tight ship. The three children always arrived at school on time. As soon as they returned home, they completed their homework, then divided up the chores, and after the family sat down for dinner together, the children studied and prayed before bed. Later in his life, Michael Jr. would describe his home situation as congenial and a place where love was central. He could not recall any instance of his parents fighting, even during hard times.

Encouraged and tutored by Alberta, Michael Sr. finished his schooling at Morehouse College just a few weeks after Alfred Daniel was born. The boys arrived in this world at the onset of the Great Depression, which swept through their city with extreme force. In Atlanta, 70 percent of Black workers were jobless by 1934. Times were difficult for everyone, and Michael Sr. assumed the pulpit at two different churches in order to help make ends meet. Members of their churches would bring food to the King family, making sure they were still well fed and supported as they provided their support and services to the community.

The King family was not rich, but they were well taken care of, and they lived with comforts that many other Black families could only dream of. Still, they did not turn a blind eye to segregation and inequality in the South. The King family was raised in lessons of social justice and progress. They were well aware that they needed to be prepared for a life where death and violence were always near.

Alberta and Michael Sr. knew the importance of teaching their children about these realities despite the privileges they were able to enjoy. They were still a Black family in danger of white supremacist violence. It did not matter how educated they were, nor did it matter how nice their home was, they too faced some of the ugliest forms of racism. Alberta and Michael had to teach their children how to stand up to injustice both in words and in practice. They also understood how essential it was to make sure their children knew their worth in a world where they would be pushed to question it.

At the age of six, Michael Jr. accompanied his father downtown. The two, who loved spending quality time together, exchanged stories and laughter as they drove to a shoe store. As soon as they entered, a white clerk approached them, not to see if they needed help, not to ask what they were looking for that day, but to remind them that they needed to go to the back of the store.

Michael Sr. replied that they were happy at the front. He said proudly, "We'll either buy shoes sitting here, or we won't buy shoes at all."

The clerk was infuriated. He looked the father and son up and down and said there were no exceptions. "You take it like everybody else, and stop being so high and mighty!" he yelled.

Michael Jr. looked up at his father, confused, since all he'd wanted was to find a new pair of shoes. Michael Sr. grabbed his son as tears began to build in the boy's eyes and walked out of the store. In the car he tried to explain the situation, but Michael Jr. was still frustrated; he just couldn't understand. It was even clearer then just how ridiculous Jim Crow was. Michael Sr. couldn't fully explain it because his bright young son was right—it simply didn't make sense.

On another day, Michael Sr. and his eldest son were driving when a white policeman began riding slowly beside them, then signaled for them to pull over. Michael Sr. realized that he'd accidentally driven past a STOP sign.

"All right, boy, pull over and let me see your license," the officer said.

Michael Sr. knew his son was watching him and quickly responded, "Let me make it clear to you that you aren't talking to a boy. If you persist in referring to me as 'boy,' I will be forced to act as if I don't hear a word you are saying." His words were incredibly risky, but Michael Sr. chose to teach his children of their worth and the need to put their fear aside to stand up for what was right.

On both occasions, Michael Jr. returned home seeking his mother's comfort. Alberta would hold him and reinforce the lessons his father had displayed. Michael Jr. would always remember his mother's teachings:

> She told me about slavery and how it ended with the Civil War. She tried to explain the divided system of the South—the segregated schools, restaurants, theaters, housing; the white and colored signs on drinking fountains, waiting rooms, lavatories—as a social condition rather than a natural order. She made it clear that she opposed this system and that I must never allow it to make me feel inferior. Then she said the words that almost every Negro hears before he can yet understand the injustice that makes them necessary: "You are as good as anyone."

In 1931 and 1933, the King family faced two losses that would change the course of their lives. On a spring day in March 1931, Christine was in the kitchen helping her grandmother make breakfast when the two heard a loud noise. First Lady Williams sent her granddaughter to see what the thump was. The little girl returned a few moments later to tell her grandmother that Granddaddy was "sleeping on the floor." Reverend Williams, Alberta's father, had suffered a stroke in the living room. After thirty-two years of marriage, Jennie Celeste had lost her husband. After thirty-seven years of having him on the pulpit, Ebenezer Baptist had lost their pastor. And at the age of twenty-seven Alberta had lost her father. Alberta, who was extremely close to both her parents, took his death in great grief. Reverend Williams's passing led Michael King to become the new head of Ebenezer Baptist, following in his father-in-law's footsteps.

The second loss came with the news of Michael's father's passing. Throughout his life, Michael's father had insisted that he'd named his son Martin after one of his brothers and Luther after his other. On his deathbed, during his final hours, he asked his son, Michael Sr., to officially change his name to what it was meant to be. After witnessing his father stop drinking and turn to the Lord before his final days, Michael Sr. fulfilled his father's wish and changed his name and his son's to Martin Luther.

*In their own ways,* these three mothers were responding to the history that shaped them and the circumstances that surrounded them. Their approach to motherhood was based on their strong beliefs and their political awareness, in addition to the lessons they had learned from the way they had been brought up. For all three women, having and raising proud children was part of their religious and political institutions. Alberta, Berdis, and Louise made decisions that were not arbitrary but instead reflected their deep awareness of their participation in larger systems.

We cannot understand the Littles, Kings, and Baldwins without understanding African American history as well as the unique backgrounds of both parents heading the household. Without knowing about Black women's struggle to take control of their ability to have children, one would have a harder time understanding the three women's decisions to have large families. Without knowing about the refusal to allow Black women to be present for their children first and the rest of the world after, it is difficult to understand why each woman accepted the need to put her children and family over her own career. Without knowing the circumstances in which the three sets of parents were raised, we lack important context in understanding the decisions each made in raising their own children.

Louise, Berdis, and Alberta give us perspectives that we can use to better understand what Black families across America faced during the 1920s and 1930s. Despite many differences, all three families faced difficulties making ends meet as a result of national economic strains. All three families faced the hardships of dealing with illness, whether physical or mental, with little support outside of their family; the best medical care was kept from Black families, leaving them in a position to hope for the best and worry about the worst without clear answers from doctors.

The Littles, Kings, and Baldwins also dealt with racial violence, unable to escape its everlasting grasp on their lives. The families dealt with these factors in unique ways, yet in some form or another they all addressed the importance of familial unity and passed down what they learned from generations before them: Louise and Earl passed down the importance of self-sufficiency; Alberta and Martin passed down the importance of social justice; and Berdis, more so than David, passed down the importance of love and acceptance for all. Finally, all three families made decisions based on their Christian faith, although their approaches differed widely.

There are far more differences between the three families than simi-larities. Many of the differences were dictated by varying levels of priv-ilege, in both economic and social capital. The families provide insight into the ways in which societal pressures seep into the fabric of every family and affect them differently depending on the support systems they have in place to stand up against such pressures. Out of the three families, the Kings had the most economic, social, and familial support; these factors allowed them to receive the best education, to live in the best conditions, and to grow even more in their faith.

The Littles had less economic and familial capital, but they did have some social support through their affiliation with the UNIA. Louise was able to provide her children with a global education as well. Earl was also able to use his own skills to literally rebuild what was taken from them. Their philosophy of self-reliance and their knowledge of several survival skills carried them forward. Out of the three families, the Baldwins had the least in terms of money and education; they were also separated from familial support. I do not believe it is a coincidence that they faced some of the unhappiest family circumstances, including violence in the home and unrecognized mental illness. Yet the Baldwins also speak to a family's ability to counteract the negative forces acting against them.

Through Berdis we witness an incredible ability to forgive, to pro-vide, and to love no matter how impossible things might seem. In fact, in the lives and decisions of all three women, we witness the undeniable role they played in shaping and sustaining their families. Had it not been for Louise's life experiences, the Little family would have had a much smaller understanding of the world. Had it not been for Alberta's life experiences, the King family would not have had the means they were able to enjoy or the maturity with which she counseled them. And had it not been for Berdis's life experiences, the Baldwins could have crumbled under the stress of discontent and resentment.

Each of the three mothers held strongly to her belief in her family's and her own inherent dignity, potential, and ability to make a lasting impact on the world. After everything they'd lived through and seen, all three mothers knew their children's lives mattered, their husband's lives mattered, and their own lives mattered, and they would not succumb to anyone or anything that told them differently.

## Part V

## Our Trials, Tribulations, and Tragedies

I am an American citizen and by God, we
all have inalienable rights and whenever and
wherever those rights are tampered with, there is
nothing left to do but fight . . . and I fight.

—FREDI WASHINGTON

As a rule, the Negro woman as wife or mother
was the mistress of her cabin. . . . Neither
economic necessity nor tradition had instilled
in her the spirit of subordination to masculine
authority. Emancipation only tended to confirm
in many cases the spirit of self-sufficiency which
slavery had taught.

—EDWARD FRANKLIN FRAZIER

The three women's lives vacillated between pain and joy. They raised their children through times of great social upheaval outside of their homes, and they also experienced tragedies within their family that rocked the foundation of their existence. But their pain shows us the strength of their continued ability to push forward. By remembering the events taking place beyond their homes—race riots, the onset of World War II, strides in African American freedom movements—we are able to see how each woman navigated loss and triumph both in and outside of her family unit. The way Alberta, Louise, and Berdis dealt with their own agony gave their children the strength to push through the suffering they would experience in the future.

In many ways, Alberta's life was the easiest in her younger years as compared with Louise's and Berdis's. Her parents were able to provide her with a stable home, a loving community, and the education they desired for her. They laid the groundwork that set her up for success and in turn provided for her children and their children after them. Alberta was able to stay in the South and thrive: she could support her husband through his journey and pass on her knowledge to her children. This is not to say that Alberta was not required to work hard and persist through her own challenges, but the generational resources her parents built for her gave her a cushion the other two women were not as fortunate to enjoy.

Alberta's father, Reverend Adam Daniel Williams, the son of a slave exhorter from Greene County, Georgia, arrived in Atlanta at the age of thirty. At the time of his arrival, he was not aware of all the incredible things he would accomplish before his death, for his family, his church, and his larger Black community. Under his and his wife's thirty-seven years of leadership, Ebenezer Baptist Church became one of the most central and influential parts of Atlanta's Black community. He took the church from a small gathering of people to one of the largest congregations in the country. He'd lived through the horrific race riot of 1906, when white mobs killed and attacked as many Black people as they could, and he'd spoken up against such injustices. He made himself known as a person who would not stand by but would make as many changes in the world as he possibly could or die trying. He and his wife were some of the earliest members of the NAACP. They led boycotts and other demonstrations, never wavering in their fight for freedom.

Alberta's mother, Jennie Celeste, had also become well-known in Atlanta for her work alongside her husband and other freedom fighters. She was born in Atlanta in 1873 as one of thirteen children. She married Adam Daniel in 1899 after attending Spelman Seminary and being the president of Ebenezer Baptist Church's Women's Missionary Society. She cared deeply about uplifting and highlighting the role women played in the Black church and in the Black freedom movement. Mrs. Williams was known and appreciated for many things, including her cooking, her fervent support of her daughter's education and musical training, her welcoming of everyone into her home (especially those who did not have a peaceful one of their own), and the respect she commanded as the pious first lady of Ebenezer Baptist for all those years.

Reverend Williams and Jennie Celeste made everything possible for Alberta and her family. Reverend King also owed much of his fortune to his father-in-law; without Reverend Williams opening his home and mentoring Reverend King, the King family would not have enjoyed the same levels of comfort. But the decade of Alberta's life taking place between the early 1930s and the early 1940s would be different. The death of her father was one of the most difficult losses of her existence.

When Reverend Williams was seventy and Alberta only twenty-seven, he suffered a fatal stroke. Alberta was devastated; her father and mother had given her everything. Her family would have to go on without his presence, holding on to the memories of his life and his works to guide them. The year of his death was the same year that nine Black boys were falsely accused of raping two white women on a train less than 150 miles away from Atlanta in Scottsboro, Alabama. Alberta, her mother, and her husband would need to remember Reverend Williams's bravery in the face of racial injustice. As more gains in Black freedom were fought for and won, more violence against Black people arose. Tactics to suppress Black advancement heightened and adapted.

Hours after the young Black men were accused, word spread and a white mob rallied around the jail where they were being held. By a stroke of luck, the mob was unsuccessful in getting to the boys, who miraculously went on to stand trial. They anxiously awaited their fate, well aware of the injustice and prejudice they would face in court. In the first set of trials, an entirely white jury convicted all of them. Only one was spared from being sentenced to death. Instead, he was given a life sentence because he was a minor. The verdict held even after one of the women recanted her testimony and a medical examination refuted the rape charge.

The Scottsboro boys became known across the world; their story incited uproar, and groups rallied together all over the United States to protest the guilty verdicts. Two landmark decisions happened along the way, one being *Powell v. Alabama* (1932), which ruled that the boys had been denied their right to counsel in violation of what they were entitled to under the Fourteenth Amendment. The second took place in 1935 when the U.S. Supreme Court overturned the guilty verdicts, ruling that the boys were denied a fair trial when Black people were systematically excluded from jury rolls. The Scottsboro case helped to fuel the rise of the upcoming civil rights movement, but it wasn't until 2013 that all the boys were posthumously pardoned by the Alabama Board of Pardons and Paroles. The nine young men spent years in and out of prison and were never able to recover from the pain of the torture they endured. One died at age thirty-nine, another killed himself, another was shot in the head by a prison guard, another was denied treatment for a disease he had been originally taking the train out of town to treat, another turned to drinking. Few of the nine were able to live stable lives following the tyrannical ordeal.

Blacks in the South, and the rest of the country, were continuing to fight for their basic human rights, like the ability to ride a train without being falsely accused of a crime or the right to a fair trial with a jury of their peers when facing accusations. Change needed to happen, and the lessons of Reverend Williams would continue to ring in the ears of the King family and motivate their own political action. In the 1930s, both Alberta and Martin became active members of the NAACP. Alberta would also go on to join the Phyllis Wheatley branch of the YWCA, named after a woman who was sold into slavery at the age of seven and went on to become the first published African American female poet in American history. Alberta was also a member of the Women's International League for Peace and Freedom. Each of these groups was dedicated to the empowerment and liberation of the most marginalized. In these organizations, Alberta carried forward her parents' legacy and fought alongside her husband and other activists for the freedom of all people.

The end of this decade brought the second in a series of tragedies Alberta would face. In 1941, her mother, Jennie Celeste Williams, died after suffering a heart attack while serving as the Women's Day speaker at Mount Olive Baptist Church. Mrs. Williams adored her daughter and her grandchildren. She played an essential role in raising the three King children. Her death was especially traumatic for the young Martin

Luther King, Jr. The loss weighed heavier on him than it did on his siblings, and he felt that God was punishing him for his sins by taking his grandmother away. The day of her death, twelve-year-old Martin had decided to skip out on homework and see a parade. When he returned home to the news of his grandmother's passing, he blamed himself and fell into a depression. His parents were able to talk him out of the guilt and grief he felt, but the whole family faced a deep sadness when Jennie Celeste passed.

Alberta's entire world was rocked by losing both of her parents by the age of thirty-seven. She was fortunate to have her own family now, one built with the same love and faith that she was raised in, but life would certainly never be the same. With the passing of her parents, Alberta and Martin Luther Sr. fully stepped into their roles as the new leaders of Ebenezer Baptist Church. Alberta went from being the adored only child of the Williams family to the revered first lady of the church, known affectionately to thousands as "Mama King."

It would be many years before the King family would experience such severe trauma again—losses that would come once more in sequence, with unimaginable intensity. They would coincide with growing racial tension, and this was not a coincidence. The King family were active members in the fight for Black humanity, which meant their losses were tied directly to the larger struggles taking place across the country. But for now, the young family thrived in the abundance of love and strength that filled the community they were continuing to build.

*When he was only* eight years old, Jimmy's heart broke as he watched his mother crying. Berdis had received news that her father, Alfred, had died. She wept as she thought of him, recalling their years out on the water together and the stories he told her about her own mother. Although they were only two states away from each other, being short on money kept Berdis from seeing her father in his last years. Now, with his passing, all she wanted was to be able to attend his funeral in Maryland. Her husband, David, didn't approve of the trip because of the cost, but Jimmy could not bear the sight of his mother's pain. Somehow, he came up with the money she needed. He helped her into the car before returning upstairs to his disapproving stepfather. He didn't care how his father felt; he was proud to have given his mother the means to properly say goodbye.

Berdis suffered her earliest tragedy when her mother died from a pulmonary hemorrhage. She came into this world without knowing her mother, and she latched on to her father and her older siblings. By the time she lost her second parent, however, she'd spent several years away from them and away from her home. Her inability to travel back and forth to see family members made their passing even harder to face. This was the case for most Great Migrants: they could return home only to say their goodbyes. Taking their chances in the North meant losing connections and much of their support system. Money was spent on surviving in the North and not returning to the places they had escaped from unless they absolutely had to.

The tragedy Berdis faced day in and day out through the 1930s and the early 1940s was her husband's worsening condition and demeanor. Jimmy described it by saying, "My mother paid an immense price for standing between us and our father. He had ways of making her suffer quite beyond our ken. . . . (We were all, absolutely and mercilessly, united against our father.)" Jimmy acknowledged the amount of suffering Berdis must have undergone all on her own, suffering that neither her children nor many of us today could ever fully know or understand. Berdis tried to protect her children from David's rage, which put her in his path of anger and violence.

About his stepfather, Jimmy would say, "He could be chilling in the pulpit, and indescribably cruel in his personal life and he was certainly the most bitter man I have ever met." The Baldwin family did not know it at the time, but David was suffering from mental illness, one that would eventually eat him from the inside out. His paranoia started to consume him so much that he did not feel he could trust anyone around him.

David's family had grown so accustomed to his odd ways—his telling people that they were "in league with the devil," his accusing his children's friends of intending to rob them, his punctuating all of his sentences with moans and hallelujahs—that they could not identify his cries for help. It wasn't until he refused to eat, out of fear that his family was trying to poison him, that they realized something more severe was happening. By this point, it was too late.

Being the victims of continued hardship and threats of violence took its toll on the minds and souls of Black people. Lacking institutional support or the means to seek individual therapy, many could rely only on each other and their churches for consultation. In cases where mental illness made them fear others and forced them to isolate themselves, there was little hope for intervention or treatment. The few facilities that existed to address Black mental illness were extremely underfunded, and they treated their patients more like prisoners. Many patients would not be given access to a bed, others would be shackled to each other, and none would receive adequate care for their needs.

After years of being experimented on and lied to, Black families rightfully questioned the intentions of any white medical professional. During this same decade when David was spiraling into the descent of his life, a study was conducted at the Tuskegee Institute in Alabama. The study involved six hundred Black men, four hundred of whom were sick with syphilis. The men were told they were being treated in order to understand their disease better and would be given free medical exams, meals, and burial insurance. Researchers originally stated that the study would last for only six months, but it ended up lasting for *forty years*. It was discovered that none of the men were being given adequate treatment, despite the fact that effective treatment became available; instead, they were unethically being studied to better understand the progression of untreated blood diseases.

Still today, many Black families, especially those with members who live with mental illness, fear what might happen if they call for help. There have been numerous cases throughout history where Black people with mental illness have been locked away or even killed by those who were called to help them. In her book *When They Call You a Terrorist: A Black Lives Matter Memoir*, Patrisse Khan-Cullors describes her brother's mental illness and the ways it has been exacerbated by the unjust criminalization and institutional abuse he's endured over the years. She states, "There are more people with mental health disorders in prison than in all of the psychiatric hospitals in the United States added up." She recounts one of her brother's mental breakdowns, where she felt that he desperately needed to get to the hospital but did not know how to get him there safely. She knew they couldn't call the police; they could rely only on their family. As a means of protecting their loved ones, many Black family members would rather endure the severity of the illness than seek outside help, moving beyond their home only as a final resort.

Berdis eventually reached this final resort and decided to have David committed. Pregnant with their ninth child, she could no longer spend energy forcing him to eat, and she could not watch him waste away. Once he arrived at the hospital, he was diagnosed with both mental illness and tuberculosis. Even the doctors were unable to get him to eat, and they were forced to feed him intravenously until he died shortly after being committed. Before David passed, Berdis urged her eldest son to pay his stepfather a visit and gain the closure he needed to let go of the hatred he'd carried for so many years. Jimmy hesitantly accompanied his aunt to the hospital, and upon seeing his weakened stepfather, he realized his mother was right: he needed to surrender any disdain. Reflecting on this moment, Jimmy later said, "I imagine that one of the reasons people cling to their hates so stubbornly is because they sense, once hate is gone, that they will be forced to deal with pain." The day after Jimmy's visit, on July 29, 1943, David Baldwin breathed his last breath. Only a few hours later, Berdis gave birth to a baby girl, whom Jimmy named Paula Maria.

Despite the hardship David had caused for his wife and his children, his death was a painful loss to endure. It was tragic to realize that much of his violence came as a result of something he did not understand, something he did not know how to control. Thinking back to the beginning of their relationship, Berdis would remember a man who had his eyes set on a better future and who genuinely wanted to provide for her and her son. Without him there, it became even more difficult to provide for nine kids all on her own as a Black woman in a racist and sexist society.

David's funeral took place a few days later, on Jimmy's birthday. The chapel was filled with David's relatives, people who hadn't seen him in years, and his children. One by one they said their last words to the body lying lifeless in the casket. Berdis was not there. She was attending to her newborn and perhaps already focusing on her new life, free from him. Years later, Berdis's grandson would describe Paula's birth as completing Berdis's solar system, with Berdis in the middle and her nine children surrounding her. He would also describe David's death as the moment that allowed Berdis's light to fully shine like the sun. She'd lost both of her parents, she was isolated in the North, away from family, and she was now a single mother of nine at the age of forty-one. She would have to do whatever she could to provide for her children, but she would, as she always had, find a way.

*In September 1931, Malcolm* remembered his home feeling filled with tension as his parents argued and discussed the Black Legion's latest threats against them. The Black Legion was a white supremacist group based in the Midwest; they were militant, made up largely of public officials, and set on terrorizing Black residents. The Black Legion had threatened the Littles for being vocal about Black rights, and their many attacks on the family caused extreme stress within the home.

Malcolm recalled his father leaving the house in anger after the argument, slamming the front door behind him. His mother, Louise, ran after her husband, calling his name. Earl turned to look at her and wave, then kept walking. Louise came back inside crying, unable to shake the feeling that something was about to happen to him. Hours passed, and when Earl hadn't returned by bedtime, Louise held her children tightly, worrying as they slowly fell asleep. The next thing Malcolm remembered was his mother screaming. He made his way downstairs to find police in the living room. Louise was going to accompany them somewhere, and Malcolm knew immediately that something terrible had happened to his father.

One officer by the name of Lawrence G. Baril had been called to the scene of a streetcar accident. There, he found a man who it seemed had almost been "cut in two." This man was Earl, and he'd been taken to the local hospital in critical condition. He was in horrendous pain for hours; "his left arm had been crushed, his left leg nearly severed from his torso." He bled to death, and when Louise arrived at the hospital, she was asked to identify his lifeless body. She was only thirty-four years old, staring at her mutilated husband, her seven young children waiting at home. The terror she must have experienced in that moment is unimaginable, but this was only the beginning of her torment.

To make matters worse—something that seemed impossible— Earl's death was ruled an accident by the Lansing coroner. An article in the local newspaper was titled "Man Run Over by Street Car [*sic*], Earl Little, 41, Fatally Hurt; Thought to Have Fallen Under Truck." The Black residents of Lansing knew better, though. This could not have been an accident. After the many threats the Littles had received from white supremacist groups, after they'd been harassed at their home and their property had been burned down, Earl's death came across as the latest development in an ongoing racist war on the family. Louise and the children were told by their fellow Black community members that the Black Legion was involved and that Earl had been shoved under the streetcar. Louise believed this to be true. She knew it was no accident: her husband had been murdered.

Malcolm recalled years later that in the aftermath of her husband's death, his mother was set on continuing to provide for her family. I am sure Louise thought of her grandmother's ability to carry on even after her grandfather passed. She too was left with seven mouths to feed. Earl had purchased two life insurance policies in order to protect his wife and children were anything to happen to him. The couple was well aware of the threats against their lives, and because they valued their independence so deeply, they had prepared for a moment like this. The smaller of the two policies was paid to Louise, but the larger one was denied her when she was told that her husband had committed suicide. Louise was also pursued by petitioners to the probate court who stated that she owed them money for past services. Some claimed they had helped with the birth of her children, others that Louise owed them for arbitrary work they had provided over the years.

With their mother doing everything in her power to make ends meet amid being denied money she was rightfully due and dealing with others hoping to capitalize on her vulnerability, the eldest children stepped up to support their younger siblings. Wilfred tried to find any job he could and used his father's gun to hunt for food. Hilda became her younger siblings' second mother and took jobs as a babysitter for other children when she could. Through their unified efforts, the Littles were able to persist for a few more years, but they were now under the careful and invasive watch of welfare workers, who would enter their house from time to time, uninvited. Over the years, many families have come to resent welfare because of its ability to take away their right to privacy and dignity. Strangers are suddenly given access to a family's home at any time of the day, and many mothers, especially mothers of color, report feeling disrespected and looked down upon when they collect the services they need for their children.

Relying on the state was a source of shame for Louise, the proud Garveyite, and Malcolm remembered his mother being even more willing to pass as a white woman in order to earn some extra money whenever possible. Yet Louise continued to hold her head high, still standing up when the white man at the store tried to cheat her at the register or speaking her mind if welfare workers tried to treat her as inferior. She was viewed as far too resistant for their liking, and over time, welfare workers started pulling Louise's older children aside to ask them questions about their mother and to tell them that she was unwell.

In the midst of all this darkness, a small beam of light appeared in 1935. Louise met a man in Lansing through mutual friends. He, like Earl, was tall, well built, dark, and handsome. He was independent and happened to be single. Louise felt that if she had a man in the household to help her provide for her children, the people from the state would go away and stop invading her family's privacy. She started to fall in love with her new beau and find some joy in her life again. She had a reason to wear her dresses again, and she laughed more than she had in years. Their relationship developed over the course of the following months. Louise was pregnant with her eighth child, Robert, when, suddenly, the man stopped coming to see her. Perhaps he became too overwhelmed by the obligation of caring for a woman and her children, with a new one on the way. He did not come back, and Louise could not believe the reality of her continued misfortune.

A severe depression overtook her. She could not provide for her children on her own, and she was degraded and disrespected by state workers who clearly did not honor her as a mother and who questioned her fitness for raising her children. She was grieving the loss of her husband and now nursing a broken heart while growing another life inside of her. Had she had access to support that did not demean her, like a therapist who could help her deal with the gravity of her losses, she could have recovered more quickly; but this was not available to her as a Black woman, and she was forced to deal with her pain—inconceivable pain—largely on her own.

The Little children were dealing with their grief as well. They had lost their father, heard the differing rumors about the circumstances of his death, experienced hunger, seen strangers come in and out of their home, heard these strangers speak about their mother in degrading ways, witnessed their mother being courted and then abandoned, and seen her lose her own sense of joy, not only once but twice. They all reacted in their own ways: the eldest did their best to act older than they were and provide for their family; others lashed out; and Malcolm started shoplifting. Louise was blamed for the burden her children were carrying and the different ways in which each of them was reacting to the trauma. A campaign to take them away from her began.

On January 3, 1939, a white male doctor by the name of E. F. Hoffman wrote a letter to the probate court for the state of Michigan. In it he recorded his observations after examining Louise. He stated, "I certify that in my opinion said Louise Little is an insane person and her condition is such as to require care and treatment in an institution for the care, custody and treatment of such mentally diseased persons. . . ." He went on to list his reasons for arriving at such a conclusion:

> Mrs. Little gives a history of maladjustment over a period of years. Began talking to herself a few years ago following the death of her husband. She has gradually lost interest in family, has had a decided change of personality and has neglected the care of the children to the point of their becoming delinquent. Recently she has given birth to a child. She has had several controversies with various agencies and is extremely suspicious of everyone. She claims people talk about her and point at her when on the

street. She claims to have been discriminated against. . . .
Diagnosis: The patient is suffering from a paranoid condition, probably dementia praecox.

Louise's experiences as a poor Black immigrant woman in a racist city were completely ignored and misunderstood. Her ability to
provide for her children for nearly a decade following her husband's
death is described as "maladjustment." Her depression is described as a
"change of personality." She is judged for the recent birth of her child,
she is punished for standing up against agencies that did not treat her
with dignity, and she is called insane for insinuating that she is discriminated against. The doctor believed she was *imagining* the discrimination she faced.

Her very logical responses to tragedy and her experiences as an
immigrant woman of color were diagnosed by a white man in such a
way that made it possible for her rights to be completely disregarded.
Louise's property was seized; her children were taken away from her,
separated, and put in foster homes. She was forced to check into the
psychiatric ward of the Kalamazoo State Hospital to treat her "dementia praecox." She would be held there against her will for *twenty-five*
years. Because she did not have immediate family old enough to demand her release from the hospital, she was given no choice but to
comply with the state's decision to have her put away.

The Kalamazoo State Hospital was overcrowded, and the doctors
who worked there had been known to go as far as performing "brain
operations" on patients to "give mentally ill recovery a chance." One
operation consisted of making "circular cuts in certain nerve tracts."
Other potential interventions included moral treatment, the most hu-
mane option of all, where patients were simply encouraged to partake
in recreational activities such as basketry, weaving, plays, and gardening; hydrotherapy, "which consisted of saturating bed sheets with either hot or cold water, then wrapping the entire body like a mummy

for several hours"; early chemical therapy, where arsenicals, mercury, and bismuth were injected into patients; insulin coma therapy, where various levels of insulin were injected until the patient went into several brief comas; and electroconvulsive therapy, which consisted of administering electric shocks that often led patients to secrete fluids from their mouths. In other words, patients were subject to various experimental treatments that were not supported by any reliable science.

I do not know what exactly Louise endured during her time at Kalamazoo. Most of her medical records at the state hospital were written by her doctors in the notes they shared with each other and the state. In one note, she was denied the visitation of her child by the hospital. A doctor wrote, "I would not advise that the child be brought to visit the mother. . . ." In another letter, it's noted that "at times she is disagreeable and resistant. . . . The prognosis in her case still is not favorable."

Louise was not granted the privilege to share her own thoughts on seeing her children, one who was less than a year old when he was taken from her, nor could she voice how she felt about her time in the hospital. Depending on whatever she faced while under the doctors' care, she easily could have developed the symptoms they diagnosed her with at the beginning of her stay. These symptoms would only have confirmed their recommendation of keeping her away from her family for longer. The murder of her husband as well as her forced institutionalization and the erasure of her voice for twenty-five years can all be read as a continued racist attack on the Little family.

*Alberta, Berdis, and Louise* were shaped by the extreme changes facing the nation as well as their own tragedies. Outside of the women's personal lives, the 1930s and early 1940s were tumultuous across the world as the name Adolf Hitler was written in every newspaper and broadcast on every radio. In 1933, as the Third Reich began its reign of terror, Black American writers and activists were quick to draw connections between Nazi dictates and American race laws. It was a proven and commonly held belief that Hitler saw America's approach to the Jim Crow laws as a model for his own eugenicist agenda.

The United States would not officially enter the war until 1941, following the attack on Pearl Harbor, and in the meantime Black Americans would celebrate landmark moments in their history. In 1935, Mary McLeod Bethune, an educator, philanthropist, and civil rights activist, established the National Council of Negro Women. As further evidence of Black women's role in advancing the movement for the liberation of Black lives, the NCNW, still around today, harnessed the power of African American women to advance their quality of life as well as that of their families and their communities.

Several Black athletes and actors also brought hope during this decade. In 1936, Jesse Owens became famous around the world when he won four gold medals at the Olympic Games in Berlin. Owens's accomplishments obliterated Hitler's belief in white supremacy. Hitler, who shook the hands of all other gold medalists, refused to shake Owens's, and Owens was also denied a visit to the White House, but his triumph gave Black Americans incredible hope. The boxer Joe Louis brought Black Americans this same feeling of victory when he became the undisputed heavyweight champion of the world after beating James J. Braddock. In 1940, Hattie McDaniel became the first African American woman to win an Academy Award, for her performance in *Gone with the Wind*. Although the part she played was stereotypical, her win still broke the color barrier in Hollywood and paved the way for actresses following in her footsteps. Alberta, Berdis, and Louise would have known the names Jesse Owens, Joe Louis, and Hattie McDaniel as symbols of Black excellence, resistance, and victory over white supremacist dictates.

By 1941, the United States would join the deadliest conflict in human history, involving more than one hundred million people from more than thirty countries. Recovering from a surprise attack that killed more than two thousand people, the United States found itself in desperate need of recruiting and training a vast military force that could stand up to three formidable enemies. All men between the ages of eighteen and sixty-four were required to register for the draft, leading 2.5 million Black men to register and once again face the hypocrisy of fighting against fascism abroad while being victims of discrimination in the country they were sacrificing their lives to protect. They continued to face segregation and discrimination while serving, and they were erased from footage following the war, further denying their contributions.

Still, the war brought several positive changes for Black Americans. Once again, labor demands increased. More minorities could work in jobs that were previously denied them. Black women were able to volunteer as nurses this time around. Many Black soldiers enjoyed more freedoms while fighting abroad than they had when back home in the United States, and this experience propelled them to fight even more fervently for their rights in America. Approximately one-third of the leaders in the upcoming civil rights movement were veterans of World War II.

*This intense period of* personal and political change and upheaval paved the way for each mother and her children to become active agents in the larger fight for Black lives. It is excruciating to even imagine experiencing the losses Alberta, Berdis, and Louise encountered throughout their lives—from the loss of their parents and husbands to the loss of their freedoms—but these were crucial moments in the development of their identities as Black women and Black mothers.

The tragedies Black women have been subject to in this country are unique as a result of their intersecting identities, and they inform Black women's varied approaches to faith and resistance. Any loss can become destabilizing when one is not afforded basic supports and instead is further victimized and blamed. In Louise's case, not only did she lose her husband and her children but she was denied dignified support and punished for her grief. This denial and punishment were made possible because of her identity as a Black woman. Yet this was also what informed the powerful wisdom she passed on to her children and anyone who knew her story. Such wisdom had the capacity to prevent the same thing from happening to her daughters and sons.

One of the quotes that appears at the beginning of this chapter comes from *The Negro Family in the United States*, authored by the sociologist Edward Franklin Frazier and published in 1939. The chapter in which it appears is titled "The Matriarchate," in reference to the matriarch trope. Another image used to control Black women, the matriarch criticizes Black mothers for emasculating their husbands and failing to fulfill their womanly duties. The matriarch is seen as an aggressive woman who works so hard outside of her home that she cannot adequately raise her children or be a submissive wife to her husband. Just like the jezebel, the mammy, and the welfare queen, the matriarch is another demeaning and untruthful depiction of Black women, meant to misrepresent them and ignore the factors contributing to their victimization.

Frazier's assertion that the Black woman in the 1930s resisted subordination to male authority is meant not as a compliment but instead as a critique of Black women's independence. He assumes that this need to care for themselves and their families is their own choice rather than a reaction to the losses they suffered as a result of structural violence and institutional racism. Frazier's quote is countered by that of Fredi Washington, who was a popular Black actress in the 1920s and 1930s. She was mixed and had fair skin. She was known not only for her roles but also for her work as a civil rights activist and a writer who refused to pass as white. Her words remind us that Black women were not granted more options beyond fighting or being defeated. When the rights she was entitled to were denied, she had no other choice but to stand up for herself, for her people, and fight. It did not matter if this choice would be read as emasculating or if this choice would be criticized; it was the only choice she was able to make.

Alberta, Berdis, and Louise all chose to fight. They fought for their dignity and their families no matter what challenge was thrown in their way. Alberta turned her grief into motivation to continue the legacy her parents passed down to her. She stepped into her role as the first lady of her church and used her talents to fully embrace and become more active in the freedom movement. Her ability to move forward became an example to her community and, perhaps most important, to her children.

Berdis chose to turn her years of caring for her husband into an opportunity to teach her children about forgiveness and unconditional love. She taught her children that it was okay to be vulnerable when she lost her father and let her children see her sadness, and when she continued to walk in optimism, they saw her strength.

Louise chose to hold strong to her ideals even when unspeakable terrors were waged against her. Even in an institution, she continued to resist and speak her truth. Her children carried forward the lessons she taught them even when they were separated from her at young ages. These lessons would later result in their successful fight to bring her back home.

## Part VI

# Loving Our Sons

We're the only race in America that has had babies sold from our breast, which was slavery time. And had mothers sold from their babes. . . . We are not fighting against these people because we hate them, but we are fighting because we love them and we're the only thing can save them now.

—FANNIE LOU HAMER

The so-called Negro Movement is a part of the attempted takeover of our country by the lazy, the indolent, the beatniks, the ignorant, and by some misguided religions and bleeding hearts, and all being led by the politicians who stay in office by appealing, remember not to reason, but to the most votes.

—BULL CONNOR

In a lecture he delivered at the University of Massachusetts in 1995, Malcolm's eldest brother, Wilfred, began by saying, "What people don't understand was that Malcolm was part of a whole, that he was part of a particular experience, part of a tradition, part of a family that resisted the corner into which America tried to push them." He continued by recounting the night that he witnessed his mother stand up to the white men who threatened her while Earl was out of town. Wilfred described it from his perspective: "My mother, she was pregnant with Malcolm at the time, and she stood there and just had no fear. . . . I never saw anybody who could tell you off so intelligently and never use a word of profanity, never cussed. When she got through, you felt like you'd been beaten up." Wilfred gave credit to Louise for her children's bravery in the face of injustice and calm in the face of chaos. He explained how her lessons from that particular night and beyond taught each of her children to walk with pride.

When the Littles came home from school, Louise would reteach them what they had been taught by their white teachers. She refused to let her children fall victim to a mentality that told them they were inferior to anybody else. She made sure they knew how Black people were standing up for their rights not only in the United States but also around the world. She would teach them lessons she'd learned from her grandparents and the Carib Indians she'd met in Grenada. Louise always had a dictionary on the kitchen table alongside daily newspaper clippings she made her children study. As Wilfred described it, "We would have to stand there and read it to her. She'd be ironing, or cooking, or whatever, but she's hearing you. And whenever you made a mistake, she'd stop you and make you go to that dictionary, look it up, 'syllablize' it, get the meaning of it, and that way you began to improve your vocabulary."

She ran a strict household that, on top of expectations around their reading and writing, also included restrictions on what they could eat. She prohibited them from eating pork and rabbit, for instance, as part of her religious beliefs. She didn't subscribe to one particular religion but instead wanted to expose her children to several different faiths. She took her children everywhere: they attended Catholic mass, congregated with Baptists, and learned from Hindus. And after every visit, they would come home and discuss their thoughts. Louise would say, "You take what you see will fit you, and the rest of it, just leave it there, but establish your own relationship with God, not a religious relationship, but a spiritual relationship with God and be true to that. . . . You'll find out that you'll do better than you'll ever do getting all hung up in these religions, and you won't be confused."

Malcolm's childhood was rich with education, but he spent his early years under the impression that his parents treated him differently from his siblings. He was the fairest of all the Little children, resembling his mother in this way, and his hair had a reddish tone. He thought his father subconsciously favored him because of this, believing that his father fell victim to the false belief that light skin was superior. Out of all the children, Malcolm was the one his father would bring to UNIA meetings, where the boy could watch his father speak out against the plight of the Black man in America. Malcolm remembered being proud of his father's crusading and militant campaigning. On the other hand, Malcolm felt his mother was harder on him because of his lighter skin. Louise would often say to Malcolm, "Let the sun shine on you so you can get some color." As he put it, "She went out of her way never to let me become afflicted with a sense of color-superiority." Louise was the disciplinarian of the family, and it seemed this was often directed at Malcolm.

This was likely because Malcolm was always more rebellious and more of a troublemaker than his siblings. He wouldn't allow others' rules to hold him back. As a child, he would cry until he got what he wanted, or he would yell out in order to avoid his mother's punishments. He knew that Louise would not want others to hear him screaming and that she would keep from disciplining him if he pretended he was in some kind of pain.

As an adult, Malcolm laughed as he remembered differences in the ways he and his eldest brother approached Louise when they wanted things. "My mother asked me why I couldn't be a nice boy like Wilfred, but I would think to myself that Wilfred, for being so nice and quiet, often stayed hungry. So early in life, I had learned that if you want something, you had better make some noise." Louise was especially strict with Malcolm because he was so much like her. She knew firsthand how dangerous things could become for someone so strong willed, so she did her best to steer his energy and intelligence in the right direction. Malcolm learned more from what he saw in Louise than what she said directly to him. He too demanded what he knew he deserved, and he stood up for himself. She had strict rules for her children because she wanted to protect them, but like her son, she was a rebel who did not let rules restrict her.

Malcolm and the rest of her children witnessed her ability to do this even after her husband's death. She continued to fight for her and her children's rights. Malcolm was younger, but Wilfred saw and understood the injustices she faced for attempting to hold on to her independence. Louise was a Black single mother in a predominantly white area; it was against all expectations for her to maintain her autonomy and continue to own her own land. Wilfred could see that the increasing visits from welfare workers had less to do with the well-being of the family and more to do with taking their family's property. Seeing that his mother was in pain, Wilfred even took her to see a psychologist, who said that "there was nothing wrong with her that rest and better nutrition could not cure." He told this to a welfare doctor who came to their home. The doctor asked for the psychologist's name, and shortly after, the psychologist recanted his statement.

Before Louise was institutionalized, Malcolm was the first of her children to be targeted for separation from the home. Because he'd started stealing, welfare workers blamed Louise for her inability to take care of him. They started planting seeds in the children's minds that their mother was "crazy," and they told Malcolm how much nicer things would be for him with a stable family who could provide for his needs. Malcolm would later state, "Right then was when our home, our unity, began to disintegrate. We were having a hard time, and I wasn't helping. But we could have made it, we could have stayed together. As bad as I was, as much trouble and worry as I caused my mother, I loved her."

Malcolm was taken away from his family first, and eventually all the Little children were placed in separate foster homes before Louise was institutionalized. Malcolm remembered Louise's final words before he was taken from her. She wanted him to remember every lesson she'd imparted, she wanted him to keep his faith, to be disciplined, but to still be able to think for himself. As her son was led away from her, she simply said, "Don't let them feed him any pig."

*Family sit-down dinners were* mandatory in Martin Luther Jr.'s home. Alberta and Martin Luther Sr. sat at the head of the table as they laughed with their children and any extended family who joined them. The dinner table was a place where Reverend and Mama King taught their children about the injustices of segregation and reminded them of the importance of doing their part in changing such inequities. The three children would sit and commune with generations of their family members as they professed their faith, shared their wisdom, and planned their next moves in their ongoing fight against oppression, all while passing good food around the table.

Christine would fondly recall such moments, saying, "Every now and then, I have to chuckle as I realize there are people who actually believe ML [as Martin was sometimes called by his loved ones] just appeared. They think he simply happened, that he appeared fully formed, without context, ready to change the world. Take it from his big sister, that's simply not the case. We are the products of a long line of activists and ministers. We come from a family of incredible men and women who served as leaders in their time and place, long before ML was ever thought of."

The love and guidance their parents gave them, paired with the comfort they could provide, allowed the King children to live joyfully, even though they still knew they were not protected from the rules of their time. They knew that they had the immense responsibility of carrying their family's legacy forward in an unjust society.

When Martin was young, he would play with the children of the white family that managed the corner grocery store. He and his friends were virtually inseparable for several years. As they grew older, the friends' parents started to create distance between the children, not allowing them to see each other. There was a clear turn of events when the boys reached a certain age where it was no longer acceptable for them to be comrades, and eventually they were officially prohibited from spending time together. Martin was shocked and hurt. He brought his pain with him to dinner that night, looking to his parents for comfort.

Alberta felt her son's agony and held back tears. She put her hand on his. She looked him in the eye and told him that he was worthy of the same respect as his friends and that he was "as good as anyone." She held him, encouraging him to feel his pain and turn it into something positive.

Martin would go to his mother with all of his concerns even as he grew up. He knew she would not only make him feel better but help him know what he could do next. She made him feel like he had control over any challenge he might face. Alberta knew her children were capable of anything they set their mind to, and she encouraged them to believe in themselves the same way. So when Christine was of an age to start attending school, a young Martin approached his mother. He wanted to start school, too. He was competitive with his sister and didn't think it was fair that she got to start without him. She was only a year and a half older, after all. Although technically too young to enroll, he reminded Alberta of everything she'd taught him. He begged his mother to let him go, to let him start on his education journey at the age of four. Proud of his desire to start learning, Alberta eventually relented and signed him up to attend with his sister. A few months later, a teacher realized he was too young and sent him home, but Alberta had supported his effort and that's what mattered most to her son.

When Martin graduated from sixth grade a few years later, Alberta bought him a brown tweed suit to celebrate the occasion. Martin wore the suit, designed to be baggy around his legs and tight around his ankles, to everything he could. He was proud of himself and proud of what the suit symbolized.

Alberta's belief in her son's abilities carried him forward through his education. When his sister graduated high school and was ready to continue on to higher education, Martin was among a group of young students who seized the opportunity to take a test that would allow successful juniors to start college two years early. At the age of fifteen, Martin was admitted to Morehouse College, following in his father's footsteps as well as those of the men on his mother's side of the family.

When they could not be together in person, Martin and Alberta would exchange letters updating each other on the happenings of the week. In much more casual language than what the world would later grow accustomed to from Martin, he would update his mother and ask her to send him things he missed or needed. One letter reads, "Dear Mother Dear: I received your letter today and was very glad to hear from you. Yesterday we didn't work so we went to Hardford we really had a nice time there. . . ." He continues in another paragraph, "As head of the religious Dept. I have to take charge of the Sunday Service. . . ." And in another: "Mother dear I want you to send me some fried chikens [*sic*] and rolls it will not be so much. And also send my brown shoes the others have worn out." Alberta was so close to each of her children, and so invested in their education, one can only imagine the joy she experienced every time she received one of their letters with updates on their whereabouts, their commitments, and their small requests for a bit of home. How happy she must have been every time she heard of their continued progress toward their goals. The King children's lives were filled with endless possibility, and Alberta beamed with pride.

*When Berdis's little boy* Jimmy grew up, he became known to the world as the acclaimed writer James Baldwin, whose brilliance, eloquence, and passion were unmatched. He unapologetically forced readers to deeply examine their society and the role each played in its making. He once said, "I never had a childhood. . . . I did not have any human identity. . . . I was born dead." His words were not only an explanation of his life but a commentary on the Black experience in America.

In many ways, Jimmy was forced to grow up faster than other children. He felt that he "never had a childhood" because he was the eldest in his family and his mother's right-hand man. To help support her and his siblings, he worked small jobs, like shining shoes, as soon as he was old enough to do so. He was sent to run errands for the family, like buying day-old bread and other groceries at lower prices. He helped to feed, change, and raise his younger siblings.

Jimmy's environment also forced him to grow up. As hard as Berdis tried, she could not shield her son from the harsh realities of poverty and discrimination. As a child, Jimmy saw friends he'd once sat next to in church turn to drugs; some became pimps and others prostitutes on the street. He was well aware that in the society he was born into, his life and those of his friends were deemed less important and less valuable than the lives of his richer and whiter counterparts. They were seen and treated as if they "did not have any human identity," denied access to opportunities, and many of them were forced to give up on their futures.

Struggling to make ends meet, the Baldwins moved from place to place all around Harlem. Everywhere they went, from their apartment on Lenox Avenue on the west to the one by the Harlem River on the east, from their place on 135th Street on the north to their home on 130th Street on the south, they experienced the effects of racism and classism firsthand. Jimmy could recall multiple times when his safety was threatened as a young Black boy and where another person made him feel inhuman.

When he was ten years old, Berdis sent him out to collect firewood for the family. He was walking down the street when suddenly he felt hands on him, pushing him into a vacant lot. Two white police officers stared down at him. They said he matched the description of a suspect they were looking for. Jimmy was terrified, and he did not resist when they searched him. When they'd tormented him enough, they left him lying there alone, flat on his back. This disregard of his rights, this denial of his dignity, pushed him to feel that as a poor Black boy in America, he was "born dead."

Yes, he was born into circumstances that forced him to grow up and a society that degraded him, but he balanced these pressures by keeping an eye on his education. Berdis made sure of this. Jimmy found joy in his schooling and love of words, just like Berdis. She knew her son was brilliant, and she would do whatever she could to support his dreams even as he helped her to raise the rest of her children. As the biographer

James Campbell put it, James used one hand "to support a baby and the other to hold a book."

Berdis and Jimmy both confronted their trials and tribulations through reading and writing. At every school that Jimmy attended, he was remembered for being exceptional. He was both the poorest and the brightest kid in school. Teachers noticed his talents, and several of them created opportunities for him to expand upon them, taking him to plays and giving him more books to read. At one school, it was said that he was the best writer of everyone in the building, including the adults, and it was clear to them where he got his talents. Gertrude Ayer, the principal of his first school on 128th Street between Fifth and Madison Avenues, attributed Jimmy's excellence to his mother:

> I remember too his mother above all other mothers. . . .
> She had the gift of using language beautifully. Her notes
> and her letters, written to explain her son's absences, etc.,
> were admired by the teachers and me. This talent trans-
> mitted through her is surely the basis of James' success. It
> is said that he too writes like an angel, albeit an avenging
> one.

Berdis could see the same drive in her son that she saw in herself. She did not know just how far his drive would take him, but she knew he *had* to write. She would support his desire to do so, no matter the cost. She would risk standing up to her husband, whom even she had to address as "Mr. Baldwin," to ensure that Jimmy could follow his passion. She'd been kept from her own by her circumstances, and she would not let the same thing happen to her son. She always reminded Jimmy of his abilities, his dignity, his worth.

Although Jimmy considered attending college, his formal education ended at the young age of seventeen. He left school in 1941, focused on helping his parents earn money for the family. He first worked with the U.S. Army, helping to build an army depot in New Jersey. He then went on to work as a railroad hand, laying track. In these experiences, he was remembered not with the same excellence as he had been in school. Instead, he was perceived as lazy—it was clear he did not have any zeal for that kind of work. He knew he was meant to write.

It would be a few years before he would formally pursue his writing full-time. He was torn between following an artist's journey, one that did not guarantee any success or resources for his family, and working mindless jobs that paid consistent money even if it wasn't very much. This inner turmoil caused him to experience multiple mental break-downs. The pressure of wanting to support his mother and his siblings made him feel guilty for even having a desire to write and travel, yet his denial of his talents, and his attempts to work in labor-intensive jobs from which he was often fired, left him feeling exhausted and un-fulfilled. But he was terrified of turning into his stepfather, a man who became so consumed with his inability to provide for his family as a Black man that he turned bitter and cold.

His personal struggle was paired with continued racist encounters that were even worse in New Jersey than in Harlem. Many of the people he worked with, both Black and white, were from the South, and they were not especially fond of his smarts. They perceived him as "uppity" and disrespectful. In addition to their perception of him, Jim Crow laws were in full effect for all Black people across the United States. Restaurant after restaurant would remind him that he was not welcome there, sign after sign would point to his lesser position. Later in life he would write the following:

> I learned in New Jersey that to be a Negro meant, pre-
> cisely, that one was never looked at but was simply at
> the mercy of the reflexes the color of one's skin caused
> in other people. . . . It was the same story all over New
> Jersey, in bars, bowling alleys, diners, places to live. I

was always being forced to leave, silently, or with mutual imprecations.

This kind of racist treatment suffocated him even more when he was further away from his writing. He became less able to control his anger without the ability to process and express it through the written word.

On his last night in New Jersey, he went to see the movie *This Land Is Mine* and, after, grab a bite to eat at a nearby diner with a white friend. Upon sitting down and trying to order, James was greeted by the waiter with the common phrase "We don't serve Negroes here." The two stood up and left the restaurant, seeming unaffected at first. But when they walked outside, something overtook Jimmy. He started walking ahead of his friend and entered a different "enormous, glittering, and fashionable" restaurant. He walked through the doors and sat at the first available seat before a waitress approached him cautiously. She repeated the words he'd heard earlier: "We don't serve Negroes here." Something boiled inside of him that he could no longer control. He knew from his mother, his teachers, and his friends that he deserved the basic right of sitting at the table. The fact that this was repeatedly denied him was no longer something he was willing to accept. He took the water mug that was sitting on the table and threw it, aiming directly at her. She ducked and the half-full mug shattered against a mirror behind her. Everyone in the restaurant stared, and then they rose and charged toward him. All he could do was run. Fortunately, he ran fast enough to avoid the dire consequences that surely would have faced him had he been caught that night.

Jimmy eventually moved to Greenwich Village. He networked with other writers and met mentors who would change his life; he'd speak onstage about his experiences at places like the Calypso café. He had returned to his writing. And eventually he was given the opportunity to travel to Paris on a writing fellowship.

The only thing he still had to do before leaving was tell his mother.

This was something he'd dreaded since graduating high school, the moment he would tell her that he was leaving to pursue a seemingly selfish endeavor, one that she herself had given up for her family. But he knew he had to "get beyond [his] private, incoherent pain" in order to fulfill whatever role he was meant to play in the world. He told his friend later that the day he told his family he was leaving was the most "dreadful" he had ever experienced. He said, "My mother had come downstairs, and stood silently, arms folded, on the stoop. My baby sister was upstairs weeping." He hoped his mother would later see how her lessons had given him the courage to leave a place that did not see him as the exceptional human being she knew him to be. He boarded his flight to Paris that evening in 1948 with only $40 in his pocket.

Jimmy spent almost a decade in Paris, and as much as Berdis missed her son, she knew he'd made the right decision. He kept in close contact with his mom the entire time—they wrote letters to each other consistently, and he especially looked forward to the birthday letter she sent every year. Berdis's children and grandchildren would say her letters were some of the most beautiful ever written.

In Paris, Jimmy had the opportunity to better understand his identity as a queer, Black American man. I haven't found any correspondence between James and his mother regarding his queer identity, but from other correspondence and research I can infer that she fully accepted her son without question. He did not hide who he was, in neither his professional nor his personal life, and he introduced those who were important to him to his mother when he could. Berdis believed in people's dignity, and her son sought experiences that aligned with his mother's embrace and love for all. He traveled around Europe, finding new friends and lovers, and he was better able to analyze American racism from a distance. Over those years, he began to build critical acclaim for his writing, yet he still felt guilty. It was no longer guilt for pursuing his calling to write but guilt for not contributing to the Black freedom struggle at home in the United States. The civil rights movement was building and he was watching it from afar. He finally felt he must return after seeing a picture of a fifteen-year-old girl by the name of Dorothy Counts.

In 1956, Dorothy became one of the first Black students to be admitted into a formerly all-white school. As she tried to enter the building on her first day, September 4, 1957, a white mob made up of both adults and children greeted her with rocks, spit, and endless insults. Some of the most iconic pictures of the growing movement consisted of Black students like Dorothy being surrounded by the terror of white supremacists while holding their heads high and continuing on their mission, not only for themselves but for their people. One such photo captured Jimmy's attention and he could not let it go. It was time for him to come home.

In 1957, Jimmy returned to the United States after being asked to report on what was happening in the South. He wrote to his family, informing them of his plans. There is no doubt that Berdis was overjoyed at the thought of seeing her son. Still, she was worried. Things were shifting, but it was still incredibly dangerous for Black people in America, especially in the places Jimmy planned to visit. He would travel first to Charlotte, North Carolina, and then to Montgomery, Alabama, where he would meet a man five years his junior named Martin Luther King.

In 1957, *Harper's Magazine* commissioned James Baldwin to write an article about what was happening in the South. While doing research for the assignment, James met Martin, who had just become the first president of the Southern Christian Leadership Conference. The SCLC was a group made up of other ministers and activists who dedicated themselves to abolishing segregation through nonviolence. In 1960, James would write Martin a letter in which he stated, "The effect of your work, and I might almost indeed, say your presence, has spread far beyond the confines of Montgomery, as you must know. . . . And I am one of the millions, to be found all over the world but more especially here, in this sorely troubled country, who thank God for you."

By this time, Martin had found his way to world fame through his work as a civil rights activist—work that began in his home from his parents' teachings and that he developed further through his studies at Morehouse College and Crozer Theological Seminary. In 1944, Martin began his freshman year at Morehouse. There he obtained a bachelor's degree in sociology in 1948, the same year he was ordained at Ebenezer Baptist. In his studies, he encountered lessons he'd learned since he was a child but didn't yet have the language for. Stemming from his grandparents' and parents' active yet peaceful approach to challenging discrimination, he found familiarity in reading works like Henry David Thoreau's "Civil Disobedience." As he put it, "Because of the influence of my mother and father, I guess I always had a deep urge to serve humanity," and in college he was able to develop the strategies and theories dedicated to making justice a reality.

At the age of nineteen, Martin graduated from college, ready to combine his desire to end racial injustice with his calling to join his family's vocation in ministry. The same year Jimmy moved to Paris, Martin enrolled in Crozer Theological Seminary, where he would go on to receive his degree in divinity in 1951. He was on an "intellectual quest for a method to eliminate social evil." He described his approach to ministry by saying, "Any religion that professes concern for the souls of men and is not equally concerned about the slums that damn them, the economic conditions that strangle them, and the social conditions that cripple them is a spiritually moribund religion only waiting for the day to be buried." Martin beautifully put words to the approaches his family had been taking to ministry, education, and social justice for generations.

Throughout his years of schooling, he was always in close contact with both his mother and his sister, writing letters to them about his progress. In one letter to Alberta, he wrote, "I often tell the boys around campus I have the best mother in the world. You will never know how I appreciate the many kind things you and daddy are doing for me." Martin's connection to his parents, especially his mom, would sustain him through his degrees and on to a life soon to be filled with both national and international demands.

In 1951, he pursued yet another degree. This time he was in Boston, where he would meet a woman who would change his life forever. He was introduced to a young singer and student at the New England Conservatory of Music by the name of Coretta in 1952. Coretta had inherited her musical talents and appreciation for art from her own mother, Bernice Scott. A gifted mezzo-soprano, Coretta dreamed of becoming a concert singer, but like that of her future mother-in-law, her path was rerouted by a Baptist preacher. Shortly after meeting Coretta, Martin wrote to Alberta telling her Coretta was to be his wife. In June 1953, this became a reality.

Things moved even faster after that. In 1954, Coretta graduated from the New England Conservatory and Martin was named head pastor of Dexter Avenue Baptist Church. On Sunday, October 31, 1954, Martin Luther Sr. preached his son's installation sermon while his sister sang "I Will Give Thanks," accompanied by Alberta on the organ. The moment, like many others, was a whole King family affair.

In 1955, Coretta and Martin brought their first child into the world, Martin received his doctorate, and Rosa Parks was arrested. Her arrest, as well as those of countless other courageous Black people who refused to give up their bus seats to white passengers, signaled the beginning of the Montgomery bus boycott as well as Martin and Coretta's official entry as civil rights leaders in the South.

While Martin's work as a civil rights leader made Alberta proud, it also terrified her. He and his family were becoming more involved than the Williamses and Kings ever had before. Her husband described her angst: "Bunch was deeply affected, of course. She grew ever more

apprehensive as her sons became rooted in the struggle and the cause."
And Martin would echo this, saying, "On the one hand I had to be
concerned about keeping my emotional and psychological balance; on
the other hand I was deeply concerned about my mother's worrying."
Although she was right to be concerned, her feelings never caused her
to doubt the rightness of her son's actions.

Alberta's fears were confirmed when, after helping to lead the
Montgomery bus boycott, Martin was arrested and put in jail as part
of a list of other intimidation tactics he would face. That same year,
Martin and Coretta's home was bombed and they began receiving death
threats. As their families had done for generations, Martin and Coretta
knew they could not buckle in the face of fear, that they must always
keep pushing for what was right and continue to live their lives as fully
as they could. Eventually, the bus boycott was successful and bus segregation laws were deemed unconstitutional in 1957. Martin continued
his involvement with the NAACP and went on to form the Southern
Christian Leadership Conference. He kept expanding his reach and
pushing his family's legacy forward.


*It would be a* few more years before Berdis's and Alberta's sons would
meet Louise's, but their meetings would also revolve around the fight
for Black lives and the men's unique roles in the civil rights movement. Just like James and Martin, who took different paths to the fight,
Malcolm found his own way. Malcolm's approach to the Black liberation movement was informed by the traumatic experiences of losing
his father at a young age and being separated from his mother and his
siblings, as well as by his mother's uncompromising strength in the face
of prejudice.

Louise was sent to Kalamazoo State Hospital when Malcolm was
only in the seventh grade. His rebellious nature and quick wit often got
him in trouble, and he eventually found himself in a nearly all-white

juvenile home after being kicked out of his school. Despite this, Malcolm performed well in school; after all, he'd been raised by a woman who prioritized an international education. He had some of the highest grades in his class (at times *the* highest) and was even elected class president at his new school. At first, he enjoyed being the only Black student. It made him feel that he stood out; it made him feel special. And for a short time it seemed he was accepted there, until he was reminded that even if he felt accepted by his teachers and his peers, they still saw him as less than, more as a class pet than a student on equal footing. This was the opposite of the lessons his mother and father had always taught him about his worth.

One of the first reminders of his position at school came in a conversation with his English teacher, Mr. Ostrowski, who asked Malcolm what he wanted his career to be. Taught by his family that he could do whatever he wanted to do and knowing that he was one of the brightest students in his class, a young Malcolm excitedly answered that he wanted to be a lawyer. His teacher replied, "Malcolm, one of life's first needs is for us to be realistic. Don't misunderstand me, now. We all here like you, you know that. But you've got to be realistic about being a nigger. A lawyer—that's no realistic goal for a nigger . . . why don't you plan on carpentry?" This bothered Malcolm deeply, and he could no longer enjoy being treated differently from his peers. In contrast with Jimmy, whose intellect had been recognized and encouraged, Malcolm realized that his ability was recognized and limited. He became more distant, less approachable, and he longed to be somewhere else.

In many ways, it can be said that the farther away Malcolm was from Louise and her teachings, the worse things became for him. While he was able to visit his mother a few times, he was no longer met by her affirmations of his worth or her exercises to expand his learning at the end of each day. With his growing discontent and his lack of her support, Malcolm would soon find himself in situations filled with danger and trouble. In 1941, he moved to Boston—a decade prior to Martin.

His half sister Ella was given custody of him, and he was ready to leave Michigan behind.

Boston was life changing for Malcolm. He found more freedom there, working odd jobs serving on railroad trains or in restaurants, shining shoes, and selling jewelry at a store. But his newly gained freedom also led to his involvement with the wrong crowds. He started consuming and selling drugs, he had his natural hair relaxed so it could lie flat on his head, and he learned the language of the streets. He became known as "Detroit Red" because of the unique color of his hair and his growing involvement with other hustlers in Boston and New York City.

After years of living a lifestyle filled with drugs and violence, Malcolm hit rock bottom. He'd orchestrated several robberies before he was caught and sent to prison. Although he was resistant at first and experienced extreme withdrawal, his ten-year prison sentence, and time spent in reformatory programs where he had a private room and access to books, allowed him to return to many of the strict practices his mother had instilled in him and his siblings.

By the time Malcolm was sentenced in 1946, four of his siblings had become devoted members of the Nation of Islam (NOI). The Black Muslim movement was founded in the 1930s at the height of the Great Depression, and it combined Black religious nationalism with ideals of Black political nationalism. Through their letters and visits, Malcolm's siblings introduced him to the NOI and their leader, Elijah Muhammad.

In these teachings, Malcolm was certainly exposed to some new rhetoric, but he also experienced a homecoming as he was reminded of his parents' own beliefs. Malcolm saw a strong and apparent connection between the Nation of Islam and his mother specifically. In one letter to his brother Philbert he wrote, "We were taught Islam by mom. . . . Everything that happened to her happened because the devils knew she was not deadening our minds. . . . All of our achievements are mom's . . . for she was a most faithful servant of Truth years ago. I praise 'Allah' for her." He also returned to a different practice Louise taught him when he was a child, the practice of writing words down from the dictionary. During his years spent on the streets, he'd lost much of the vocabulary he once knew, so once he was sober, he found comfort and reformation in a dictionary he was provided with.

After six years in prison, Malcolm was released and sent to live with his oldest brother, Wilfred. He had fallen in love with the teachings of Elijah Muhammad, and he made it his mission to do whatever he could to expand the reach of the Nation of Islam, quickly becoming one of their most prominent ministers.

In 1957, Malcolm received word that one of his New York temple members, Johnson Hinton, had been savagely beaten by police and taken into custody without adequate medical care. Malcolm sprang into action, going to the precinct with other members and demanding that Hinton be taken to the hospital. When the police noticed Malcom and the crowd that followed him, refusing to disperse, they agreed to send Hinton to the emergency room. Malcolm stood with his head high among his members, and when he was satisfied, he dispersed the crowd with a slight wave of his hand. He was unafraid, composed, and dignified in the face of racism and denigration, just as Louise was when she'd held Malcolm in her womb. This would become a key moment in history, one that gained Malcolm, as well as the Nation of Islam, international attention and put Malcolm and his family in harm's way. But, as we know, this was not the first time Malcolm or his family members were threatened by groups aiming to hold them down. He would not be scared into submission; it was in his blood to resist.

## Part VII

# Losing Our Sons

I didn't see right away, but there was an important mission for me, to shape so many other young minds as a teacher, a messenger, an active church member. God told me, "I took away one child, but I will give you thousands." He has. And I have been grateful for that blessing.

—MAMIE TILL-MOBLEY

In essence, the Negro community has been forced into a matriarchal structure which, because it is so out of line with the rest of the American society, seriously retards the progress of the group as a whole, and imposes a crushing burden on the Negro male and, in consequence, on a great many Negro women as well.

—DANIEL PATRICK MOYNIHAN

In the summer of 1955, a young boy from Chicago named Emmett visited his uncle in Mississippi. Although he attended a segregated school in the North, there was nothing that could prepare him for the level of segregation he would experience in the South. On August 28, he was kidnapped from his uncle's home after being accused of flirting with and harassing a white woman named Carolyn Bryant. Two white men, Bryant's husband and brother, took him to the Tallahatchie River, where they had him strip before beating him, nearly to death, gouging his eye out, shooting the child in the head, and throwing his body, which was tied to a seventy-five-pound cotton-gin fan with barbed wire, into the river. Three days following the heinous attack, Emmett's body was recovered, but it was mutilated to such a horrible extent that the only way he could be identified was by an engraved ring he wore.

This is not how Emmett Till's story ends. When his body was recovered, officials wanted to bury him immediately, but his mother, Mamie Till, demanded that her baby's body be sent home to her in Chicago. Her beautiful son was just visiting family in the South for the summer; he was supposed to return home to her alive. There are no words to describe the heartbreak she experienced when she saw her boy. Yet somehow, through her pain, she knew she needed to do more than mourn her son—she knew his life could not be lost in vain. Mamie

Till demanded that her son have an open-casket funeral so that the world could see what racism and racists had done to him.

The world took notice, making Emmett Till a household name for decades to come and forcing a deeper evaluation of Jim Crow. While the men who murdered Emmett were deemed "not guilty" by an all-white jury, many consider Emmett Till's murder—and, more important, his mother's decision—to be one of the primary catalysts of the civil rights movement.

Almost ten years after Emmett's tragic death, James Baldwin released *Blues for Mister Charlie* in the young boy's honor. In the play, he confronts the harsh realities of American racism while leaving his audience with hope for change. This was one of the many ways that James showed who raised him. He faced his pain and sadness the way Berdis taught him to, saying, "We are walking in terrible darkness here, and this is one man's attempt to bear witness to the reality and the power of light." James saw it as his duty to "bear witness to the truth," and he spent his years in the civil rights movement writing books, essays, poems, and plays, fulfilling this duty. He constantly reminded his audiences that the story of the American Negro was the story of America. He traveled around the world speaking not only against racial segregation but also against homophobia and America's involvement in the Vietnam War. Although he played a prominent role in writing, speaking, and organizing protests as a member of the Congress of Racial Equality, he considered himself not a leader or a spokesperson but a witness.

James spent much of his time traveling for his career, and he worried about leaving his mother and his siblings. He dealt with his guilt by writing to Berdis as often as he could, reassuring her that he was "still in the service of some power for good beyond himself, that his mission was sacred," as his dear friend David Leeming, a philologist and professor, put it. In one letter to his mother, James said that he felt the "responsibility to learn humility . . . publish the truth, sparing no one." James and Berdis's constant correspondence with each other allowed him to explore this mission and calling. He dedicated many of his works to Berdis, and in one such poem, titled "The Giver," he writes:

*If the hope of giving*
*is to love the living,*
*the giver risks madness*
*in the act of giving.*

He ends the poem with *"I cannot tell how much I owe."* Berdis was the ultimate giver: she humbly gave without asking for anything in return. And like her son, she was happy to be in the background as a supportive observer rather than considering herself the leader or the star of the show. James was aware of this and he acknowledged everything she had done to give him what he needed.

When James was away from home, he longed for his mother and his siblings. When he was trying to work out an idea, when he felt the need to explain his commitments, when he met someone of importance to him, he would write to his mom. So, when he was honored with one of his first writing awards, from the National Institute of Arts and Letters, acknowledging the importance of his contributions to the world, it was fitting for Berdis to accept the honor on his behalf.

One can only imagine the depth of pride Berdis experienced when reading one of her son's works or seeing him speak on television. Her firstborn, the boy she'd given her all to provide for, the son who stood by her side through all of her pain, was now taking what he learned from her and helping millions of people. In her letters back to her son, she offered her love and support. She also voiced her concerns about Jimmy's drinking and smoking and reminded him of the need to keep his faith. Most important, she stressed the necessity of avoiding, at all costs, the road of racial or personal hatred.

James's works most commonly referenced when speaking to his immense influence on the civil rights movement are *Notes of a Native Son*, published in 1955; *Nobody Knows My Name*, published in 1961; and *The Fire Next Time*, published in 1963. All of his works blended stories from his own life with his comments on the state of the nation. In *Notes of a Native Son*, James tackled issues of race in America and Europe through a collection of ten essays. Before the book begins, he includes a section titled "Autobiographical Notes," where he writes, "[I] Also wrote plays, and songs, for one of which I received a letter of congratulations from Mayor La Guardia. . . . My mother was delighted by all these goings-on, but my father wasn't; he wanted me to be a preacher." James often spoke of his mother's encouragement of his career standing in opposition to his stepfather's disappointment.

In *Nobody Knows My Name*, James builds on his reflections in *Notes* by continuing his examination of race and reflecting on the role of the writer. Here too we see a blend between the autobiographical and social commentary. The title refers not only to the erasure of identity all Black people faced in America but also to the one he felt he faced from the moment he was born as an "illegitimate" child. He was given his mother's last name when he was born, and because of the way society works, without his father's name he was treated as though he lacked identity.

*The Fire Next Time* became an instant national bestseller and positioned James as a passionate voice of the civil rights movement. In it, he writes a letter to his nephew about the realities of being a Black boy in the United States. In one powerful section he says, "I *know* the conditions under which you were born, for I was there. . . . Your grandmother [Berdis] was also there, and no one has ever accused her of being bitter. I suggest that the innocents check with her. She isn't hard to find. Your countrymen don't know that *she* exists, either, though she has been working for them all their lives." James is telling his nephew and the rest of his audience about his mother's influence as well as the lack of credit and recognition she deserved but was denied. He's also saying that everyone would gain more knowledge if Berdis were asked to share her wisdom after all she'd witnessed. All three of these works are now classics in American history, and they show how influential Baldwin's mother was on his career.

*The Fire Next Time* was published in 1963, the same year that James met Attorney General Robert F. Kennedy, won the George Polk Memorial Award, led a civil rights demonstration in Paris, and participated in the March on Washington. It was an exciting year, to say the least. That summer, James invited his family to join him for a trip to Puerto Rico to celebrate his birthday. Berdis had never flown and had a deep fear of flying, but she wouldn't dream of ignoring the call to see her eldest son. Berdis and her other children joined James. When they arrived, James asked for their help with a play he was working on, titled *Blues for Mister Charlie*. Together they read the first two acts, each of them playing one of the roles. He cast Berdis as Mother Henry, and he later told his brother that he was so impressed by her beautiful performance, he strongly considered the possibility of having her play the role for him on Broadway.

*In 1957, Alberta was* named "Mother of the Year" by the *Atlanta Daily World* newspaper. Over the years, she was acknowledged by many as one of the prominent "mothers of the movement." It was clear to those who knew her, her own work, and her dedication to her husband's and children's work that she had made many sacrifices for the Black freedom movement. She was a well-educated woman who, like Berdis, constantly gave of herself to others without asking for anything in return. She'd sacrificed her career for her family, and she supported them on their journeys. She coached her husband through his schooling and comforted her children through each challenge and accomplishment. Alberta did all of this while still maintaining her power and agency. She volunteered with various organizations committed to social justice, all while leading the church choir. These commitments were not always easy to balance, but she saw them as her way to continue the work that her parents and her ancestors before them had started.

After doing everything in her power to support each of her children on their unique paths, Alberta found herself apart from all of them in their early adult years. She could not help worrying about them, and through many sleepless nights, she found herself praying for their safety. If she could have, she would have kept her kids at home, but she knew the world needed them.

Between in-person visits, Alberta and Martin Sr. would stay up-to-date with their children's educations, careers, marriages, and growing families through regular phone calls and letters. Christine, Martin (called "M.L." by his family), and Alfred Daniel ("A.D.") knew the importance of keeping their mother posted on their lives to ease her concerns, concerns that were growing alongside the dangers they faced in the 1950s and 1960s. In addition to the phone calls and letters, Alberta could follow her eldest son on television and on the covers of magazines and newspapers.

Alberta witnessed her boy, the one with the sensitive heart, the one who begged her to start school early and wore his sixth-grade graduation suit with such pride, take national and international stages. He was sharing the lessons she'd taught him with his audiences. Although she wanted to protect him, she knew there was nothing she could do beyond supporting him. She could not keep him from what God had in store for his life. She beamed with pride and voiced her support in her letters to him; she prayed with him over the phone. Alberta would often tell her husband that she would never fail to stand by her son, no matter how hard it was for her to see and imagine what could happen to him and his family.

In January 1956, Alberta and Martin Sr. received word that something had happened to Martin and Coretta's home in Montgomery. Martin was away for a meeting, and Coretta and their newborn, Yolanda, were at home alone when a bomb went off. Coretta and her daughter were safe, but the shock left Alberta distraught and weakened, bringing the danger her son and his family were constantly in to the forefront of her mind. She couldn't even bring herself to accompany her husband and Christine when they drove to see Martin and Coretta the next day. The stress was often too much for her, and Martin would later say, "My mother too had suffered. Like all parents, she was afraid for her son and his family. After the bombing she had had to take to bed under doctor's orders, and she was often ill later."

Martin would pay the cost of long-distance phone calls to check in with his mother. He knew that "if Mother could hear my voice on the telephone she would be temporarily consoled." Alberta's husband confirmed this; he could see that his wife was torn apart by the threats on their son's life. As he described it, "Each moment he was away, out of touch with her, became an eternity of waiting for the next indication of any kind that he was alright." Martin's commitment to the nonviolent movement, which constantly put him in harm's way, was the source of Alberta's deepest pride *and* pain.

During the 1950s, Martin spent much of his time outside of Atlanta. After finishing his degree, finding the love of his life, and leading successful nonviolent demonstrations, he became recognized internationally for his ability to move audiences through his words. Speeches such as "Give Us the Ballot" advocated for African American voting rights, while books such as *Stride Toward Freedom* provided a personal account of the movement he and his colleagues in the fight were building.

Martin found himself in a constant tug-of-war between the love and hate he received from his nation. On the one hand, he was adored by many and awarded for his efforts, he sat in meetings with presidents and other world leaders, and he had influence over their decisions. On the other hand, he was constantly threatened, called the "most notorious liar in the country," and jailed multiple times.

After the bombing of his home in 1956, he found himself in danger again in 1958. Alberta and Martin Luther Sr. received word that something was wrong and that this time Martin was at Harlem Hospital in New York City (the same hospital where James was born years earlier) undergoing emergency surgery. During a signing for his book, he was approached by a woman named Izola Ware Curry. Martin was looking down when she approached him and asked if he was Martin Luther King. When he replied in the affirmative, she plunged a letter opener directly into his chest. He was rushed to the hospital, and the following morning *The New York Times* ran an article stating that if he'd sneezed between the time of the stabbing and the surgery, he would have died from a punctured aorta. Alberta was in agony and wanted her son to come home right away.

Her prayers were answered when, in 1960, Martin, Coretta, and their children did indeed return to Atlanta so he could continue his work with the Southern Christian Leadership Conference. To his parents' delight, Martin also accepted his father's invitation to be co-pastor of Ebenezer Baptist Church with him. The church Alberta's parents built was now being led by her, her husband, and her eldest son.

Alberta had her son back home in Atlanta for the time being, but danger pursued him. In 1962, he was arrested at a prayer vigil, the same year he was assaulted by a member of the American Nazi Party. A twenty-four-year-old by the name of Roy James attacked Martin as he led an SCLC meeting. During his trial, Roy James bragged about being a lieutenant in the American Nazi group and he proudly pleaded guilty to the assault. He was sentenced to only thirty days in prison and charged a $25 fine. Even with her son closer to home, Alberta could not protect him from dangers like this kind of police intimidation and other white supremacist violence. His assailants bragged about hurting him, having no shame for their wrongdoings.

Alberta's worry was outweighed only by her love and pride for her son. Despite the many times she received bad news, pushing her to the brink, more often than not, when word arrived about Martin it was about something that made her joyful and proud of the son she'd raised.

The following year, in August 1963, Alberta, Martin Luther Sr., and their eldest, Christine, tuned in to watch Martin deliver one of his many speeches. Christine had come down with the flu and her parents did not feel up to traveling all the way to Washington, D.C., to see Martin speak. Instead, they all watched him on TV together while sitting in Alberta and Martin's family room. They watched in awe as their son addressed the world, telling them about his dream. Martin's words rang through their hearts: "I have a dream that my four little children will one day live in a nation where they will not be judged by the color of their skin but by the content of their character. . . . Let freedom ring from Stone Mountain of Georgia. . . . Black men and white men, Jews and Gentiles, Protestants and Catholics, will be able to join hands and sing in the words of the old Negro spiritual: 'Free at last! Free at last! Thank God Almighty, we are free at last!'" These were the teachings with which Alberta had raised her son.

Martin's family sat in silence as pride welled in their hearts and tears welled in Alberta's eyes. They knew this speech would go down as one of the most powerful in history. Their quiet astonishment was suddenly interrupted by the phone. Call after call came through from loved ones all around the country sharing their excitement and joy. These were the moments that balanced Alberta's deep fear for her son's life with happiness and hope. He was so clearly doing what God called him to do, and she would never stand in the way of that.

In early 1964, Alberta's son was named *Time* magazine's "Man of the Year," his face on the cover for the whole world to see. The year ended with Martin being awarded the Nobel Peace Prize. Alberta was jubilant; she wanted to see Martin accept the award in person, but she was not sure how they could afford tickets to Norway. Then, one Sunday after church, Martin asked Alberta and Christine to meet him in his office. Without their knowledge, he'd asked friends if they would be willing to help cover some of the travel costs for his family to be there with him when he received such an incredible recognition. He knew he could not accept an award, one that honored the work his family had started, on his own. Martin's friends happily obliged, pulling enough money together for his wife, parents, and siblings to travel and attend the ceremony. Alberta and Christine were overjoyed; they could not wait to tell the rest of the family. They returned home and immediately began planning for the trip of a lifetime. In the weeks that passed between hearing the news and boarding their flight, they planned their outfits, organized their itinerary, and made arrangements for the church to continue operating while they were away.

The day arrived: December 10, 1964. Alberta's son was about to become the youngest man and only the second African American to receive the most prestigious award on the planet. Her strong and curious boy had taken the lessons she'd instilled in him, combined them with his own experiences and education, and made an indelible mark on his community, his country, and all of humanity. Before leaving their hotel on that cold morning, Alberta busied herself to keep from crying. She looked at Martin and decided to focus on his clothes. The knot in his tie needed to be perfect, so she fiddled with it until it looked just right. She brushed his shoulders with her hands, making sure there were no wrinkles in his formal morning suit.

Later that day, the King family would sit at the grand event held in the Aula Hall at Oslo University, among a sea of white faces. Alberta could no longer keep from crying. She let the tears fall down her cheeks as her son spoke: "I accept this award today with an abiding faith in America and an audacious faith in mankind."

In between being on the cover of *Time* magazine and accepting the Nobel Peace Prize, Martin met another influential civil rights leader. This young man had reached out to Martin several times before they actually met, inviting him to participate in meetings and sending him articles from the Nation of Islam. Because they disagreed on their approach to solving the "race problem," Martin never accepted the invitations, but on March 26, as Martin wrapped up a press conference, he would meet this other young activist, who had recently reached a turning point in his own career.

"Well, Malcolm, good to see you," Martin said.

"Good to see you," Malcolm responded. "I am throwing myself into the heart of the civil rights struggle."

*Louise was imprisoned and* silenced during her twenty-five years at Kalamazoo, but her children, who became adults while she was away, carried forth both her and her late husband's legacy. Malcolm kept the spirit of his parents alive even after his father was murdered and while his mother was locked away. He became one of the most notable men in history.

Garveyites like Louise and Earl as well as members of the Nation of Islam promoted Black unity, Black pride, and Black autonomy. They refused to assimilate to whiteness, and they proclaimed Black to be beautiful; they celebrated their natural features and hair; they saw themselves as possessing their own worth separate from their white counterparts. Both also promoted the importance of Black people relying on their own efforts and their own economy. The only major difference between the two was that Garveyism veered more toward Christianity while the NOI veered toward Islam; yet in this, they also shared similarities in their devotion to strict religious practices.

Given these parallels, it was natural for Malcolm to become a leader in the Nation of Islam in the same way that both his parents had become Garveyite leaders. He carried his parents' legacy as he grew various temples across the country promoting radical Black pride, recovery from drug abuse, pursuit of education, and Black ownership as well as Black autonomy. Malcolm had been raised in these ideals, and he could take from the many lessons his parents taught him to grow the movement. When he taught new NOI members the importance of keeping a strict diet, he thought of his mother's instructions about pork; when he explained the importance of owning land, he thought of his parents' lessons around property in the various cities they'd lived; and when he pushed for history to be reevaluated from a different perspective, he remembered Louise's teachings being different from what the white man had taught him in school.

Following Johnson Hinton's savage beating and his brave confrontation with the police, Malcolm, who changed his last name to X in order to "replace" the "white slavemaster name of Little," became known around the globe. This caused him to be loved by his community and feared by many outside of it, just like his parents. He joined Martin Luther King, Jr., on the FBI's list of "key figures" who warranted significant surveillance. He suffered an increase in harassment from police and others who feared the rise in popularity of the Nation of Islam. This was not the first time Malcolm had experienced threats on his life. He'd grown up with them. He'd seen his parents face them, he'd watched as his mother stood tall while she was constantly under the eye of the state. In keeping with the example Louise provided for him, he refused to be deterred from his radical activism. He would commit himself to the larger cause of Black independence while still living his life, finding both joy and love.

In 1956, Malcolm met a woman by the name of Betty Sanders when she joined a nursing school friend for a visit to the Harlem NOI temple. Beautiful and intelligent, Betty was the adopted daughter of two activists who also preached the importance of self-reliance. She'd experienced Jim Crow as a child, and she continued to face racism in her own education and career. Black nurses were given assignments that were far worse than those given to their white counterparts. They were also subject to harassment from white patients. When Betty met Malcolm and heard him speak, she felt connected to him and his message. She started to visit the temple regularly and converted to Islam months after they met. Two short years later, the young couple got married after Malcolm proposed to Betty over the phone. They would create a large family together, similar to the family Malcolm grew up in, bringing six daughters into the world.

In 1960, Malcolm established *Muhammad Speaks*, a newspaper that promoted the message of the NOI similar to the way the *Negro World*, the newspaper Louise wrote for, promoted the message of Garveyism. *Muhammad Speaks* was crucial to the growth of the Nation of Islam, especially after the release of a documentary titled *The Hate That Hate Produced*. While the documentary brought more awareness to the NOI, it also led many to view their beliefs as violent and negative. The documentary caused Malcolm's relationship with the country and the world to lie between both intrigue and fear. He became one of the most sought-after speakers of his time, yet he was constantly criticized by those who aligned themselves more with Martin Luther's promotion of nonviolence. Malcolm was seen by many as being too radical, and he was painted in opposition to Martin. Malcolm was to Martin what Garvey was to the NAACP in the 1920s. While the world tried to put them on opposite sides, each was essential to the progression of the movement for Black lives. They were not against each other's aims, they simply differed in their approach to a shared goal.

After a life of constant changes and losses, Malcolm was shaken once again when a series of events led to his departure from the NOI. In a matter of months he discovered that his leader was an adulterer; he was vilified for comments he made in regard to President John F. Kennedy's assassination and was silenced by the organization he gave everything to help build. Malcolm's world spun around him. He was only being true to himself when he boldly spoke up against Elijah Muhammad's actions and when he shed light on the violence that took place in the United States on a daily basis, but he was punished for speaking his mind. He was silenced by the paper he himself established, and he eventually parted ways with the NOI and Elijah Muhammad.

Malcolm decided to form two of his own organizations. Muslim Mosque Incorporated was a religious organization, and the Organization of Afro-American Unity was a secular group that furthered the message of Pan-Africanism. The OAAU built on the global, Pan-African education Louise instilled in Malcolm. He'd been inspired by her teachings, passed down to her from her grandparents, as well as by traveling around the world on his mission to better understand global civil rights movements.

He was trying to move on with his life in the face of overwhelming pressure and instability, just as his parents had taught him to do, but he knew he was in danger. Malcolm predicted that he would be assassinated either by one of his former NOI peers or by the FBI or both. It was this feeling that caused him to open up and tell his story to the writer Alex Haley. In 1963, he allowed Haley to start keeping a record of his life, from Malcolm's perspective.

*The Autobiography of Malcolm X*, which begins with the story of Louise confronting the Ku Klux Klan while she was pregnant with Malcolm, was released in 1965. Just a year before, Malcolm had received news from his siblings that he'd never expected. What he heard on the other line was something he'd given up on for years. He hadn't thought it was possible, so he'd buried his hope for it somewhere deep inside. His mother was finally coming home. Louise was being released from Kalamazoo. Her other children's efforts and insistence that their mother was well enough to be with them were eventually rewarded after twenty-five long years.

In one of his many conversations with Alex Haley, Malcolm described his emotions prior to Louise's release: "Ever since we discussed my mother, I've been thinking about her. I realized that I had blocked her out of my mind—it was just unpleasant to think about her having been twenty-some years in that mental hospital. . . . I simply didn't feel the problem could be solved, so I had shut it out. I had built up subconscious defenses." Being separated from his mother was painful for Malcolm, so painful that he'd had to block out the thought of her just to keep moving forward. He felt helpless when he couldn't find a way to bring her home.

After twenty-five years of being separated from them, Louise sat with her children for a meal. She hugged each of them. She stared at them, proud of who they had all become. They were just babies when they'd been taken away and now they were all older, married and with children of their own. Malcolm later told Haley about their emotional reunion: "We had dinner with our mother for the first time in all those years! She's sixty-six, and her memory is better than mine and she looks young and healthy. She has more teeth than those who were instrumental in sending her to the institution." Malcolm and his siblings all reported that once Louise was home with them, she made a complete recovery from the supposed "symptoms" for which she'd been institutionalized to begin with.

In 1965, Malcolm's life was looking up. His mother was finally free, he was approaching his work with newfound wisdom, and his wife was expecting twins. Yet the war that was brewing against him only continued. After he returned from a trip to London, his family's home in East Elmhurst, Queens, was firebombed. The incident must have conjured up old memories for Malcolm, as he was awakened once again in the middle of the night to a shocking boom before smelling the smoke, seeing the flames, and running to gather his family. Following the attack, Malcolm said, "I'm not surprised that it was done. It doesn't frighten me. It doesn't quiet me down in any way or shut me up." His family fled from the attack unharmed, just as his mother and father had been able to do during his childhood.

Like his parents, Malcolm would not be stopped easily; he would not be scared into submission. His enemies were all too aware of this. So long as he was alive, he would continue his work, unafraid.

On February 21, Malcolm delivered his opening remarks at an OAAU rally in Harlem, with his pregnant wife and children sitting in the front row of the audience. A ruckus erupted from the crowd. Two men were arguing, and people turned toward them to see what was going on. Suddenly, shots rang out through the room and Malcolm fell to the ground. Betty cried out in agony while the rest of the four-hundred-person audience scrambled, trying to run out of the Audubon Ballroom.

Malcolm was pronounced dead upon his arrival at Columbia-Presbyterian Medical Center. Bullets had pierced his chest, shoulder, arms, and legs.

Betty lost her husband, six daughters lost their father, and only a year after being released from Kalamazoo, Louise tragically lost her son again. This was her little boy, the one who took after her in both his looks and his attitude, the one who stood for what he believed in, the one who wouldn't give up until he got what he wanted. The little boy who would carefully tend to his peas and sit by his garden, staring up at the sky and dreaming about his future. A brilliant boy who became a man willing to bravely stand for his people and continuously learn from both triumphs and trials. At only thirty-nine years of age, Malcolm had so much more life to live. Louise thought she would have time to make up for all the years they'd missed together, the years that had been robbed from them; but she had lost her son, and this time it was for good.

Louise's son was gone, but in his short time on this earth he did what she taught him to do. He left his mark in the hearts and minds of millions as he challenged white supremacy as no one else could and liberated others from its grasp. In the days that followed his murder, thousands of people traveled to Harlem to mourn the loss of Malcolm, a man who gave his life so courageously for the cause of Black freedom. A few months after he passed, his autobiography was released, and shortly after, Betty gave birth to the couple's last two daughters. Just like Louise, Betty would be left to raise her children without their father.

*After Malcolm was brutally* assassinated, many turned to Martin Luther King, Jr., for his thoughts. The two had been painted as polar opposites: one as a nonviolent leader and the other as a "dangerous" radical. Martin wrote:

> He was an eloquent spokesman for his point of view and no one can honestly doubt that Malcolm had a great concern for the problems that we face as a race. While we did not always see eye to eye on methods to solve the race problems, I always had a deep affection for Malcolm and felt that he had the great ability to put his finger on the existence and root of the problem.

Martin knew how deeply they both cared about their community, even if they differed in their approaches.

As the 1960s continued, it seemed that Martin could not and would not be stopped from his mission to spread the message of nonviolence, to stand for those who had been pushed to the margins, and to display that change was fully within reach. Following his acceptance of the Nobel Peace Prize, Martin specifically continued fighting alongside his comrades invested in gaining the right to vote for African Americans. One of the most famous demonstrations of solidarity in American history, because of both the violence marchers faced and their resolve to keep going despite the violence, came in Selma, Alabama, in 1965. On March 7, six hundred people, led by Martin Luther King, Jr., set out from Selma toward Montgomery, the state capital. Their peaceful demonstration was not allowed to go very far before it was attacked by state troopers wielding weapons of war. They used whips, tear gas, and nightsticks to beat the nonviolent demonstrators. This extreme brutality was caught on camera and it captured the attention of viewers around the world. Hundreds flew to Selma to join hands with Martin and his fellow marchers. Two days later, undeterred and with even more support, Martin led two thousand people over the Edmund Pettus Bridge, forcing state troopers to step aside.

Martin participated in as many marches and demonstrations as he could, traveling around the country, often accompanied by Coretta. He wanted to maintain his involvement and use his own gifts of oration and organization to keep others' spirits up and advise on strategy. His younger brother, A.D., began to join him as well.

Alberta was proud of her sons and their crucial roles in the movement, but still she feared for their lives. Martin was given more airtime and influence because of how moving his words could be and how effectively he could bring people together. This scared Alberta even more. After dinner at the King household one night, as they sat on their patio and watched the sun set, Martin turned toward Alberta and said, "Mother, there are some things I want you to know." He continued,

"There's a chance, Mother, that someone is going to try to kill me, and it could happen without any warning at all.

"But I don't want you to worry over any of this. . . ." He came closer to her side. "I have to go on with my work, no matter what happens now, because my involvement is too complete to stop."

Alberta's eldest son had just told her that he might be killed soon but that she should not worry. The request was impossible. She must have known there was nothing she could do to stop him. Alberta's sons both returned to their work and did their best to reassure her that they were fine by calling her almost daily. Martin Sr. would fondly remember the phone calls Alberta shared with the two of them, hearing them laugh, seeing her smile, and finding comfort, even if for only a short moment.

On April 4, 1968, Alberta received two calls from her sons before noon, and she found herself in good humor as she drove with her husband to church for a Thursday evening celebration of life for a member of Ebenezer who had recently passed. She knew Martin planned on delivering some words that night in Memphis as a follow-up to his "I've Been to the Mountaintop" speech from the night before.

As the two pulled up to their church, their car was blocked from entering by a driver in front of them who ceaselessly honked her horn and yelled something neither Alberta nor Martin Sr. could understand. They looked at each other, confusion on their faces. Something was wrong, but they did not know what. When the woman eventually pulled away and allowed them to park, the two rushed into the church building to turn on the radio. The words they heard stopped them in their tracks.

Memories rushed into Alberta's head as she thought of her eldest son. She thought of the way he came home looking to her for guidance; she thought of holding him in her arms and doing her best to protect him from and prepare him for the world outside of their home.

No matter how much she had done, no matter all the lessons she had taught him, no matter how many resources she had given him, she was hearing words she'd been dreading for years: "Dr. Martin Luther King, the apostle of nonviolence in the civil rights movement, has been shot to death in Memphis, Tennessee." Martin Sr. turned to Alberta, whose face was covered with tears; she cried in silence, unable to make any noise. After all the time she had spent worried sick about her boy, her worst fears had become reality. Her son, her precious and peaceful son, was gone, taken away from this world in an act of pure hatred and violence.

Just five days later, Martin Luther King, Jr., was buried in Atlanta. Thousands of people lined the streets to mourn their fallen prince. Activists, preachers, and artists at the height of their careers were in attendance to pay him due honor for his work on their behalf. Martin Sr. described it as a "funeral that gathered up America's attention for a day. One day in exchange for so many others." The suffering Alberta experienced in losing Martin was unimaginable, but she wanted to be there for her loved ones. She did her best to hold herself together, and she focused on supporting her daughter, daughter-in-law, and grandchildren. Her husband would later say, "I came to admire my wife's great personal strength during this period. She suffered enormously but never neglected to be available to others in the family who needed her."

Alberta and Martin grieved their eldest son, but they knew that he'd made the most of his mere thirty-nine years on earth and that he was now sitting with his heavenly Father. They knew they needed to continue with their own lives, that they still had work to do. In the midst of their pain, they held on to their loved ones tightly, especially their children and grandchildren.

Following Martin Jr.'s passing, A.D. was installed as the co-pastor of Ebenezer Baptist. Then, only fifteen months after Martin's assassination, in the early hours of a morning in July, Alberta and Martin Sr. received a call from their grandson.

A.D.'s son was flustered and scared; he kept saying there was trouble at the house and he needed them to get there quickly. Alberta, afraid of what they would see upon their arrival, could not bring herself to get in the car. She could not stand any more tragedy, so Martin Sr. left her at home and rushed to his youngest child's house. He got there at the same time as the fire truck and ambulance. But they were all too late. A.D. had mysteriously drowned in his pool, and he could not be resuscitated.

Alberta and Martin lost not one son but two. They were deprived of answers as to what had actually happened to either of them. To this day, it is unclear who shot Martin Luther King, Jr., and the King family never found out exactly how A.D., who was a good swimmer, drowned. Alberta and Martin Sr. were distraught, but they did not want hate to enter their hearts. If it did, their sons' deaths would be in vain. They needed to keep faith and hope alive for the rest of their family, especially their grandchildren, who were now fatherless. They needed to keep the light shining that they'd passed to their children and that their lost children had now passed back to them.


*Some say that by* the 1960s, Malcolm, Martin, and James found themselves more in line with one another than they ever had before. They'd come to appreciate each other's differing roles in the larger movement, and they'd grown in their respect for one another. Kenneth Clark, an interviewer who had spoken to the three separately on different occasions, had even arranged for them all to sit down in conversation together for the first time on February 23, 1965. Of course, the meeting never took place, as Malcolm had been assassinated only two days earlier.

Malcolm's death caused profound inner turmoil for James. As David Leeming put it, "When reporters arrived to interview Baldwin on the night of the assassination, they found a man in deep distress. He spoke in rhetorical terms they had difficulty following." James shouted, "You did it! It is because of you—the men who created this white supremacy—that this man is dead. You are not guilty, but you did it! . . . Your mills, your cities, your rape of a continent started all this." In James's opinion, this was another product of the "white problem," a plague that denied Black people their humanity. Malcolm's death, along with several other major losses for the Black civil rights movement, began to disillusion James, and although he continued to participate through his writing and his speeches, his message began to take a more somber tone and he found a closer allegiance with Malcolm's "righteous anger."

On April 4, 1968, James sat by a swimming pool in Palm Springs, listening to an Aretha Franklin record, when he received a call telling him of Martin's assassination. He dropped his phone and immediately began to weep. Martin had been murdered, and James, the master of language, couldn't find the words to mourn his friend. He made his way to Atlanta to attend the funeral and honor the mark Martin had left on their world.

James continued in his resolve to bear witness to the works of his friends. Through the seventies and early eighties he wrote the classics *No Name in the Street*, *If Beale Street Could Talk*, and *Just Above My Head*. He went on living his life fully, with both joy and pain, spending his time mostly outside of the United States with partners and friends.

In 1986, James returned to France from London in a depressed mood. He lacked interest in any new projects, and he couldn't bring himself to eat or drink nearly anything. He confided in a friend that he could barely swallow but that he refused to see a doctor. His friend called for help anyway, and James was taken to the closest hospital, where he was diagnosed with cancer of the esophagus. Although a laser treatment improved things temporarily and allowed him to eat and drink again, James worried this might be his end. He threw his energy into writing a play, *The Welcome Table*, which would become his final work.

He did not let his friends or family know just how serious his condition was. He even continued to work on his play until his final week of life. By July 1987, his body began to deteriorate. The cancer had spread to his lungs and he was running out of time, but he still wrote to his loved ones as if he were fine. He even asked one of his friends to interview the widows of Medgar Evers, Malcolm X, and Martin Luther King, Jr., in his stead for a project he was planning to start working on.

By November, James was nearly unrecognizable: his already small frame had lost significant weight, he had an IV in his arm, and he could barely sit up in bed. On November 26, James insisted that he wanted a "real Thanksgiving dinner," and knowing this might be his last chance to do so, he wanted to talk to his mother over the phone. He was happy and comforted to hear her voice. Berdis knew her son was dying. She and her eldest son were so close that even though he tried to hide it, she could hear that he was weakened and his time was coming. The call was long and sad, and when it was over, tears streamed down Berdis's face. Her heart was heavy; she did not think she would live to bury her boy, the boy who had stood by her side his whole life, who'd inherited her talents and changed people's lives with them.

Jimmy spent his last days surrounded by friends and his brother David. He reminisced with them as he grew weaker by the hour. A few days after his phone call with Berdis, on November 30 to be exact, James was drifting away, barely able to open his eyes anymore. David kissed his older brother on the forehead and said, "It's all right, Jimmy, you can cross over now." When James breathed his last breath, David walked into a different room and put on a record. "Amazing Grace," and the sounds of James's loved ones mourning filled the house.

James's body was flown back home to Harlem for a celebration of his life and his burial. His coffin was draped in black and the procession of his loved ones was led by Berdis. She was pushed down the aisle in a wheelchair as she sobbed while drums played in the background. Her mourning echoed throughout the church, and her cries were remembered by those in attendance above all else.

Although Berdis's son went on to live a much longer life than Louise's and Alberta's, she still was not spared the pain of burying him. She'd lost her firstborn, her right hand, her little Jimmy, who would do anything to give back to her what she had given to him. Maya Angelou, Toni Morrison, and Amiri Baraka were among several of the visionaries and leaders who delivered heartfelt tributes in honor of their brother. They were dear friends of Jimmy's who had come to know Berdis as well. Berdis's son's funeral, just like Malcolm's and Martin's, was attended by thousands whose lives had been forever changed by his works.

*In 1965, the American* sociologist Daniel Patrick Moynihan released *The Negro Family: The Case for National Action.* In his report, Moynihan highlighted the economic plight Black Americans were facing and he argued for national interventions. While he believed he was doing something in service to the Black community, by calling attention to the disparities they faced, his report caused more harm than good. Immediately following its release, Black civil rights leaders criticized Moynihan for his perpetuation of stereotypes that implied Black people were mentally inferior and prone to violence. His observations lacked an informed analysis of the role violence *against* Black people played in the challenges they encountered Moynihan also implied that most of the blame for Black struggle in the United States should be placed on the matriarchal structure of Black households. He said that Black families were falling behind white families because Black women were leading their homes.

Moynihan's report followed a pattern that unfortunately is still in place today, one that is quick to blame Black mothers and fails to give them credit for their ability to persist, provide, and create new possibilities for their children despite attacks against them. To this day, Black mothers are vilified, told to do better with less, blamed when they cannot make ends meet, but never thanked when they miraculously do. Reflecting on this reality and the intention behind it, the activist, scholar, and poet Alexis Pauline Gumbs writes, "Those of us who nurture the lives of those children who are not supposed to exist, who are not supposed to grow up, who are revolutionary in their very beings are doing some of the most subversive work in the world. If we don't know it, the establishment does." Gumbs describes Black women and children as the "generators of an alternative destiny," a destiny that defies the limits that have intentionally and strategically been placed on us.

In Berdis, Alberta, and Louise, one can see even more clearly just how flawed Moynihan's assumptions were. These women are just three of the countless examples of Black mothers who allowed their children to thrive even when all odds were stacked against them—Black mothers who created new visions for the world through the abundant love with which they raised their children. They had to believe in something their larger world said was impossible, that they and their children held the power to move mountains.

For many Black activists, the plight Black mothers face was and is a driving force in their work. Nowhere can the denial of Black humanity be seen more clearly than in the treatment of Black mothers and their children throughout U.S. history. Black women are the only people who have legally been deemed the givers of nonlife, the givers of property, and as Fannie Lou Hamer puts it, Black people are the only ones who have had babies sold from their mothers and mothers sold from their babies. Her words shine a light on the way in which this has propelled Black people to work on behalf of the salvation of the United States, committing themselves to use their pain to inspire change.

In James, Malcolm, and Martin we witness the direct connection between their heroic work and their mothers. They carried their mothers with them in everything they did. Contrary to previous tellings, these men were not individuals who were born ready to change the world; they are instead part of a larger whole, part of a generational bank of knowledge that was passed on to them. They were products of what their families and environments taught them, and very specifically what their mothers taught them through both their words and their actions. All three men were well aware of this. They saw their mothers as their primary guides even when they were away from them and even, in Malcolm's case, when they were separated from them at a young age. These men gave credit to their mothers and had a deep understanding that they could not be who they were without the lessons they inherited.

While all three women were incredibly proud of their sons' works, they found themselves in another tug-of-war. Just as the way they needed to survive when their humanity was denied time and time again, so they had to push against the fear of losing their children as they entered the battlefield, attempting to change the country in ways previously unseen. These women, like so many Black mothers before and after them, were forced to sacrifice their children for a larger cause.

Louise, Alberta, and Berdis were focused on teaching their children the way to survive in a world that would deny them their humanity, to give them the tools they had picked up along the way. These women taught their children, in the best way they knew how, to maintain their sense of worth and inherent dignity even if they were going to hear the opposite beyond their homes. Could they have known just how far these lessons would take their boys? The three mothers may not have viewed their approach to parenting as radical, but in seeing the effect their love and lessons had on their sons and on the world as a result, one cannot deny the revolutionary power of their motherhood.

## Part VIII

# The Circumstances of Our Death

I saw my mother's face again, and felt, for the first time, how the stones of the road she had walked on must have bruised her feet.

—JAMES BALDWIN

The mother is the first teacher of the child. The message she gives that child, that child gives to the world.

—MALCOLM X

It is something like the mother giving birth to a child. While she is temporarily consoled by the fact that her pain is not just bare meaningless pain, she nevertheless experiences the pain. In spite of the fact that she realizes beneath her pain is the emergence of life in a radiant infant, she experiences the agony right on.

—MARTIN LUTHER KING, JR.

By the mid-1970s, as American citizens witnessed the culmination of the Vietnam War, after rising tension and bloodshed both abroad and at home, Alberta and Martin Luther King, Sr., had brought three children into the world and seen the arrival of twelve grandchildren as well as one great-grandchild. Their own descendants carried the family legacy of promoting peace and social justice with Christian faith at the core of their work, a legacy passed on to Alberta by her parents and their parents before them.

Although the couple suffered the tragedies of losing both their sons, they could sit with a sense of full gratification as they reflected on the accomplishments of their children. Their eldest became an assistant professor of education at Spelman College, following directly in her mother's footsteps; their middle child, the Nobel laureate, was known and will continue to be known all over the world as a leader of the nonviolent movement for racial justice; and their youngest did his own part in fighting for civil rights while leading his congregations in joining the rise of Black liberation. Their grandchildren would also carry the torch forward for future generations. Alberta and Martin, having suffered unimaginable losses, still could do nothing but thank the Lord for their family and the everlasting impact they had already made on their nation and the world. They could not be more proud of their daughter, and whenever they mourned the loss of their sons, they were comforted seeing Martin's and A.D.'s works continue to inspire, giving them a presence that could never be fully extinguished.

Alberta Christine Williams King is best known for being the mother of the revered Dr. Martin Luther King, Jr. She veered away from the spotlight and preferred to support from the background. She was humble and eager to help others on their journeys, especially her family members. She was most proud of the family she built, thankful for the blessings of a happy marriage that led to children, grandchildren, and great-grandchildren. In accepting one of the various awards and recognitions she received over the years, she thanked her husband and children, who helped her "earn the credentials of wife and mother," credentials she saw as some of the highest anyone could accomplish. Others might have seen her quitting her career in order to be a wife and mother as too great a sacrifice, but Alberta saw her decision as part of fulfilling her life's greatest honor.

While Alberta was most proud of her role as a wife and a mother, one who stood by her family through their own missions, her legacy extended far beyond these roles. As an educated Black woman who received her training in the public schools of Atlanta, Spelman Seminary, Hampton Institute, and Morris Brown College, she was able to use her privileges to lead, organize, and encourage others. She did this for her husband, her children, and the children of her children, as well as members of her community. As an extremely talented musician, Alberta touched the lives of each of her students as she passed her gifts on to them.

Even though she could no longer teach in the public school system after getting married, she continued to be a powerful instructor. She was the organist director of Ebenezer Baptist for thirty years, from 1932 until 1962, and the organist for the Women's Auxiliary to the National Baptist Convention from 1950 until 1962. She also reestablished the Ebenezer choir, which she directed for several decades. Her choirs were one of the main reasons so many people from all walks of life came to visit Ebenezer as a tourist destination, a religious staple in the South, and a living monument of the civil rights movement. The choir was even selected to perform at events around the country including the premiere of *Gone with the Wind*.

Beyond education and music, Alberta cared deeply about the role women played in organizing and activism. She founded the Women's Council of Ebenezer Baptist and was its president for several years. She was a life member of the National Baptist Convention's Women's Auxiliary, an active member of the Phyllis Wheatley branch of the YWCA and the NAACP, and a member of the Women's International League for Peace and Freedom. All of her work earned her several recognitions and awards over the years: in addition to being named "Mother of the Year" by the *Atlanta Daily World*, she was also recognized for her work by the Business and Professional Women of the National Baptist Convention, the National Beauty Culturists' League, Sigma Gamma Rho Sorority, and many more.

As natural as teaching was to her, Alberta never stopped being a student. She was open to what her children, students, and community could teach her, and she deeply enjoyed traveling to new places. Believing that all humans deserve equal rights, she took trips all over the United States, Europe, and the Caribbean with the goal of continuing to grow in her knowledge and better understand the lives of different people outside of Atlanta. In them she saw more of their similarities than their differences.

Alberta's work did not stop when she got married, it did not stop when she became a mother, it did not stop when her heart was weighed down by anxiety over the danger her children faced, it didn't even stop when she buried her sons. Alberta used her family teachings, her own training, her love for her family, her deepest pain, and her desire to educate to touch the lives of others and, by doing so, to live a full life. Loved ones said, "Her teachings of unshakable faith and love for mankind were instrumental in shaping the nonviolent movement which has changed the course of history."

Most Sundays in the King house followed a similar pattern. Martin and Alberta woke up in preparation for church: she would ready herself to play the organ, while he would go over his sermon. Sometimes they would briefly discuss Alberta's growing concern for Martin Sr.'s travels. Since their sons' passing, he'd been speaking at colleges and churches around the country, not seeing any need for retirement even at seventy-five years of age. Alberta could see how tired he was, and again she lost sleep as her concerns grew for the safety of another member of her family. After all the loss they'd experienced, it was difficult for Alberta not to imagine the worst scenario anytime her husband left for one of his lectures. As Martin described it, "She carried that burden that only mothers can know, the burden that comes with losing children of whatever age. That her sons were grown when they passed and had lived extraordinary lives didn't minimize the feeling that they were still her babies when they were taken away."

On the morning of June 30, 1974, Martin rose before Alberta and looked at her as she slept. He thought about her unmatched strength and was comforted that she was finding rest, even if only temporarily. He drove to church alone, knowing his wife would arrive only a little later. After greeting various church members on his way in, he sat in his office to go through the mail that had accumulated during the week he'd been traveling. He suddenly found himself feeling restless with a desire to walk around the church and decided to go downstairs to walk past the rooms in the church basement. These were buzzing with Sunday school classes and bright young faces, but he felt another presence, too, as he saw faces passing by him that he did not recognize. This was not out of the ordinary, as visitors came to Ebenezer from all corners of the world, but something about this specific unfamiliarity felt wrong to Martin. There was a group of young men who looked tense. They smiled without warmth or happiness. One particular set of eyes watched Martin as he was turning to go back to his study.

Now back in his office, he tried to push the feeling of discomfort away. He could hear the sound of the organ in the background, putting him at ease. This meant that his wife, his Bunch of Goodness, had arrived and was playing her beautiful melodies. Martin made his way into the main sanctuary, greeted by the blooming organ sounds. The seats were filled as usual, and late arrivals craned their necks to find any remaining space in the pews. In the crowd, he could see some of his family members and he started to walk toward his daughter, Christine. On his way, he took a moment to turn toward the platform where the organ sat. He stared at his wife again as she played her instrument softly. Memories of their life together flashed before his eyes.

A voice suddenly yelled out from the crowd, interrupting Martin's thoughts. "I'm taking over here this morning!" the unfamiliar voice declared. A gunshot sliced through the air and Alberta cried out. Her hands were now on her face and her fingers were filled with blood.

In total shock, Martin looked toward the man. He saw the same eyes that haunted him earlier that morning, now flagrantly filled with anger. All Martin could think to do was get as close as he could to the love of his life. He started on his way toward her when he heard more shots ring out and saw Alberta falling forward, holding her side. People were scrambling to get out of the church alive; many tried pulling Martin with them, but all he could say was, "I can't leave here without Bunch!"

Alberta and Martin's grandson Derek tackled the assailant, but not before Alberta and several others had been severely injured. Ambulances and police rushed to the church and Martin raced behind the ambulance, which carried Alberta to Grady Memorial Hospital. The memories of their shared life continued to flash before him. When he was able to see Alberta, she tried to talk, but all she could utter were gasping sounds as she was rolled away. Only a few minutes later, Martin was approached by a young doctor saying words that were all too familiar: "I'm sorry, Reverend King, we just couldn't save her. All of us tried, but it was just too late."

Alberta's daughter, Christine, who'd become so strong after being inconsolable in her earliest moments, described her mother's passing as the worst day of her life. She remembered being eager to get to church because Alberta would be reuniting with the choir she'd established forty years earlier. Christine would now work to fill—as much as she could—the hole her mother's death created in their family. She comforted her father, her children, her nieces and nephews; she now carried forward not only the legacies of her brothers but that of her mother as well.

Alberta's life was honored by two celebrations. One took place on Tuesday, July 2, at Spelman College's Sister Chapel and the other on July 3 at Ebenezer Baptist. Her funeral fittingly began with an organ prelude and included the hymns "All the Way My Savior Leads Me" and "For All the Saints Who from Their Labors Rest." Performers whom Alberta had taught and mentored over the years came back to honor their teacher. In her obituary it was said that she "immortalized herself through her students" and that "the musical inspiration that flowed from her permeated the church, the city of Atlanta, the nation, and the world." Just as her sons' works immortalized them, so too did Alberta's teachings. The church overflowed with visitors who wanted to pay their respects to the mother of the movement. The first Black mayor of Atlanta, Maynard Jackson, delivered a touching tribute. The funeral program was printed on pink paper because, as Martin described it, "Bunch was music and pink is the color of music." The final words printed on the program read:

> Servant of God well Done, Rest from you love employ;
> The battle is fought, the victory's won, enter thy Master's
>   joy.
> A voice at midnight came, she started up to hear;

*A mortal arrow pierced her frame, she fell but felt no fear.*

*The pains of death are past; labor and sorrow cease;*

*And life's long war-fare closed at last, her soul is found in*
*    peace.*

*Soldier of Christ, well done; praise be thy new employ;*

*And, while eternal ages run, rest in thy Savior's joy.*

*Amen.*


*Louise lived for twenty-six* more years after losing her son Malcolm. This was the same amount of time she'd been kept from her children during her institutionalization at the Kalamazoo State Hospital. The little girl from Grenada, the one who dreamed of traveling the globe, the one who could not wait for her chance to join the fight for Black lives, lived an incredible and long life filled with both sorrow and jubilation, loss and triumph.

She lived through all of the events of the early 1900s. She then witnessed the formation of the Black Panther Party—a revolutionary organization with ideological links to both Garveyism and the Nation of Islam. Louise also lived to see the end of the Vietnam War, the election and reelection of President Ronald Reagan, the first launch of the space shuttle, and the United States invasion of her homeland. She would likely have heard of a Black director by the name of Spike Lee, who released his first feature film, *She's Gotta Have It*, in 1986. Just a year after her passing, this same director would create a masterpiece tribute to her own son. She might have watched one of the very first episodes of *The Oprah Winfrey Show*, and maybe she heard of the passing of the novelist and playwright James Baldwin. Some of these specifics cannot be confirmed, but they represent the incredible range of events Louise lived through and alongside in her ninety-seven years of life.

Louise, with her almost century on this earth, would leave an indelible print on the lives of millions, most of whom are still unaware of her name. She was a feminist grassroots community activist whose works present a model for others to follow. Her activism helped to push forward the causes of Black nationalism, Pan-Africanism, and the African diaspora as a whole. As the educated and radical woman she was, she became a crucial member of the Marcus Garvey movement. She and her husband brought attention to an area of the United States that has often been forgotten in tellings of Black revolutionary history. While much of history has focused on the South and the East Coast, Erik McDuffie, professor of African American Studies at the University of Illinois at Urbana-Champaign, explains that Louise's commitment to the Midwest serves as a reminder of its, and its people's, importance. Out of the claimed two million members of the Garvey movement, Louise was reported as being one of Garvey's closest confidantes. Her eldest son, Wilfred, recalled Louise writing letters on Garvey's behalf and even helping to shelter him in their home when he was being pursued by the FBI. This act was a risky one, but Louise did not let fear control her. Wilfred also remembered his mother receiving letters from other leaders of the movement filled with gratitude for her contributions to their shared cause.

For those who worked closely with her, she provided an example of someone who was unafraid to stand up against traditional notions of gender and race. Like other prominent women in the Garvey movement, she challenged patriarchy and racism by taking control of her narrative and involving herself in the heart of the organization. Although women were not allowed to be presidents of UNIA chapters, Louise used her position as the Omaha UNIA secretary to influence the decisions and directions of the branch.

Louise was aware of the need to be in control of her own narrative, despite others relentlessly trying to take this agency away. This self-assurance was made clear in the way she explained and presented herself to her children and, later, her grandchildren. The simple fact that her kids knew of her encounter with members of the Black Legion, whether they were alive to witness the moment or not, displays Louise's desire for her children to truly know who she was as a radical activist. Every time she taught them to rely on their own skills, to be aware of the happenings of the world for themselves, to question any teachings that taught them they were inferior, she was practicing her activism.

Her children witnessed her strength every time she stood up to her husband; she was unafraid of his intensity and would not be silenced in her own home. They bore witness to her resistance when welfare workers began showing up and challenging her ability to raise her children. She fully believed that her institutionalization in Kalamazoo was a form of incarceration and state punishment for her desire to live as a free, single, immigrant Black woman.

The lessons she taught her children would eventually secure her freedom once again. The Littles would not give up on the fight to have Louise released, no matter how long it might take. For twenty-plus years they pursued her liberation, until finally they were successful and Louise was allowed to return home. This return would not be the end of her hardships, however, as she would quickly face the devastating loss of her son. Following his assassination, Louise would also hear the many misunderstandings of her son's mission; Malcolm was certainly celebrated by his followers, but he was also hated by anyone who rejected his unapologetic pursuit of Black freedom.

The state continued to attack the Little family well after Louise's release from Kalamazoo. In 1997, her family received a "Petition for Reimbursement" that stated the Little family owed the state more than $13,000 for the treatment Louise received while she was in their "care." She'd been institutionalized against her will and then posthumously charged for it. The petition read, "The said Louise Little has certain relatives who are liable for his/her support and for the expenses paid and to be paid by the state of Michigan for the care and maintenance of said patient in said hospital." It continued, "Your petitioner verily believes that said relatives have been and are possessed of means sufficient and adequate to reasonably enable them to contribute at least in part to the care and maintenance of said patient in said hospital and to reimburse the said State and County for the expense paid and to be paid by them, but they have neglected so to do."

Just as the attacks persisted, the resistance of the Little family did as well. Louise's children had been taught by her, Earl, and through them their ancestors, and they were not going to succumb to the threats of the state now. Each of her children and grandchildren would find their own way to continue the legacy they were born into. Her sons Wilfred Little, Philbert Little, and Reginald Little, like their brother Malcolm, played important roles in the Nation of Islam as ministers in Michigan.

Her eldest son, Wilfred, who was the first in the family to join the NOI, became a well-known community activist who would continue to share his family's story with countless audiences around the country for years to come. Although audiences most often invited him to speak specifically about his brother Malcolm, Wilfred began many of his talks reminding them where Malcolm came from. He shared several stories about their parents and focused heavily on the lessons their mother taught them. In one lecture he spoke about his mother's ability to combat any source that told her children they were "less than." As he recalled:

> My mother didn't want us to fall victim to that, so she would teach us at home when we came home from school. We would give her what we had learned that day, and she would then reteach it to us and give it to us in a way where it would do away with some of those negative things they had incorporated in there . . . and I never remember a time when we ever felt that because we were black, we were something inferior to anybody else.

Another of Louise's sons, Robert Little, the first in his family to graduate from college, also took inspiration from his mother's ability to nurture future generations in the way he and his siblings were nurtured and pursued his career in social work and family caregiving. He went on to become the commissioner of New York City's Child Welfare Administration. Robert would say, "I came to the business on the receiving end," referencing his family's history with welfare and foster care systems. He received praise over the years for decentralizing welfare bureaucracies, including counseling and training in youth services, and increasing subsidies for the adoption of disabled children.

Louise's sons certainly carried the torch passed on to them, but her work in grassroots activism is even more apparent in her daughters' and granddaughters' lives. Her daughter Yvonne Woodward became the first Black telephone operator in Lansing and, later, the first one in Grand Rapids. She never converted to Islam like her brothers, but she was committed to building self-sustaining Black communities. She wanted to pass on her mother's lessons around landownership and Black unity to as many people as she could. In the 1960s, Yvonne moved to a historically Black town in central Michigan called Woodland Park. There she purchased her own land, established a community grocery store, and built a public park in the center of town. She spoke out against racism and was intent on protecting her family's story and setting the record straight on anything that misrepresented them. Several of Yvonne's family members moved to Woodland Park to join the beautiful, independent Black community she built. Her mother, Louise, even spent her final years there surrounded by her beloved children and grandchildren.

Following her institutionalization and the attempted rupture of their family, Louise no longer participated in direct activism and organizing and instead spent her last quarter of a century living a private life surrounded by her loved ones. She did not speak publicly about her life

story, she never wrote a book, she didn't even comment on the assassination of her son, but she grieved privately and shared her story with
the youngest and newest members of her family. Her grandchildren
are well aware of her life's work and her importance in raising their
parents. They have also been committed to keeping her alive through
their talks and activism. Attallah Shabazz, Malcolm and Betty's eldest,
says that she is her grandmother's keeper, and she honors Louise each
day through her own work as a diplomat and an author.

As Yvonne's daughter Deborah Jones says, "The history of
Grandma Little is so important to Black women." It is a simple statement but one that holds immense power. Imagine if every Black
woman knew the story of the girl who was born out of a potentially
tragic situation, who carried her West African ancestry with pride,
who learned the stories of her people, who went on to become an
activist and a close confidante of one of the most recognized revolutionaries in history, who then gave birth to her children, one of whom
continues to touch the hearts of millions decades following his murder.
Louise was a woman who bravely challenged white supremacy and a
woman who refused to be silenced. Her story, alongside Alberta's and
Berdis's and those of countless other Black mothers, are so important
to all of us. They allow us to see the possibilities in our own lives no
matter what we go through and no matter what we're told we can or
cannot be.

Louise never returned home to Grenada, but her descendants
found themselves wanting to learn more about her and their own
roots. Many of them traveled, and continue to travel, back to Grenada
to reestablish a family connection there and gain a more profound
appreciation for her.

Louise passed away in 1991 after living happily in Woodland Park
for her final years. Her life was honored by her family in a private
memorial service in Grand Rapids. There is no tombstone in place for
one to visit, as Louise expressed her desire to be cremated instead. Her

ashes were scattered across the Woodland Park area, symbolizing the final release of the shackles she fought against for more than ninety years.

*The Baldwin home, sitting* on West Seventy-first Street between Columbus Avenue and Broadway, was named a historic landmark in June 2019 for its importance as James Baldwin's residence. What many do not know today, however, is that to the Baldwin family, this was not James's home but his mother's. He spent much of his time there, but he had purchased it for Berdis. It had always been his dream to buy a home for her, and he fulfilled this honorable goal in 1966. In the four-story building one could find his youngest sister, Paula, living on the first floor, another sister, Gloria, on the third floor, and his mother, Berdis, on the second floor in the middle of the two. Her placement in the middle of the shared home was symbolic of the central role she played in her family.

Berdis's home became a headquarters for the Baldwins. The first floor was almost always booming with conversation, music, and visitors, and the second floor was filled with the aroma of Berdis's cooking. She loved keeping her loved ones full and would sit on a chair close to her kitchen so she could move in and out of it to check on her dishes and bring them out as soon as they were ready to share.

James brought all of his close friends to the house on Seventy-first Street, where they too could partake in the company, cooking, and conversation. It was in this home that he introduced the likes of Toni Morrison, Maya Angelou, and Marlon Brando to his mother, who welcomed each of them and many more, as her own children. These three luminaries spoke highly and affectionately of Berdis whenever they talked about her son, their dear friend. It was also in this home that her grandchildren would form some of their most vibrant memories and come to learn that Grandma Berdis was the central focal point of the

Baldwin family. Her grandchildren might not have always known how renowned their uncle Jimmy was, especially when they were young, but they all saw their grandmother as the most important member of their family.

Her grandchildren were all devastated when they heard of their uncle's passing, but they were absolutely heartbroken when they heard their grandmother's cries at his funeral. As they all sat in the grand cathedral, feeling overwhelmed by the sheer number of people present, they were haunted by their grandmother's weeping, which persisted throughout the service; at one point it was all anyone could hear. For many of her grandchildren, it was the first time they'd seen Berdis cry, seen her show anything other than her contagious positivity and bright light.

After James's death, Berdis continued to push forward and be there for her growing family, attending her other children's and grandchildren's events, including the eighth-grade graduation of one of her grandsons just a few weeks following the funeral. She did not want to miss a single moment that mattered in their lives, and she maintained close contact with all of them—just as she had with Jimmy—when they moved away to pursue their passions, degrees, and careers. Her children and grandchildren looked forward to and could always count on their annual birthday card from Berdis. She seemed never to forget a single one. In her letters, she would stay consistent with the lessons she had always taught them and would center her birthday wishes on the importance of love. This tradition is now one that her daughter Barbara is proud to continue.

Berdis's life revolved around her family, and her family revolved around her life. She spent the years between Jimmy's death and her own forming more memories with her children and reconnecting with her loved ones on the Eastern Shore. When Berdis was in her home in New York, she constantly had people around who basked in her presence and did whatever task or chore they could just to honor her. She was in good health and could easily complete these things on her own, but her loved ones were eager to take care of her needs.

Each summer, she would travel to her home state of Maryland, where she still had relatives whom for years she couldn't afford to visit. She was making up for time she'd lost with them, living a life of love and freedom that had been previously hindered by her late husband. Her grandchildren would even get dropped off at different times throughout the summer and they would sit with her as she watched her daytime soap operas and cooked her famous meals; sometimes they would just sit quietly on the porch together listening to the sounds of the Eastern Shore.

Similar to Alberta, Berdis would mourn the loss of two of her sons during her lifetime. David took after his mother's creative spirit and was a raconteur, actor, and painter. He was named after Berdis's late husband and was the sibling who spent the most time with James, especially in his final years. He passed away in 1997, ten years after his eldest brother. David's funeral was held in the same place as his brother Jimmy's, the Cathedral Church of Saint John the Divine in New York City.

Following the tragedy of David's passing, Berdis moved to Washington, D.C., with her daughter Gloria. They moved to a historically Black neighborhood where Berdis would spend the last two years of her life. She was in relatively good health all through her near century of living on this earth. She was taken to the hospital a few times but never for anything drastic. Her body and mind remained strong up until her peaceful passing in the winter of 1999.

A celebration of her life was held in the same place as her late husband's funeral, Abyssinian Baptist Church, on March 5. The church was founded in 1808 by free Ethiopian seamen and allied Black parishioners who left the First Baptist Church in protest of their racial segregation practices. Abyssinian Baptist was only a few steps away from the hospital where Berdis had given birth to her first son, James, seventy-five years earlier. It was a fitting location to honor the daughter of a seaman and another mother of the movement.

Berdis's ceremony was led by Pastor Calvin O. Butts III, still the church's pastor to this day. Many of her children and her grandchildren spoke in remembrance of the woman who'd raised and guided them, while hymns including "Precious Lord" and "Blessed Assurance" were sung.

Her grandson Trevor's tribute read, "Berdis's song thundered against their beating hearts: LOVE ONE ANOTHER, LOVE ONE ANOTHER, TEACH YOUR FRIENDS TO LOVE ONE ANOTHER. How we struggled to sing like our Berdis." These words spoke to the value Berdis lived her life by, love, and the immense difficulty most would have in doing so given everything she had endured. This was her most magical quality, her ability to love and spread love, no matter the circumstance, the person, or the pain she was experiencing.

Her children and grandchildren were determined to carry on her legacy and share her teachings. Many of them followed in her artistic footsteps. Her youngest daughter, Paula, for example, has chosen to dedicate her life to the creation of art and introducing children to the creative process. She has become known in Baltimore for the clay figures she molds that celebrate Black culture and Black womanhood. The eyes of her sculptures stand out as resembling those of her mother and famous brother.

Gloria, the daughter Berdis lived with the longest and in her final years, is the literary executor of the Baldwin estate. In her role, she officially holds her family's legacy. Aisha, Gloria's daughter and Berdis's granddaughter, is now a celebrated author, educator, and public speaker who has traveled the world honoring her uncle's legacy, one that she sees as inextricably linked to Berdis. Trevor, another of Berdis's grandchildren, also plays a key role in keeping both his uncle and his grandmother alive. Of his uncle Jimmy, he once wrote, "Like most of God's creatures, the first woman he loved was his mother. Grandma Berdis was an oracle and the purest source of love I've ever known."

Her family honors her every two years by bringing together as many relatives as possible for a reunion somewhere in the Eastern Shore. During these reunions they pay homage to Berdis's place of origin, they reconnect and forge the bonds she demanded they maintain, they sometimes meet new extended family members they didn't know before, and each time they are together they learn something new about their mother and grandmother. Even if they didn't have the chance to meet her before her passing, her great-grandchildren also celebrate her name, role, and importance.

Berdis was laid to rest in a double plot shared with her eldest son, Jimmy, at the Ferncliff Cemetery and Mausoleum in New York. The double plot was purchased when James passed away, and it waited for Berdis's time to join him. The black plaque with gold lettering that sits on their grave serves as a final reminder of the complete interconnectedness of their lives. In the lower left corner is James's name and in the lower right is Berdis's; above both, in big letters at the very top, it reads, "Baldwin."

*In the lives of* Louise, Alberta, and Berdis exists a record of the United States and Black American history, through the eyes of Black women over a century. Among the three of them, they lived through the elections of nineteen U.S. presidents, World War I, World War II, the Great Depression, the Cold War, the space race, and even the Monica Lewinsky scandal. They were alive for key events in Black history, including the formation of the NAACP, the beginnings of Black sororities and fraternities, the Red Summer, the Harlem Renaissance, the Great Migration, the lynching of Emmett Till, the civil rights movement, the brutal attack of Rodney King, and so much more. And of course, they did not just live to see these moments, they played active roles in them.

They birthed and raised three of the most prominent champions of human rights to ever walk the earth. It is clear that Malcolm, Martin, and James were all part of a legacy much larger than themselves, and they had their mothers to thank, not only for their lives but for the direct instruction on how to survive in the world while actively changing it. Martin even used the notion of motherhood as a metaphor for every time he felt the pain of risking his life for the sake of his nation. A mother fully experiences the agony of bringing a child into the world, yet she is consoled by the life she has created.

The lives and legacies of Louise, Alberta, and Berdis teach both the similarities and the differences among three Black women. All three were selfless and forced to shift their own passions for the sake of their families. This was not something any of the three regretted; instead, it was something they made work for themselves and for their children. It is another example of how they persevered with heads held high in the face of circumstances unique to their identities as Black women and mothers.

Louise, Alberta, and Berdis were committed to helping their children find their own paths and giving them the tools to pursue the rights they deserved. In each of them we find a manual on how to survive and persist in a country that stacks all the odds against you. We also see that the world is changeable and waiting on our instruction. Malcolm X's quote at the beginning of this chapter points to the ways in which a mother's lessons are the ones that will determine the trajectory of the child's life and that child's contributions to the world. In a Black mother's teachings lies a world beyond what currently exists. These lessons defy laws that say you are less than, they peek into the future and assure us there are other possibilities, and they make it clear that we are the ones who will usher in the change.

The lives of Louise, Alberta, and Berdis also celebrate the diversity of Black womanhood. All had different approaches to survival and their definitions of what it meant for each of them and their family members to thrive. For Alberta, fulfillment for herself and her children rested completely in their Christian faith and was paired with their pursuit of education in order to better their own situation as well as that of their larger community. For Louise, surviving meant never allowing fear to keep you from speaking the full truth, never being afraid of what you might lose in the fight for what was right. For Berdis, living life to the fullest centered around being able to find love and joy for yourself no matter how hard others tried to take it away from you.

Each had distinct understandings of being Black, of being women, and of being mothers. Yet all three defied objectifying and stereotypical notions of Black womanhood and motherhood. While in some ways all three women could be seen as adhering to more traditional notions of wife and mother, all three made the role their own. Yes, they all primarily cared for their husbands and children, but they also pushed back against traditional gender roles. Alberta, being more educated than her spouse, supported him in rising closer to *her* level. Louise refused to be treated as less than when she lost her husband. Berdis found more liberation as a single mother and never sought a traditional marriage again. The three mothers were all aware of their independence and worth despite what society would have them believe.

The fact that each woman lived a very full life despite losing their sons speaks to their resilience and their view of their own worth. All three spent their remaining years encircled by those they loved the most, they did what made them happiest, and they educated the next generation of their families. Family members who outlived the three women speak with reverence about them as continued pillars in their lives. What is even more pertinent evidence of their legacy, however, is the way in which their actions affect countless people who may never even know their names.

Black mothers are rarely given the honor and recognition they deserve. Their contributions are taken for granted, and while they are at times acknowledged, they are not seen with the admiration they should engender. As James Baldwin's words read at the beginning of this chapter, it must become common practice to think of the stones each Black mother walks upon and imagine the bruises they've left on her feet. We must highlight the experiences of Black mothers and appreciate their ability to bring life no matter how often it is denied them. Their humanity is removed when they are forgotten, when they are not given the credit they earned, and when their names fade from history.

Civil rights icon Marian Wright Edelman once wrote, "Black mothers have always been ready and willing to do whatever it takes to transform the world for our children," and I am saying it is now time that we give them their due recognition in return. Through honoring Alberta, Louise, and Berdis, learning their stories, and keeping their names alive for years to come, we can give them back the gift of recognition they deserve. We must also honor Black mothers who are *currently* doing the work to transform our world. May they be seen, may they be celebrated, and may they be thanked while they are still alive to hear it.

# Our Lives Will Not Be Erased

A woman loves her children. That is a given in
our society, reinforced at every conceivable turn.
And a black woman is the mother to the world.
Look at our history—all the babies we've raised.
Our own and other people's.

—MARTHA SOUTHGATE

Just as mothers can become the ideological
vehicles for hierarchy and dominance, they
are uniquely positioned to lead both visionary
and opposition strategies to it. With the right
supports, mothers from underrepresented
communities can help lead the way to new forms
of governance, new approaches to the economy,
and an enlightenment of civil society grounded
in fundamental human rights. In fact, they
always have.

—MALKIA A. CYRIL

I cannot fully express just how much hurt and frustration the erasure and misrecognition of women and mothers, especially Black women and mothers, causes me. In my own life I've experienced others demeaning me and questioning my abilities simply because I am a Black woman. How many times have men threatened my sense of safety, hollering at me from their cars? How many times have I heard I was given an opportunity only because of the color of my skin? How many times has another person's looks or comments tried to make me question my worth? I cannot say; there have been too many.

I also cannot tell you how many times people have been surprised by my intellect and my successes because they assume my biggest accomplishment was marrying my husband. My own work has often been hidden behind his, not for lack of his appreciation but because we still live in a world where women of color are not fully seen. Now that I am a mother, this erasure takes place on new levels. I have stood at events right next to my husband while he was congratulated on the birth of "his" son. I could list pages of examples from my own life, but this book is about Alberta, Louise, and Berdis. I mention these moments now to simply say this work is personal for me. I am tired of Black women being hidden, I am tired of us not being recognized, I am tired of being erased. In this book, I have tried my best to change this for three women in history whose spotlight is long overdue, because the erasure of them is an erasure of all of us. Denying a person recognition is not only frustrating and hurtful, it is violent because it denies their existence, their power, their imprint on the world. It claims it is okay to treat them as less than, as unworthy of being seen, as not needing protection, love, or respect.

The crucial contributions Alberta, Louise, and Berdis made to their families have been ignored for decades and were largely unappreciated while they were alive. They were not given the credit they deserved for the ways in which they fought for their families and the ways in which their love allowed not only for their survival but for the progression of Black freedom at a national and even international level.

Such erasure made writing this book a difficult feat. Finding many of these details was like finding a needle in a haystack. Stories of their lives were scattered mostly in margins and footnotes because very few cared to document anything about these women. I have done my best to piece together their stories while regretting that there is so much more that we may never know about their incredible existence. I hope that this book is only part of our recovery of their stories. Just as I was able to build on the little that was out there, I hope others will build on this as well.

What is most revelatory in the lives of these three women was their ability to push against, break down, and step over each and every challenge that came their way. They saw themselves and their children as being worthy of life, worthy of rights, and worthy of grace. Through this radical acknowledgment of their own selves, they survived, and they joined Black American women around the country who contributed to the strides and accomplishments of their larger community.

Simply believing they were entitled to the right to live, despite what they were told from the moment they were born, they gave of themselves to a larger movement for Black freedom. I believe this gift they granted all of us was not something that happened unintentionally.

Instead, it is evident that Alberta, Berdis, and Louise provided guidance and strategies to fight and survive, at least for their own children. Alongside the other Black women of the twentieth century, both famous and unknown, they believed not only in their own lives but in ours as well.

Alberta, Berdis, and Louise defined for themselves what it meant to be women, to be Black women, and to be Black mothers. In doing so, they opened possibilities of self-definition for their children and the people their children would touch. Alberta found her identity as a Black woman in a more conservative role; she had a strong presence, but she was content with staying in the background of her husband and her children. Alberta was stern yet quiet and soft-spoken. She emphasized the importance of her children working hard and following their paths with dignified discipline. Louise cared deeply about speaking her truth and doing so loudly. She fought against traditional notions of what was expected of her as a Black woman. She traveled on her own when she was only a teenager, she was a proud activist, she was unafraid to disagree with her husband, and she was not intimidated by threats of direct violence or by state officials. Berdis cared deeply about fostering her own creativity and that of her children. She encouraged them to follow what they loved, even putting herself in the path of her husband's rage to allow this. It may seem that Berdis kept her head lower than Louise, but she too was very capable of being on her own, traveling as a teenager as well, supporting herself as a single mother, first of one and later of nine.

While all three women showed immense strength and in many ways could be described as "the strong Black woman" who did not need others to support them, when we look at their lives more deeply we see their willingness to express vulnerability. Black feminists have discussed the dangers of the strong Black woman stereotype for years, pointing to the problems that arise when everyone else assumes that

Black women can somehow sustain more pain, that Black women must be tough no matter what struggles come our way, that it is on us to be the backbone of our families and our larger communities. For many, this trope has become a source of pride, and they are happy to wear the badge of honor, putting everyone else's needs ahead of their own. However, the lives of Alberta, Berdis, and Louise display a balance between unparalleled strength and an acceptance of their own fragility, and therefore their humanity.

Their self-perceptions and abilities translated into their unbelievable capacity to maintain their hope and their faith no matter what was thrown in their way. They continued to pursue opportunity, they continued to see worth in their own existence at all costs even through their unspeakable losses. When they lost their sons, they chose to continue living; when Berdis and Louise lost their husbands, they were determined to keep pushing and provide as much as they could for their children. Whenever tragedy struck or another challenge presented itself, each of them mourned yet persisted in their pursuit of life.

All three women also sought support. Alberta, Berdis, and Louise formed communities around themselves and their families. Alberta continued what her parents built by highlighting the importance of her church community. She always played an active role in the affairs of the church and became a sister and mother to many far beyond her biological family. Louise found community among other activists when she first moved to Canada. She continued to find community in each place that she and her husband moved to and especially relied on a close group of friends after losing Earl. One couple even took care of some of her children when Louise was institutionalized. Berdis also found community in her church when she was far away from the Eastern Shore and unable to afford visits home. Later in her life, she reconnected with her family members and embraced all of her children's partners and friends, providing a space for their community of artists and activists in her home. All three women were capable of being fully independent, yet they sustained themselves by depending on connection with others.

Although it seems that none of the three women cared deeply about formal recognition whether within their families or outside of their homes, each was intentional in passing on her views to her children. All three were aware of the need to share what they'd gained over the years. They did not write books or keep a close record of their own lives, but they cared more about passing on their lessons to their children and grandchildren directly. Even though Berdis never published her writing, she gifted her family members with letters filled with lessons on how to live. Louise was not presented with the same opportunity as her husband to speak in front of audiences, yet she held class in her kitchen for her children on a daily basis. Out of the three, Alberta had the most opportunity for public exposure, but she was still known as the "quiet one," who preferred to gift her knowledge through her closer connections with her children at home and her students.

Alberta's, Berdis's, and Louise's lives, legacies, and lessons are crucial for all Black women, especially today. Black women and Black mothers continue to face blockades in our pursuit of dignity for ourselves and our children, as well as challenges in our desire to be treated as human beings with basic needs. While the faces and forms of oppression have changed, even if only slightly at times, Black women today rely on the knowledge of those who came before us to continue to survive, thrive, and create new realities.

Black women have influenced the fabric of this nation in countless ways: decades ago, writers such as Zora Neale Hurston, politicians such as Shirley Chisholm, and activists like Fannie Lou Hamer offered inspiration to all of us. Today, Black women are leaders in all realms. In sports, we have record breakers like Serena Williams and Simone Biles. In politics, women such as Kamala Harris, Maxine Waters, and Stacey Abrams are running, winning, and leading in the highest offices. In entertainment, Beyoncé, Janet Mock, Tracee Ellis Ross, and hundreds of others inspire millions of fans. In academia, we find examples in Patricia Hill Collins, Kimberlé Williams Crenshaw, and Brittney Cooper. And Alicia Garza, Opal Tometi, and Patrisse-Khan Cullors are activists standing with and for all of us as they force our country to wake up. So many other Black women, famous and less famous, are reaching new heights, excelling in their fields, and standing as a clear sign of Black women's ability to succeed in spite of the obstacles we encounter.

Still, disregard for Black women's lives remains prominent. Media portrayals of Black women frequently represent opinions that deem us as less worthy of respect, love, and protection. One can take any famous Black woman as an example and follow the trail of comments and threats she must deal with no matter what position of power she has obtained.

In 2018, Serena Williams, the professional tennis superstar and business mogul, was given three code violations after a game she lost to Naomi Osaka, another legend in the making. In frustration, she reacted similarly to other athletes, breaking her racket and calling the umpire a "thief." Unlike others, she was criticized and fined for her anger. Criticisms took on a clear racist and sexist tone in an attempt to control a Black woman's display of emotion. In a long list of comments and memes that mocked Serena came one cartoon that portrayed her as an overweight baby throwing a tantrum. In the drawing, she was given an oversize nose and oversize lips. Even her hair was portrayed differently than Serena had worn it that day, showing her with bigger, poofier hair, signaling popular views that Black women's natural hair lacks professionalism. The stance of the cartoon figure resembled that of an animal. In short, the image, published in an Australian newspaper, was wrought with stereotypical representations of Black women that aim to demean them and police their behavior.

This is a common experience for famous Black women, including our beloved former First Lady Michelle Obama, who was once called an "ape in heels." The experiences of the non-famous Black women and mothers are even worse because they are not given the same platform to speak out against such attacks, nor are they backed by hordes of fans willing to defend their honor. Other Black women face portrayals of their inferiority in the workplace, at school, when they seek public assistance, and when they attempt to advance beyond cycles of poverty. Only recently, in the summer of 2019, did California become the first state to deem discrimination based on natural hairstyles illegal. Up until this point, Black people have lost jobs because of their hair, been sent home from school, and been demeaned publicly. Whether it is an attack on Black hair, the belief that the darker one's skin is the less worthy one is, or the perpetuation of stereotypical tropes that degrade Black women, media portrayals and popular representations of Black women have continued to be used as fuel to justify abuses against us.

Many times these abuses happen within Black communities. According to a 2017 report by the Institute for Women's Policy Research titled "The Status of Black Women in the United States," Black women are more likely to experience domestic violence than white, Latina, and Asian/Pacific Islander women. The report also showed that 40 percent of Black women have experienced intimate partner violence during their lifetimes and were two and a half times more likely to be murdered by men than their white counterparts. Ninety percent of these victims knew their murderers. According to the Institute on Domestic Violence in the African American Community, pregnant Black women are eleven times more likely to die owing to domestic violence than pregnant white women.

The reasons for these disparities are complex, stemming from the intersectional oppression Black women face. Black women often feel the need to protect the men in their lives from police violence and therefore are less likely to report their victimization. Additionally, due to a lack of resources to support Black women, such as employment and wage disparities, they find themselves in positions of financial dependence on men more often. Another prevalent reason for this disparity relates to the continued lack of mental health resources available for Black families.

This desire to protect their loved ones from police violence, the circumstances that force Black women to be financially dependent on others, and the lack of mental health support for their perpetrators as well as for themselves as victims can be seen clearly in the discussion of mass incarceration in the United States. It is well-known that the United States has a dangerous obsession with incarceration, boasting the largest prison population in the world. According to CNN, more people are behind bars in the United States than are living in many major cities.

In 2017, Black women were imprisoned at twice the rate of white women. This is not because Black women commit more crimes but because Black women are less likely to be able to post bail or pay for qualified legal representation; they are also more likely to be given harsher sentences when they act in self-defense or when they attempt to find loopholes in the system to give their children better opportunities. Here, I am referring to several examples of Black mothers who have been put behind bars for falsifying their addresses in order to enroll their children in better school districts. While this is actually a common occurrence across the nation, when Black parents are caught doing it, they receive harsh punishment.

Even when they are not the ones behind bars themselves, Black women feel the greatest burden that results from the grossly disproportionate incarceration of Black men. They are the ones who take on the fees and fines associated with the incarceration of a loved one, whether these are court fines, charges associated with phone calls, or the costs of other needs for loved ones who are imprisoned. According to the Ella Baker Center for Human Rights, the average debt for court-related fines and fees in 2018 was $13,607. The median income of African American households was only $41,361 that year and $36,959 for households headed by African American females. While one in four women in the United States has a loved one behind bars, according to Essie Justice Group, one in two Black women has a loved one who is incarcerated. Many Black American women find themselves paying much of their income to the state as a result of the incarceration of their partners, children, and other family members.

These forms of structural racism expose Black women to various stressors that negatively impact their health, both emotionally and physically. It becomes especially clear how Black women are being hurt by institutional discrimination when we focus on the current Black maternal health crisis. Black women suffer disproportionate maternal mortality rates. They experience some of the highest rates of death associated with pregnancy and childbirth. They are three to four times more likely to experience a pregnancy-related death than white women, and these facts span income and education levels. The National Committee for Responsive Philanthropy points to various factors contributing to this terrifying disparity, showing how it stems from the marginalization of Black women. They state that "maternal health care operates in systems that inherently undervalue Black lives." Black women are more likely to be uninsured, exposed to environmental risks, receive subpar medical care, and experience racial bias from health-care providers that allow them to be ignored or dismissed by doctors and nurses.

For these reasons, many Black women seek the help of doulas and midwives, who can advocate for them in a system that does not provide the protections they deserve and are entitled to. Unfortunately, another injustice that Black mothers face is a lack of support for their desire to work with doulas and midwives. These health-care experts are viewed as less skilled and their services are not usually covered by insurance even though research has shown that they reduce mortality and harmful outcomes for birthing parents and children.

If Black women are able to survive the dangers associated with pregnancy and childbirth, they and their children are still forced to endure the constant threat of violence. Black women and girls are victims of overpolicing, brutality, and sexual harassment far more often than their white counterparts. Black trans women in particular are disproportionately victims of fatal violence. The murder rate of Black trans women was more than seven times as high as that of the general population in 2016.

In recent years, with the availability of recording devices and social media, the violence Black women face in and outside of our larger community has become more visible and apparent. In the spring of 2019, a twenty-two-year-old Black trans woman named Muhlaysia Booker was found dead, lying facedown on a road in Dallas just one month after video footage appeared capturing a brutal attack she endured. The video showed a group of Black men stomping, punching, kicking, and insulting her while she lay helplessly on the ground. She survived that attack before being shot and killed only a few weeks later. In June 2020, another extremely disturbing video came to light depicting twenty to thirty men beating Iyanna Dior, a Black trans woman, outside of a convenience store in Minneapolis while calling her homophobic and transphobic slurs.

Other videos have surfaced showing mostly white men, who are often police officers, tackling Black women, Black mothers, and Black girls or aiming their guns at them. These videos display the illogical escalation that occurs when Black women either follow orders, ignore unwarranted threats, or stand up against what they know is unfair treatment.

In 2015, Sandra Bland was driving in Prairie View, Texas, when she harmlessly forgot to signal a lane change. She was pulled over by an officer who, as shown in a recording, removed her from her car, threw her to the ground, and arrested her. Three days after being arrested, she was found hanging in her jail cell, and her death was ruled a suicide. Her family and others across the country have continued to question these suspicious circumstances, especially after witnessing on the video the unwarranted violence with which she was treated. Again in 2015, a video went viral displaying the attack of a young Black girl by a school security guard who threw her from her desk to the ground. In 2016, another name emerged in newspaper headlines when a young Black mother, Korryn Gaines, was shot in her home when police officers came to serve her a warrant in relation to a traffic violation. Such displays of violence against Black women and girls are commonplace and highlight the persistent lack of protection granted to them.

The stories of Black mothers who have lost one of their children at the hands of state violence have also become commonplace. While there is more of an effort to acknowledge such heroines in our community and to revere them for their strength, the world has grown far too accustomed to accepting that it is some kind of inevitable burden for Black women to carry. In 2016, Beyoncé was applauded for bringing four special guests with her to the MTV Video Music Awards. Their names are Sybrina Fulton, Gwen Carr, Lezley McSpadden, and Wanda Johnson, and their experiences are similar to that of Mamie Till. Sybrina Fulton's son, Trayvon Martin, was shot and killed by a self-proclaimed "neighborhood watchman" on his way back to where he was staying during a short visit in Sanford, Florida. Trayvon was seventeen years old. Gwen Carr's son, Eric Garner, was choked to death by New York City police officers after he was suspected of selling single cigarettes from packs without tax stamps. The forty-four-year-old father of six children and three grandchildren uttered the words "I can't breathe" eleven times during the attack before he died. Lezley McSpadden's son, Michael Brown, was fatally shot by an officer in Ferguson, Missouri, where his body was left in the street for four hours. The eighteen-year-old had just graduated from high school and was days away from attending technical school. Wanda Johnson's son, Oscar Grant III, was killed by an officer in Oakland, California, during the early morning hours of New Year's Day in 2009. The twenty-two-year-old was handcuffed, restrained, and then shot in the back.

Black mothers continue to be reminded of the belief that their lives and those of their children are worth less than others'. While these four mothers have been given due recognition for their pain and persistence, there are countless more stories just like these that simply haven't received the same level of international attention, yet again highlighting the erasure Black women face. This is especially the case in the stories of Black mothers who have lost their daughters in similar circumstances.

Melissa Harris-Perry speaks to the erasure of Black women when she uses the term "misrecognition." She states that all "citizens want and need more than a fair distribution of resources: they also desire meaningful recognition of their humanity and uniqueness." *Sister Citizen*, *But Some of Us Are Brave*, *Eloquent Rage*, *When They Call You a Terrorist*, *Killing the Black Body*, and several other books, fictional and nonfictional, written by Black women provide companions to understand the importance of fighting erasure in our attempts to combat all the other obstacles in place for Black women to be allowed to live their fullest lives.

*Alberta, Berdis, and Louise* offer guidance for our modern struggles as Black women and Black mothers. Knowing their stories, acknowledging their humanity, and recognizing their existence allow us to apply their strategies of survival and creation in our own lives. Beyond the personal healing each of us can gain from their inspiring journeys, they also carry guidance for activism, education, and policy. It is in the recognition of Black women's unique stories that the entire nation can find a path forward that is inclusive and beneficial for all its citizens.

The lessons of Alberta King, Berdis Baldwin, and Louise Little have never been more important for us to observe and hold on to than right now. They offer us, Black women, a refuge that confirms our own existence and a manual on different ways to fight, different ways to survive, and different ways to re-create our world. They offer our nation a political agenda with the lives of the most marginalized at the forefront. They show how policies that would have made their lives easier, that would have protected and supported them, are still needed today. Because of this, they hold the key to many of the political debates and cycles of oppression paralyzing the United States.

In the stories of these three mothers, we see the need for protection against domestic abuse that doesn't involve the police. Black women need to know when and where they can seek help if they find themselves in relationships that threaten their security. These three life stories display clear needs for access to health care that includes mental health coverage. All three women could have benefited greatly from even a small amount of grief counseling. It is also obvious that more economic support would have removed several barriers to their sense of safety. Had they been given an economic floor such as a universal income to meet their most basic needs, they could have avoided several hardships that came with needing to work jobs that did not guarantee their well-being. Furthermore, if they'd had access to bolsters such as universal childcare or universal preschool, they could have earned more for their families or continued to advance in their careers or had some time to rest and breathe. Additionally, they would not have been forced to leave their children alone at home. Their stories also address the need for prison reform, including the need to eliminate the cash bail system and costs associated with communicating with loved ones behind bars. We are supplied with even further proof of the need to establish stringent gun restrictions that could have prevented not only Alberta's death but that of her son and Louise's son as well. Their stories are also a reminder of the need to prioritize reproductive justice in our organizing efforts. Advances in each of these areas continue to be desperately needed and would make a lasting impact on the nation as a whole.

*As I record the* stories of these three women, the United States is led by a man with a record of sexual misconduct and harassment, one who proudly upholds ideals of white supremacy, is more than comfortable with obstructing justice and reversing progress, and uses social media to build on his disgraceful behavior. Day after day, the news is filled with his latest attacks on the freedoms of American people, both those born in the country and those who have immigrated here. He represents the worst ills and fears plaguing American mentalities.

President Donald Trump's treatment of women of color, specifically, plainly shows what happens when we are misrecognized and disrespected. He is a symbol of the enduring presence of the patriarchy, classism, racism, and xenophobia Alberta, Berdis, and Louise all faced. His attacks on four Democratic congresswomen, Alexandria Ocasio-Cortez, Ayanna Pressley, Ilhan Omar, and Rashida Tlaib, are prime examples. Trump has called the four women "a very Racist group of troublemakers who are young, inexperienced, and not very smart." This comment followed his statement that they should each "go back" to the "crime infested places from which they came," even though all but one of the women were born in the United States. Furthermore, he has encouraged his supporters in their own dangerous beliefs surrounding people of color especially.

While his commentary has been shocking to some, women of color expected nothing less from him, and they warned the nation through their own votes back in 2016. Ninety-six percent of Black women voted for Hillary Clinton, the highest percentage of any group in the country. On the other hand, 53 percent of white women voted for Donald Trump. Under his administration, children have been separated from their parents and held unconstitutionally in camps where their basic needs are ignored, hate crimes have spiked to record levels, thousands of people have died from COVID-19 who could have lived under better national leadership, and he has risked starting multiple international wars, just to name a few of the issues. It is clearer now than ever before that we must listen to women of color and take guidance from what their stories teach us about what is necessary for progress rather than regression. Black women ushered in a new era in U.S. history when they ensured a Democratic victory in the 2020 presidential election by delivering battleground states like Georgia and Pennsylvania. Black women have proven once again that we hold the key to the future, we continue to fight for ourselves, our children, and our nation.

Alberta, Berdis, and Louise teach their modern readers that there is no single way to be a Black woman and no single way to be a Black mother. In their lives we find validation for the many different ways in which Black women choose to live and to bring life into this world. Through their uniqueness, they directly challenged assumptions, stereotypes, and categorizations that aimed to objectify and reduce them, and studying their lives gives us the gift of doing the same for ourselves today. These different approaches to Black womanhood contribute to the larger fight for our shared liberation.

Alberta, Berdis, and Louise teach us the importance of passing our unique gifts on to others. They all practiced some way of sharing their stories that allowed this book to be possible. Louise practiced the tradition of oral history, sharing her truth with her children and grandchildren. Berdis left her mark through her letters that traveled across the country and the world, following her descendants. Alberta made an imprint through fostering other people's talents, and her tutees would remember her anytime they sang or played their instruments. All three women have lived far beyond their time on this earth.

With this in mind, we must do a better job of recording our stories and sharing our truths, not only with our immediate networks but with as many people as possible. It is only a disservice when we hide ourselves, when our children do not know what we have gone through and how we survived it, when we allow others to define who we are. Written records of our contributions are crucial for sustained community strength and shared knowledge. The stories of Alberta, Berdis, and Louise can bring us new breath: by learning the lessons they offered us, even long before they became literal mothers, we can continue to find meaning in our own struggles and accomplishments.

These three women bring me incredible inspiration and hope; through honoring their existence and worth, I have affirmed my own. Yet their lives speak to more than what we, Black women, can gain from their stories in order to persist in our own journeys; they speak also to the role of the communities and society we find ourselves in. Their stories are not only about how as Black women we can protect ourselves and our families but also about how others, including our loved ones and even policy makers, can and *should* protect us. While it is true that Alberta, Berdis, and Louise lived powerful and influential lives despite a lack of additional support, we should not accept the challenges they faced as if they were unavoidable. Such challenges have hurt and even killed far too many of us. We should instead honor their journeys and use them as guidance for making life easier for all Black women and mothers moving forward.

At the heart of this writing is the constant tug-of-war we Black women face and our best attempts to find balance despite this. We are deemed "less than" when we are forced to be "more than." We are reminded over and over again that we are viewed and treated as objects without the need for dignity or protection, that we are less intelligent, less beautiful, less able; and as a result, we push ourselves to always be more, working harder than those around us to pursue our goals. This balancing act of being told the opposite of what we know about ourselves and acting with such a dichotomy in mind leads to our ability to produce life even when it is denied us. Our lives consist of fighting for ourselves and our communities in response to the attacks we face, pushing against the sources that deny our existence.

Black motherhood, in and of itself, is liberating and empowering; it is the lack of support we need that can make the experience oppressive and draining. Being a Black mother should not be seen as a journey one embarks on and endures on her own. Friends and partners, when they are present, should share in carrying the load Black mothers hold on their shoulders. Rather than standing in awe of Black mothers and simply commenting with deference on their incredible strength, others should stand with them and lighten their burden. Partners should participate equally in the home and in supporting Black mothers with their own dreams. Public officials should listen to what Black mothers say they and their community members need. It is time for the honor many quietly pay to Black mothers to become as loud as Alberta's choir, as consistent as Berdis's love, as strong as Louise's fight.

*We may be Black* women and mothers who choose to be on the front lines, sacrificing our bodies, protesting, marching, and speaking loudly for our cause, like Louise. This Black woman is willing to break the law, to harbor a fugitive, and to put her name in writing on messages for the movement, and she appears unafraid of what she might lose in the process. No matter how many attacks she endures mentally, emotionally, and physically, she stands tall in who she knows she is, and she hopes that she's done enough to prepare her children to do the same even without her. From her, we learn strategies for surviving as an activist and understanding what it means to be part of something larger than ourselves and our family.

We may be Black women and mothers who choose instead to be leaders in our churches and/or educate our closer community, like Alberta. We may dedicate our lives to our students, knowing that in each of them lies the future. Perhaps we are Black women who volunteer extensively in our communities, organizing community gatherings and fundraising money and resources for the less fortunate, while remaining proud of our roles as wives and mothers. Alberta also speaks to the well-educated Black woman who does not seek fame or recognition. She does not see herself as possessing more value as a result of her privileges but instead uses her training to share opportunities with everyone she is able to connect with. From her, we learn strategies for living as a humble community leader, one who takes on more traditional feminine roles and uses these to share her talents.

We may be Black women and mothers who dedicate ourselves fully to our families and who focus almost all of our love and attention on our children and the friends they bring into our families, like Berdis. We may be those who recognize how difficult the world can be for our children outside of the home, and therefore we equip our family with as much care and support as we can muster, praying that if they feel this at home, they will go on to spread that love in their own relationships, creating a never-ending ripple. This Black woman cannot shelter her children from all the dark truths that people bring with them, but she makes sure to be the consistent light her children need. From Berdis, we learn strategies for thriving as the committed leaders in our households, seeing them as the places where everything begins.

We may relate to one woman more than the other two, or maybe we see ourselves as a combination of all their strengths and weaknesses. Regardless, we find guidance in each of their approaches and their own abilities to adapt across time and space.

Finally, each of the three teaches us that wherever we come from, outside of the United States, a big city, or a small village—no matter where we live, the East Coast, the Midwest, or the South—and no matter our level of education or varying levels of access to resources, we have much to offer: each of us carries the potential to transform the world. These women did so through their own actions and through raising sons who became internationally recognized for their transformative power. They teach us that we possess inherent worth, and we must recognize that worth in each other. We are likely very different from one another, but we can still offer each other affirmation and guidance. We must take pride in ourselves, in our children, and in our shared mission for each person to be granted the basic right to live life with dignity, happiness, and recognition.

## Author's Note

When I set out to write this book, I knew it was going to be challenging, but this journey has highlighted the immense difficulties of composing historic accounts in ways that I did not predict. I tasked myself with telling Alberta's, Berdis's, and Louise's stories in the absence of being able to interview them. Each woman was a member of a family that scholars and researchers have hurt time and time again with misrepresentations. I was forced to reckon with the question of what is and is not true in history and who gets to decide this. From the difficulty in finding details on lives that were deemed less worthy of documentation to the desire to show the utmost respect to living loved ones of the three women and the inconsistencies that come with memories and historical records written primarily by men, I faced several hard decisions.

But there are always hard decisions in valuable work. These challenges further spoke to the women's humanity and complexity, and I am proud to present a book that honors them. I am hopeful that this work will raise their names as key figures in history whose lives are worth knowing, studying, and continuing to learn about. By presenting the stories of three women who would otherwise have been mostly forgotten and erased I am not only recognizing them but also recognizing those like them: other people who have been marginalized and other people who have been forgotten. Through piecing together evidence of their lives, I am hopeful this new knowledge will help others and our society continue to grow.

## *Acknowledgments*

I want to begin by thanking the person who has, in a way, created this book with me. From feeling his kicks as I sifted through archives, to hearing his small breaths as he slept on my chest while I edited chapters, I am thankful for my beautiful boy, Michael Malakai, and his company on this journey. I of course am grateful for my own strong, brilliant, and beautiful mother, who has always taught me to believe in myself and to defy expectations. Mom, I thank you for your sacrifices. I am blessed to be in a marriage filled with support, respect, and love. Michael, my husband, thank you for always believing in me and for listening to my reflections and ramblings as this book came together. I must also thank the three women who raised him, my mom-in-law, aunt-in-law, and Nana, who are extraordinary examples of mothers who overcome every obstacle and create possibilities for their children and grandchildren.

I am grateful for my father, who has told me stories about revolutionary queen mothers since I was born, reminding me constantly of my own worth and strength. My incredible aunt Kathryn has inspired me in more ways than I can summarize here, but she is an amazing mother and historian who motivated me to revisit stories we've been told and think of those who have been forgotten. My sister, Lydia, has always wholeheartedly supported my growth and learning, and now that we are both mothers, I seek her wisdom even more often than before. My brother, Isak, has been there every single step of the way, imagining the future with me, allowing me to believe that my dreams are possible. Whenever I feel doubt, he lifts me up, reminding me of my abilities and making me smile. My sister-in-law, Mariah, has never failed to give me the deepest encouragement and love.

My friends and mentors have been my cheerleaders and confidants. Elle, Shay, and Megan, thank you for being by my side since middle school. Ceslee, Jessica, Kaela, Bana, and Daphne, thank you for talking through ideas with me, for checking in on me, for comforting me through the hard moments, and for celebrating the great ones. Eden, Milton, and Mia, thank you for reading drafts of my writing and for giving me such thoughtful feedback. Gerald, Farris, and Lange, thank you for the best pep talks and for always being my thought partners. Pastor and First Lady Shields, Christie and Joe, Mary and Willie, Heidi and Richard, Jane and Jerry, Lisa and Pete, I cannot thank you enough for your prayers, support, comfort, and encouragement.

I am eternally grateful for the scholarship, scholars, and researchers who made this work possible. I would not have been able to complete my Ph.D. at Cambridge without the Gates Cambridge Scholarship. My Ph.D. supervisors, Dr. Mónica Moreno Figueroa and Dr. Arathi Sriprakash, supported this project from the very beginning. My fellow Gates scholars, especially Patricia, Lily, Nick, and Parker, gave me a community while I was away from home. Professor Garrett Felber graciously shared all of his files on Louise with me. Aaron Horner of the Edward H. Nabb Research Center in Maryland located marriage and death certificates for me. Researchers at the King Library and Archives department of the King Center shared everything they could find about Alberta with me. Regina Roberts dug through databases with me as I pieced together the context behind each decade of the women's lives. Without research and writing done by Professor Erik S. McDuffie, David Leeming, Jessica Russell, and Dr. Christine King Farris, this book would have been only a fraction of its length.

I owe my deepest gratitude to the family members of the three mothers who were willing to speak with me. I do not take for granted their generosity in sharing some of the most personal details of their lives. I sincerely hope I have made them proud.

I am forever grateful to my agent, Julia Kardon, for believing in my writing. Thank you, Julia, for representing me so passionately and for being there for all of my questions. I am grateful to my editor, Bryn Clark, for building this book with me and making the process so fun! I could tell from our very first conversation that this work would be in the best of hands with you. I am thankful for Arabella Pike and Jo Thompson's feedback and encouragement. I cannot thank my copy editor, Sona Vogel, and production editors, Lisa Davis and Bethany Reis, enough; thank you for confirming the painstaking details and catching my mistakes. These incredible people, alongside the rest of the HG Literary, Flatiron, and Williams Collins families, have been an absolute pleasure to work with. I thank them all for recognizing the importance of this research and helping me to share it with the world.

From the bottom of my heart, I thank each and every person who picks up this book. Thank you for taking the time.

Last but never least, I thank God—who sees each and every one of us.

# Bibliography

"About Abyssinian Baptist Church." New York: Abyssinian Baptist Church. https://abyssinian.org/about-us.

"About NACWC." Washington, D.C.: National Association of Colored Women's Clubs, 2019. https://nacwc.com/history.

Adkins, Lenore T. "These African-American Women Helped in World War I." Share America, Bureau of Global Public Affairs. Washington, D.C.: U.S. Department of State, February 27, 2020. https://share.america.gov/these-african-american-women-helped-in-world-war-i.

"African American Experience." Atlanta: A National Register of Historic Places Travel Itinerary, National Park Service. Washington, D.C.: U.S. Department of the Interior. https://nps.gov/nr/travel/atlanta/africanamerican.htm.

"African Americans in World War II." Boston: The History Place, 1999. https://historyplace.com/unitedstates/aframerwar/index.html.

Alberta King's funeral program. Provided to researcher by the Martin Luther King, Jr., Research and Education Institute at Stanford University.

"Alberta Williams King General Information," a list of biographical data, recognitions, and awards provided to the author by the King Library & Archives researchers at The Martin Luther King, Jr. Center for Nonviolent Social Change, Inc.

Alfred Jones/Leah Bevans Somerset County Circuit Court Marriage Record, September 24, 1886, 103.

Alfred Jones/Mary F. Berkley Somerset County Circuit Court Marriage Record. December 30, 1905. 304–05.

Allen, Ivan. *Atlanta from the Ashes*. Atlanta: Ruralist Press, 1929.

Als, Hilton. "The Enemy Within: The Making and Unmaking of James Baldwin." *New Yorker*, February 9, 1998.

Alter, Alexandra. "A James Baldwin Book, Forgotten and Overlooked for Four Decades, Gets Another Life." *New York Times*, August 20, 2018.

Amadeo, Kimberly. "Unemployment Rate by Year Since 1929 Compared to Inflation and GDP: U.S. Unemployment Rate History." The Balance, Economy Stats: Unemployment, 2019. Updated July 2, 2020. www.thebalance.com/unemployment-rate-by-year-3305506.

Amann, Peter H. "Vigilante Fascism: The Black Legion as an American Hybrid." *Comparative Studies in Society and History* 25, no. 3 (1983): 490–524. https://jstor.org/stable/178625.

*Amsterdam News.* "The Life and Time of Yvonne Little Woodward, Malcolm X's Youngest Sister." March 12, 2020. http://amsterdamnews.com/news/2020/mar/12/life-and-time-yvonne-little-woodward-malcolm-xs-yo.

Anderson, Carol. *White Rage: The Unspoken Truth of Our Racial Divide.* New York: Bloomsbury, 2016.

Anderson, Harold. "Black Men, Blue Waters: African Americans on the Chesapeake." *Maryland Marine Notes* (March–April 1998): 1–3, 6–7. www.mdsg.umd.edu/sites/default/files/files/MN16_2_BlackMenBlueWaters.PDF.

Anderson, Mary Louise. "Black Matriarchy: Portrayals of Women in Three Plays." *Negro American Literature Forum* 10, no. 3 (1976): 93–95. https://jstor.org/stable/3041323.

Angelou, Maya. "My Brother Jimmy Baldwin." *Los Angeles Times*, December 20, 1987.

Anonymous [southern white woman]. "Experiences of the Race Problem." *The Independent* 56, March 17, 1904, 593.

Associated Press. "Deputy Who Tossed a S.C. High School Student Won't Be Charged." *New York Times*, September 2, 2016.

Austin, David. *Fear of a Black Nation: Race, Sex, and Security in Sixties Montreal.* Toronto: Between the Lines, 2013.

Bailey, Greg. "This Presidential Speech on Race Shocked the Nation . . . in 1921." *Narratively*, October 26, 2016. https://narratively.com/this-presidential-speech-on-race-shocked-the-nation-in-1921.

Baker, Peter C. "The Tragic, Forgotten History of Black Military Veterans." *New Yorker,* November 27, 2016.

Baldwin, James. "The *Black Scholar* Interviews: James Baldwin." *Black Scholar* 5, no. 4 (December 1973–January 1974): 33–42. https://jstor.org/stable/41065644.

———. *Blues for Mister Charlie: A Play.* New York: Dial Press, 1964.

———. "The Dangerous Road Before Martin Luther King." *Harper's Magazine*, February 1961. https://harpers.org/archive/1961/02/the-dangerous-road-before-martin-luther-king.

———. *The Fire Next Time.* Harmondsworth, UK: Penguin Books, 1964.

———. "The Giver (for Berdis)." In *Jimmy's Blues and Other Poems.* Boston: Beacon Press, 2014.

———. *Go Tell It on the Mountain.* New York: Alfred A. Knopf, 2016.

———. *Nobody Knows My Name.* New York: Vintage Books, 1993.

———. *Notes of a Native Son.* Boston: Beacon Press, 1955.

Baldwin, Lewis V. *There Is a Balm in Gilead: The Cultural Roots of Martin Luther King, Jr.* Minneapolis: Fortress Press, 1991.

Baldwin, Trevor. "James Baldwin: My Uncle and His Love Life." *Huffington Post*, July 30, 2014. Updated September 29, 2014. www.huffpost.com/entry/james-baldwin-my-uncle-an_b_5634524.

Balfour, Lawrie. *The Evidence of Things Not Said: James Baldwin and the Promise of American Democracy.* Ithaca, NY: Cornell University Press, 2001.

Banks, Nina. "Black Women's Labor Market History Reveals Deep-Seated Race and Gender Discrimination." Washington, D.C.: Economic Policy Institute, February 19, 2019. https://epi.org/blog/black-womens-labor-market-history-reveals-deep-seated-race-and-gender-discrimination.

Bazian, Hatem. "Islamophobia, Trump's Racism and 2020 Elections!" *Islamophobia Studies Journal* 5, no. 1 (2019): 8–10. https://jstor.org/stable/10.13169/islastudj.5.1.0008.

Beauboeuf-Lafontant, Tamara. *Behind the Mask of the Strong Black Woman: Voice and the Embodiment of a Costly Performance.* Philadelphia: Temple University Press, 2009.

Berdis Emma Jones Baldwin funeral program, Friday, March 5, 1999. In author's possession.

Berg, Herbert. *Elijah Muhammad and Islam.* New York: New York University Press, 2009. https://jstor.org/stable/j.ctt9qgjgq.

Berry, Cecelie S., ed. *Rise Up Singing: Black Women Writers on Motherhood.* New York: Harlem Moon, Broadway Books, 2004.

Biondich, Sarah. "The Golden Age of Bronzeville: Milwaukee's African-American Heritage." *Milwaukee Color.* Milwaukee: Shepherd Express, August 26, 2009. https://shepherdexpress.com/around-milwaukee/golden-age-bronzeville-milwaukee-s-african-american-heritage.

Black, Edwin. *War Against the Weak: Eugenics and America's Campaign to Create a Master Race.* Washington, D.C.: Dialog Press, 2003.

"Black Family Income." *The African American Population.* Black Demographics, 2018. https://blackdemographics.com/households/african-american-income.

"Black Women's Maternal Health: A Multifaceted Approach to Addressing Persistent and Dire Health Disparities." Washington, D.C.: National Partnership for Women & Families, April 2018. www.nationalpartnership.org/our-work/health/reports/black-womens-maternal-health.html.

Blain, Keisha N. "These Overlooked Black Women Shaped Malcolm X's Life." *Time* magazine, February 24, 2020.

Blakemore, Erin. "The Fair-Skinned Black Actress Who Refused to 'Pass' in 1930s Hollywood." *History*, A&E Television Networks, updated February 14, 2020. https://history.com/news/fredi-washington-black-actress-hollywood-jim-crow-era.

Blinder, Alan. "Alabama Pardons 3 'Scottsboro Boys' After 80 Years." *New York Times*, November 21, 2013. www.nytimes.com/2013/11/22/us/with-last-3-pardons-alabama-hopes-to-put-infamous-scottsboro-boys-case-to-rest.html.

Bloome, Deirdre, and Christopher Muller. "Tenancy and African American Marriage in the Postbellum South." *Demography* 52, no. 5 (2015): 1409–30. https://doi.org/10.1007/s13524-015-0414-1.

Bolster, W. Jeffrey. *Black Jacks: African American Seamen in the Age of Sail.* Cambridge, MA: Harvard University Press, 1997.

Bradford, Sarah H. *Harriet Tubman: The Moses of Her People*. New York: Published for the author by Geo. R. Lockwood and Son, 1886.

Brandt, Allan M. "Racism and Research: The Case of the Tuskegee Syphilis Study." *Hastings Center Report* 8, no. 6 (1978): 21–29. https://jstor.org/stable/3561468.

Braswell, Sean. "When America Forgot All About Its Black WWI Soldiers." OZY, April 29, 2020. https://ozy.com/true-and-stories/when-america-forgot-all-about-its-black-wwi-soldiers/90207.

Brempong, Arhin. "The Role of Nana Yaa Asantewaa in the 1900 Asante War of Resistance." *Ghana Studies* 3 no. 1 (2000): 97–110. https://doi.org/10.1353/ghs.2000.0004.

Britter, Eric V. B. "Grenada." In *Encyclopædia Britannica*. Chicago: Britannica Group. www.britannica.com/place/Grenada.

Brown, DeNeen L. "Martin Luther King Jr. Met Malcolm X Just Once. The Photo Still Haunts Us with What Was Lost." *Washington Post*, January 14, 2018. www.washingtonpost.com/news/retropolis/wp/2018/01/14/martin-luther-king-jr-met-malcolm-x-just-once-the-photo-still-haunts-us-with-what-was-lost.

Campbell, James. *Talking at the Gates: A Life of James Baldwin*. London: Faber and Faber, 2008.

Campbell, John. "Work, Pregnancy, and Infant Mortality Among Southern Slaves." *Journal of Interdisciplinary History* 14, no. 4 (1984): 793. www.jstor.org/stable/pdf/203466.pdf?seq=1.

Carew, Jan. "Malcolm X's Mother in Montreal: A Pioneering Educator." In *Re/visioning: Canadian Perspectives on the Education of Africans in the Late 20th Century*, edited by Vincent D'Oyley and Carl James. North York, Ontario: Captus Press, 1998.

———, and Malcolm X. *Ghosts in Our Blood: With Malcolm X in Africa, England, and the Caribbean*. Chicago: Lawrence Hill Books, 1994.

"Caribbean Migration." *In Motion: The African-American Migration Experience*. New York: Schomburg Center for Research in Black Culture. http://inmotionaame.org/print.cfm;jsessionid=f830332711589949968546?migration=10&bhcp=1.

Carroll, Charles R. *"The Negro a Beast," or "In the Image of God."* St. Louis: American Book and Bible House, 1900.

Carter, LaShonda, and Tiffany Willoughby-Herard. "What Kind of Mother Is She?: From Margaret Garner to Rosa Lee Ingram to Mamie Till to the Murder of Korryn Gaines." *Theory & Event* 21 no. 1 (2018): 88–105. https://muse.jhu.edu/article/685971.

Casares, Aurelia Martin, and Christine Delaigue. "The Evangelization of Freed and Slave Black Africans in Renaissance Spain: Baptism, Marriage, and Ethnic Brotherhoods." *History of Religions* 52, no. 3 (2013): 214–35. https://jstor.org/stable/10.1086/668659?seq=1.

Cecelski, David S. *The Waterman's Song: Slavery and Freedom in Maritime North Carolina*. Chapel Hill: University of North Carolina Press, 2001. https://jstor.org/stable/10.5149/9780807869727_cecelski.

Chan, Melissa. "Officer in Eric Garner Death Fired After NYPD Investigation. Here's What to Know About the Case." *Time* magazine, updated August 19, 2019. https://time.com/5642648/eric-garner-death-daniel-pantaleo-suspended.

Chaudhury, Yasmin. "Honoring African American Women Who Served in the Army Nurse Corps in World War I." United States World War One Centennial Commission. Washington, D.C.: Doughboy Foundation. https://worldwar1centennial.org/index.php/communicate/press-media/wwi-centennial-news/4046-honoring-african-american-women-who-served-in-the-army-nurse-corps-in-wwi.html.

Chavez, Nicole, and Faith Karimi. "California Becomes the First State to Ban Discrimination Based on Natural Hairstyles." CNN, updated July 3, 2019. www.cnn.com/2019/07/03/us/california-hair-discrimination-trnd/index.html.

Child, Benjamin S. *The Whole Machinery: The Rural Modern in Cultures of the U.S. South, 1890–1946.* Athens: University of Georgia Press, 2019.

Clark, Kenneth B., James Baldwin, Martin Luther King, Jr., and Malcolm X. *The Negro Protest: James Baldwin, Malcolm X, Martin Luther King, Talk with Kenneth B. Clark.* Boston: Beacon Press, 1963.

Clayton, Gina Endria Richardson, Lily Mandlin, and Brittany Farr. "Because She's Powerful: The Political Isolation and Resistance of Women with Incarcerated Loved Ones." Los Angeles and Oakland, CA: Essie Justice Group, 2018.

Clegg, Claude Andrew, III. *An Original Man: The Life and Times of Elijah Muhammad.* New York: St. Martin's Press, 1997.

Collins, Merle. "A Caribbean Story: Grenada's Journey—Possibilities, Contradictions, Lessons." *Caribbean Quarterly* 60, no. 1 (2014): 23–41. https://doi.org/10.1080/00086495.2014.11672511.

Collins, Patricia Hill. *Black Feminist Thought: Knowledge, Consciousness and the Politics of Empowerment.* New York: Routledge, 2000.

———. "Gender, Black Feminism, and Black Political Economy." *Annals of the American Academy of Political and Social Science* 568, no. 1 (2000): 41–53. www.jstor.org/stable/1049471?seq=1.

———. "Learning from the Outsider Within: The Sociological Significance of Black Feminist Thought." *Social Problems* 33, no. 6 (1986): S14–S32. https://doi.org/10.1525/sp.1986.33.6.03a00020.

———. "Shifting the Center: Race, Class, and Feminist Theorizing About Motherhood." In *Mothering: Ideology, Experience, and Agency,* edited by Evelyn Nakano Glenn, Grace Chang, and Linda Rennie Forcey. Milton Park, Oxfordshire, UK: Taylor & Francis Group, 2016, 45–65. https://doi.org/10.4324/9781315538891-3.

———, and Sirma Bilge. *Intersectionality.* Cambridge, UK: Polity Press, 2016.

Collins, William J., and Robert A. Margo. "Race and Home Ownership: A Century-Long View." *Explorations in Economic History* 38, no. 1 (2001): 68–92. https://doi.org/10.1006/exeh.2000.0748.

Cone, James H. *Martin & Malcolm & America: A Dream or a Nightmare.* Maryknoll, NY: Orbis Books, 2001.

Cooper, Brittney. *Eloquent Rage: A Black Feminist Discovers Her Superpower.* New York: St. Martin's Press, 2018.

Cox, Edward L. "Fedon's Rebellion 1795–96: Causes and Consequences." *Journal of Negro History* 67, no. 1 (1982): 7–19. https://jstor.org/stable/2717757.

Crenshaw, Kimberlé. "Mapping the Margins: Intersectionality, Identity Politics, and Violence Against Women of Color." *Stanford Law Review* 43, no. 6 (1991): 1241. https://jstor.org/stable/1229039?seq=1.

Cronon, E. David. *Black Moses: The Story of Marcus Garvey and the Universal Negro Improvement Association.* Madison: University of Wisconsin Press, 1998.

Cummings, John, and Joseph A. Hill. *Negro Population in the United States, 1790–1915.* New York: Kraus Reprint, 1969.

"Current Deal Island, Maryland, Population, Demographics and Stats in 2020, 2019." SuburbanStats.org. https://suburbanstats.org/population /maryland/how-many-people-live-in-deal-island.

Cyril, Malkia A. "Motherhood, Media, and Building a 21st-Century Movement." In *Revolutionary Mothering: Love on the Front Lines*, edited by Alexis Pauline Gumbs, China Martens, and Mai'a Williams. Toronto: Between the Lines, 2016.

Daniels, Douglas Henry. *Pioneer Urbanites: A Social and Cultural History of Black San Francisco.* Berkeley: University of California Press, 1990.

Davidson, Charles. "Transportation Has Long Fueled Atlanta." Atlanta: Federal Reserve Bank of Atlanta, July 13, 2017. https://frbatlanta.org /economy-matters/regional-economics/2017/07/13/transportation-has -long-fueled-atlanta.

Davis, Angela. "Racism, Birth Control, and Reproductive Rights." In *Feminist Postcolonial Theory: A Reader*, edited by Reina Lewis and Sara Mills. New York: Routledge, 2003.

Davis, Angela Y. *Blues Legacies and Black Feminism: Gertrude "Ma" Rainey, Bessie Smith, and Billie Holiday.* New York: Vintage Books, 1998.

"Deal Island Historic District." Maryland's National Register Properties, Maryland Historical Trust. Crownsville: Maryland Department of Planning. https://mht.maryland.gov/nr/NRDetail.aspx?NRID=1501&COUNTY =Somerset&FROM=NRCountyList.aspx.

Decker, William A. *Northern Michigan Asylum: A History of the Traverse City State Hospital.* Traverse City, MI: Arbutus Press, 2010.

deVuono-Powell, Saneta, Chris Schweidler, Alicia Walters, and Azadeh Zohrabi. "Who Pays?: The True Cost of Incarceration on Families." Oakland, CA: Ella Baker Center for Human Rights, Forward Together, and Research Action Design, 2015. https://ellabakercenter.org/sites/default/files /downloads/who-pays.pdf.

Dillon, Elizabeth Maddock, and Sarah Connell. "African American Women in Advertising." Literature and Digital Diversity, Department of English. Boston: Northeastern University, 2020.

Donovan, Roxanne A., and Lindsey M. West. "Stress and Mental Health: Moderating Role of the Strong Black Woman Stereotype." *Journal of*

*Black Psychology* 41, no. 4 (August 2015): 384–96. https://doi.org/10.1177 /0095798414543014.

Douglass, Frederick. *My Bondage and My Freedom*. New York: Auburn, 1855.

Doyle, Dennis. "Slums, Race and Mental Health in New York (1938–1965)." *Palgrave Communications* 4, no. 1 (2018). https://doi.org/10.1057/s41599 -018-0068-x.

DuMonthier, Asha, Chandra Childers, and Jessica Milli. "The Status of Black Women in the United States." Washington, D.C.: Institute for Women's Policy Research, June 7, 2017. https://iwpr.org/publications/status-black -women-united-states-report.

Dunbar-Nelson, Alice. "Women's Most Serious Problem." *Messenger* 9, no. 3 (March 1927): 73.

Dunbar-Nelson, Alice Moore. *Masterpieces of Negro Eloquence*. New York: Bookery Publishing Company, 1914.

"Earl and Louise Little." *American Experience*. Public Broadcasting Service. Boston: WGBH Educational Foundation, 2001. https://pbs.org/wgbh /americanexperience/features/garvey-little.

Earl Little certificate of death, Michigan Department of Health.

Ebenezer Baptist Church. "Our History." Atlanta: Ebenezer Baptist Church. https://ebenezeratl.org/history.

Edmondson, Mika. *Power of Unearned Suffering: The Roots and Implications of Martin Luther King, Jr.'s Theodicy*. Lanham, MD: Lexington Books, 2017.

Edwards, Griffin Sims, and Stephen Rushin. "The Effect of President Trump's Election on Hate Crimes." Rochester, NY: SSRN, revised January 31, 2019. https://papers.ssrn.com/sol3/papers.cfm?abstract_id=3102652.

Edwards, Linda McMurry. *To Keep the Waters Troubled: The Life of Ida B. Wells*. New York: Oxford University Press, 2000.

Elliott, Diana B., Kristy Krivickas, Matthew W. Brault, and Rose M. Kreider. "Historical Marriage Trends from 1890–2010: A Focus on Race Differences." San Francisco, CA: Annual Meeting of the Population Association of America, 2012. www.census.gov/content/dam/Census/library/working -papers/2012/demo/SEHSD-WP2012-12.pdf.

Equal Justice Initiative staff. "Lynching in America: Confronting the Legacy of Racial Terror." 3rd ed. Montgomery, AL: Equal Justice Initiative, 2017. https://lynchinginamerica.eji.org/report.

―――. "Targeting Black Veterans: Lynching in America." Montgomery, AL: Equal Justice Initiative, February 13, 2020. https://eji.org/reports /targeting-black-veterans.

Ewbank, Douglas C. "History of Black Mortality and Health Before 1940." *Milbank Quarterly* 65, supp. 1 (1987): 100. https://doi.org/10.2307/3349953.

Farris, Christine King. *My Brother Martin: A Sister Remembers Growing Up with the Rev. Dr. Martin Luther King Jr.* Columbus, OH: Zaner-Bloser, 2013.

―――. *Through It All: Reflections on My Life, My Family, and My Faith*. New York: Atria Books, 2009.

Feimster, Crystal. *Southern Horrors: Women and the Politics of Rape and Lynching*. Cambridge, MA: Harvard University Press, 2011.

Felber, Garrett. "Black Nationalism and Liberation." *Boston Review*, August 30, 2016.

Field, Douglas, ed. *A Historical Guide to James Baldwin*. New York: Oxford University Press, 2009.

Fishel, Leslie H., Jr. "The Negro in the New Deal Era." *Wisconsin Magazine of History* 48, no. 2 (1964): 111–26. https://jstor.org/stable/4634026.

Foster, Hannah. "Black Star Line (1919–1923)." BlackPast, September 17, 2019. https://blackpast.org/african-american-history/black-star-line-1919-1923.

Foster, Sarah, and Wei Lu. "Atlanta Ranks Worst in Income Inequality in the U.S." Bloomberg Economics. Bloomberg, updated October 10, 2018. https://bloomberg.com/news/articles/2018-10-10/atlanta-takes-top-income-inequality-spot-among-american-cities.

Foster, Thomas A. "The Sexual Abuse of Black Men Under American Slavery." *Journal of the History of Sexuality* 20, no. 3 (2011): 445–64. https://doi.org/10.1353/sex.2011.0059.

Fox, Margalit. "Izola Ware Curry, Who Stabbed King in 1958, Dies at 98." *New York Times*, March 21, 2015, 21. www.nytimes.com/2015/03/22/us/izola-ware-curry-who-stabbed-king-in-1958-dies-at-98.html.

Franklin, John Hope, and August Meier, eds. *Black Leaders of the Twentieth Century*. Champaign: University of Illinois Press, 1982.

Frazier, E. Franklin, and Anthony M. Platt. *The Negro Family in the United States*. Notre Dame, IN: University of Notre Dame Press, 2001.

Gardell, Mattias. *In the Name of Elijah Muhammad: Louis Farrakhan and the Nation of Islam*. Durham, NC: Duke University Press, 1996.

Garvey, Marcus. "Aims and Objects of Movement for Solution of Negro Problem." [Originally published by the Universal Negro Improvement Association, 1924.] In *The Making of African American Identity*, vol. 3, *1917–1968*. Research Triangle Park, NC: National Humanities Center, 2011. http://nationalhumanitiescenter.org/pds/maai3/segregation/text1/marcusgarvey.pdf. http://nationalhumanitiescenter.org/pds/maai3/index.htm.

Gates, Henry Louis, Jr. "What Was Black America's Double War?" *The African Americans: Many Rivers to Cross*. Public Broadcasting Service. Newark, NJ: WNET, September 19, 2013. https://pbs.org/wnet/african-americans-many-rivers-to-cross/history/what-was-black-americas-double-war.

Geary, Daniel. "The Moynihan Report: An Annotated Edition; A Historian Unpacks *The Negro Family: The Case for National Action* on Its 50th Anniversary." *Atlantic*, September 14, 2015.

"Ghastly Deeds of Rioters Told." *Chicago Defender* 14, no. 31 (August 2, 1919).

Giddings, Paula J. *Ida: A Sword Among Lions: Ida B. Wells and the Campaign Against Lynching*. New York: Amistad, 2009.

Gillon, Victoria D. "The Killing of an 'Angry Black Woman': Sandra Bland and the Politics of Respectability." Eddie Mabry Diversity Award, 2016. https://digitalcommons.augustana.edu/mabryaward/3.

Ginzberg, Lori D. *Elizabeth Cady Stanton: An American Life*. New York: Hill and Wang, 2009.

Glenn, Gwendolyn. "Dorothy Counts-Scoggins Honored at High School She Integrated in 1957." *All Things Considered*, hosted by Michel Martin. Washington, D.C.: National Public Radio, June 16, 2019. www.npr.org/2019/06/16/733248960/dorothy-counts-scoggins-honored-at-high-school-she-integrated-in-1957.

Goldin, Claudia. "Marriage Bars: Discrimination Against Married Women Workers, 1920's to 1950's." Cambridge, MA: National Bureau of Economic Research, October 1988. https://doi.org/10.3386/w2747.

Goldman, Peter. *The Death and Life of Malcolm X*. Urbana: University of Illinois Press, 1979.

Gov.gd. "Biography: Theophilus Albert Marryshow." St. George's: National Portal of the Government of Grenada, 2009.

Gray, Richard, and Owen Robinson, eds. *A Companion to the Literature and Culture of the American South*. Malden, MA: Blackwell Publishing, 2004.

Green, Susan. "Violence Against Black Women—Many Types, Far-Reaching Effects." Washington, D.C.: Institute for Women's Policy Research, July 13, 2017. https://iwpr.org/violence-black-women-many-types-far-reaching-effects.

Greenberg, Cheryl Lynn. *To Ask for an Equal Chance: African Americans in the Great Depression*. Lanham, MD: Rowman & Littlefield, 2009.

Greenidge, Kerri K. *Black Radical: The Life and Times of William Monroe Trotter*. New York: Liveright, 2019.

Greenidge, Kerri. "The Radical Black Newspaper That Declared 'None Are Free Unless All Are Free.'" *Guardian*, January 3, 2020. www.theguardian.com/us-news/2020/jan/03/boston-guardian-william-monroe-trotter-newspaper.

Gregory, Ted. "Forgotten War Nurses Keep Their Story Alive." *Chicago Tribune*, May 28, 2001.

"Grenada." *Encyclopædia Britannica Almanac 2010*. Chicago: Britannica Digital Learning, 2010, 291.

Griffith, D. W., director. *The Birth of a Nation*. Hollywood: D. W. Griffith Productions, 1915.

Gross, Kali Nicole. "African American Women, Mass Incarceration, and the Politics of Protection." *Journal of American History* 102, no. 1 (2015): 25–33. https://doi.org/10.1093/jahist/jav226.

Grosvenor, Ian, Nicola Gauld, and Garry Stewart. "Stories of Omission: Conflict and the Experiences of Black Soldiers." Voices of War and Peace, 2018. https://voicesofwarandpeace.org/wp-content/uploads/2018/10/storiesofomission-guide_rd.pdf.

Gumbs, Alexis Pauline, China Martens, and Mai'a Williams, eds. *Revolutionary Mothering: Love on the Front Lines*. Toronto: Between the Lines, 2016.

Gumbs, Alexis Pauline. "m/Other Ourselves: A Black Queer Feminist Genealogy for Radical Mothering." In *Revolutionary Mothering: Love on the Front Lines*, edited by Alexis Pauline Gumbs, China Martens, and Mai'a Williams. Toronto: Between the Lines, 2016.

GWLI Staff. "Woodrow Wilson and the Women's Suffrage Movement: A Reflection." Washington, D.C.: Wilson Center, June 4, 2013. https://wilsoncenter.org/article/woodrow-wilson-and-the-womens-suffrage-movement-reflection.

Hamer, Fannie Lou. "We're On Our Way." Speech delivered at mass meeting in Indianola, Mississippi, September 1964. In *The Speeches of Fannie Lou Hamer: To Tell It Like It Is*, edited by Maegan Parker Brooks and Davis W. Houck. Jackson: University Press of Mississippi, 2011.

Hampton, Robert, Joyce Thomas, Trisha Bent-Goodley, and Tameka Gillum, eds. "Facts About Domestic Violence & African American Women." Institute on Domestic Violence in the African American Community. St. Paul, MN: University of Minnesota School of Social Work, 2015. http://idvaac.org/wp-content/uploads/Facts%20About%20DV.pdf.

Hampton, Robert L., Jaslean J. LaTaillade, Alicia Dacey, and J. R. Marghi. "Evaluating Domestic Violence Interventions for Black Women." *Journal of Aggression, Maltreatment & Trauma* 16, no. 3 (2008): 330–53. https://doi.org/10.1080/10926770801925759.

Hancock, Ange-Marie. *The Politics of Disgust: The Public Identity of the Welfare Queen*. New York: New York University Press, 2004.

Handy, Gemma. "The Caribbean Honours Its Overlooked WWI Soldiers." BBC News, November 7, 2018. https://www.bbc.com/news/world-latin-america-46110120.

Harmon, Steven. "Sister of Malcolm X Dies at 73." *Grand Rapids Press*, July 23, 2003.

Harold, Christine, and Kevin Michael DeLuca. "Behold the Corpse: Violent Images and the Case of Emmett Till." *Rhetoric & Public Affairs* 8, no. 2 (2005): 263–86. https://doi.org/10.1353/rap.2005.0075.

Harper, Frances Ellen Watkins. *A Brighter Coming Day: A Frances Ellen Watkins Harper Reader*. Edited by Frances Smith Foster. New York: Feminist Press at the City University of New York, 1990.

"Harriet Tubman." National Park Service. Washington, D.C.: U.S. Department of the Interior, 2019. https://nps.gov/people/harriet-tubman.htm.

Harris, David E., Anne-Lise Halvorsen, and Paul F. Dain. "Stealing North: The Jim Crow South and Richard Wright." In *Reasoning with Democratic Values 2.0: Ethical Issues in American History*, vol. 2, *1866 to the Present*. New York: Teachers College Press, 2018, 91–95.

Harris-Perry, Melissa V. *Sister Citizen: Shame, Stereotypes, and Black Women in America*. New Haven: Yale University Press, 2011.

Hart, Jamie. "Who Should Have the Children?: Discussions of Birth Control Among African-American Intellectuals, 1920–1939." *Journal of Negro History* 79, no. 1 (1994): 71–84.

Hartman, Saidiya. *Lose Your Mother: A Journey Along the Atlantic Slave Route*. New York: Farrar, Straus & Giroux, 2007.

Hartmann, Betsy. *Reproductive Rights and Wrongs: The Global Politics of Population Control*. New York: Harper & Row, 1987, 93–113.

Hayden, Sara. "Michelle Obama, Mom-in-Chief: The Racialized Rhetorical Contexts of Maternity." *Women's Studies in Communication* 40, no.1 (2017): 11–28. https://doi.org/10.1080/07491409.2016.1182095.

Hendrick, George, and Willene Hendrick. *Black Refugees in Canada: Accounts of Escape During the Era of Slavery.* Jefferson, NC: McFarland & Co., 2010.

Henry, Frances, and Dwaine Plaza, eds. *Carnival Is Woman: Feminism and Performance in Caribbean Mas.* Jackson: University Press of Mississippi, 2020.

Henry, Linda J. "Promoting Historical Consciousness: The Early Archives Committee of the National Council of Negro Women." *Signs: Journal of Women in Culture and Society* 7, no. 1 (1981): 251–59. https:/jstor.org/stable /3173527?seq=1.

Hietala, Thomas R. *The Fight of the Century: Jack Johnson, Joe Louis, and the Struggle for Racial Equality.* New York: M. E. Sharpe, 2004.

History, Art & Archives, U.S. House of Representatives, Office of the Historian. "World War I and the Great Migration." *Black Americans in Congress, 1870–2007.* Washington, D.C.: U.S. Government Printing Office, 2008. https:// history.house.gov/Exhibitions-and-Publications/BAIC/Historical-Essays /Temporary-Farewell/World-War-I-And-Great-Migration.

History.com editors. *"Plessy v. Ferguson." History*, A&E Television Networks, October 29, 2009. Updated February 21, 2020. https://history.com/topics /black-history/plessy-v-ferguson.

"The History of Georgia in WWI." Georgia World War One Centennial Commission, United States World War One Centennial Commission. Washington, D.C.: Doughboy Foundation, October 2018. https://worldwar1centennial .org/index.php/georgia-ww1-history-page.html.

Hobbs, Allyson. *A Chosen Exile: A History of Racial Passing in American Life.* Cambridge, MA: Harvard University Press, 2016.

Hoffman, E. F. Physician's certificate, State of Michigan, 1939.

Hohn, Maria. "African-American GIs of WWII: Fighting for Democracy Abroad and at Home." *The Conversation*, February 9, 2017. https:// theconversation.com/african-american-gis-of-wwii-fighting-for -democracy-abroad-and-at-home-71780.

Holpuch, Amanda. "Beyoncé Brings Mothers of Four Black Men Killed in the US to MTV VMAs." *Guardian*, August 28, 2016. www.theguardian.com /culture/2016/aug/29/mtv-vmas-2016-beyonce-brings-mothers-of-four -black-men-killed-in-the-us-to-awards.

Horton, James Oliver. *Landmarks of African American History.* New York: Oxford University Press, 2005, 131.

Howell, Elizabeth A. "Reducing Disparities in Severe Maternal Morbidity and Mortality." *Clinical Obstetrics and Gynecology* 61, no. 2 (2018): 387–99. https://ncbi.nlm.nih.gov/pmc/articles/PMC5915910.

Hull, Akasha (Gloria T.), Patricia Bell Scott, and Barbara Smith, eds. *All the Women Are White, All the Blacks Are Men, But Some of Us Are Brave: Black Women's Studies.* New York: Feminist Press at the City University of New York, 2015.

Hull, Gloria T. *Color, Sex & Poetry: Three Women Writers of the Harlem Renaissance*. Bloomington: Indiana University Press, 1987.

———. "Researching Alice Dunbar-Nelson: A Personal and Literary Perspective." *Feminist Studies* 6, no. 2 (1980): 314. https://doi.org/10.2307/3177745.

Hunter, Tera W. *Bound in Wedlock: Slave and Free Black Marriage in the Nineteenth Century*. Cambridge, MA: Belknap Press of Harvard University Press, 2017.

Hurston, Zora Neale. *Zora Neale Hurston: A Life in Letters*. Edited by Carla Kaplan. New York: Anchor/Doubleday, 2003.

"Interview Excerpts of Philbert Little." *American Experience*. Public Broadcasting Service. Boston: WGBH Educational Foundation, 1994. www.pbs.org/wgbh/americanexperience/features/malcolmx-interview-excperts-philbert-little.

Inwood, Joshua F. J. "Sweet Auburn: Constructing Atlanta's Auburn Avenue as a Heritage Tourist Destination." *Urban Geography* 31, no. 5 (2010): 573–94. https://doi.org/10.2747/0272-3638.31.5.573.

Jackson, Carlton. *Hattie: The Life of Hattie McDaniel*. Lanham, MD: Madison Books, 1990.

Jackson, Van. *On the Brink: Trump, Kim, and the Threat of Nuclear War*. Cambridge, UK: Cambridge University Press, 2019.

"James Baldwin Residence." New York: NYC LGBT Historic Sites Project, 2017. https://www.nyclgbtsites.org/site/james-baldwin-residence.

Jennings, Thelma. "'Us Colored Women Had to Go Through A Plenty': Sexual Exploitation of African-American Slave Women." *Journal of Women's History* 1, no. 3 (1990): 45–74. https://doi.org/10.1353/jowh.2010.0050.

Jerkins, Morgan. "The Forgotten Work of Jessie Redmon Fauset." *New Yorker*, February 18, 2017. www.newyorker.com/books/page-turner/the-forgotten-work-of-jessie-redmon-fauset.

Johnson, Charles S. *Shadow of the Plantation*. Chicago: University of Chicago Press, 1934.

Johnson, Kecia R., and Karyn Loscocco. "Black Marriage Through the Prism of Gender, Race, and Class." *Journal of Black Studies* 46, no. 2 (2015): 142–71. https://www.jstor.org/stable/24572942?seq=1.

Johnson, Michael P. "Smothered Slave Infants: Were Slave Mothers at Fault?" *Journal of Southern History* 47, no. 4 (1981): 493–520. https://jstor.org/stable/2207400?seq=1.

"John Wesley Methodist Episcopal Church." Maryland Historical Trust. Crownsville: Maryland Department of Planning. Last updated October 2, 2003. https://mht.maryland.gov/secure/medusa/PDF/Somerset/S-372.pdf.

Jules-Rosette, Bennetta. *Josephine Baker in Art and Life: The Icon and the Image*. Urbana: University of Illinois Press, 2007.

*Kalamazoo Gazette*. "Brain Operations Give Mentally Ill Recovery Chance." March 18, 1945.

Kalamazoo State Hospital medical superintendent note, April 27, 1939.

Kalamazoo State Hospital medical superintendent note, September 24, 1940.

Kaltenbach, Chris. "Kobi Little Elected President of Baltimore NAACP." *Baltimore Sun*, October 6, 2018. www.baltimoresun.com/maryland/baltimore-city/bs-md-naacp-president-20181006-story.html.

Kann, Drew. "5 Facts Behind America's High Incarceration Rate." CNN, updated April 21, 2019.

Kaplan, Erin Aubry. "Mother, Unconceived." In *Rise Up Singing: Black Women Writers on Motherhood*, edited by Cecelie S. Berry. New York: Harlem Moon/Broadway Books, 2004.

Kasinsky, Renee Goldsmith. "Child Neglect and 'Unfit' Mothers." *Women & Criminal Justice* 6, no. 1 (1994): 97–129. https://doi.org/10.1300/J012v06n01_06.

Kay, Marvin L. Michael, and Lorin Lee Cary. "'The Planters Suffer Little or Nothing': North Carolina Compensations for Executed Slaves, 1748–1772." *Science & Society* 40, no. 3 (1976): 288–306. https://jstor.org/stable/40401956.

Kearney, Belle. *A Slaveholder's Daughter*. New York: Abbey Press, 1900.

Khan-Cullors, Patrisse, and Asha Bandele. *When They Call You a Terrorist: A Black Lives Matter Memoir*. New York: St. Martin's Press, 2018.

King, Coretta Scott, and Barbara Reynolds. *My Life, My Love, My Legacy*. New York: Picador, 2018.

King, Martin Luther, Jr. *The Autobiography of Martin Luther King, Jr.* Edited by Clayborne Carson. New York: Warner Books, 2001.

———. "Give Us the Ballot." MLKJP, GAMK, Martin Luther King, Jr., Papers (Series I-IV). Atlanta, Georgia: Martin Luther King, Jr., Center for Nonviolent Social Change.

———. *Stride Toward Freedom: The Montgomery Story*. New York: Harper & Row, 1964.

King, Martin Luther, Sr. *Daddy King: An Autobiography*. Boston: Beacon Press, 1980.

Klein, Christopher. "Last Hired, First Fired: How the Great Depression Affected African Americans." *History*, A&E Television Networks, April 18, 2018. Updated August 31, 2018. www.history.com/news/last-hired-first-fired-how-the-great-depression-affected-african-americans.

Krech, David, Richard S. Crutchfield, and Egerton L. Ballachey. *Individual in Society: A Textbook of Social Psychology*. New York: McGraw-Hill, 1962.

*Lansing State Journal*. "Man Run Over by Street Car." September 29, 1931.

Larson, Charles R. "James Baldwin Bearing Witness to His Times." *Washington Post*. April 16, 1989. www.washingtonpost.com/archive/entertainment/books/1989/04/16/james-baldwin-bearing-witness-to-his-times/520ae19d-0bc6-4dbe-9aa3-55dbdf4478d1.

Leah Hester Jones certificate of death. Maryland State Archives.

Leeming, David. *James Baldwin: A Biography*. New York: Alfred A. Knopf, 1994.

Lehr, Dick. "The Racist Legacy of Woodrow Wilson." *Atlantic*, November 27, 2015. https://theatlantic.com/politics/archive/2015/11/wilson-legacy-racism/417549.

Lentz-Smith, Adriane. *Freedom Struggles: African Americans and World War I.* Cambridge, MA: Harvard University Press, 2011.

Letter from James Baldwin to Martin Luther King, Jr., May 26, 1960. Stanford, CA: Martin Luther King, Jr., Research and Education Institute, Stanford University. https://kinginstitute.stanford.edu/king-papers/documents/james-baldwin.

Letter to Berdis Baldwin from James Baldwin, January 19, 1977. Gift of the Baldwin family. Washington, D.C.: Smithsonian National Museum of African American History and Culture.

Letters from Malcolm to Philbert and Henrietta Little, 1948–1952. Copies of documents provided to the author from Dr. Garrett Felber's Malcolm X collection, box 3, folder 1.

Lewis, David Levering. *W. E. B. Du Bois: Biography of a Race, 1868–1919.* New York: Henry Holt & Co., 1993, 511.

"Liberated Africans." https://liberatedafricans.org.

Linder, Douglas. "The Trials of 'the Scottsboro Boys.'" Kansas City: University of Missouri School of Law, 2007. https://ssrn.com/abstract=1027991.

Ling, Peter J. *Martin Luther King, Jr.* London: Routledge, 2002.

Linhorst, Donald M. "A History of Powerlessness." In *Empowering People with Severe Mental Illness: A Practical Guide.* New York: Oxford University Press, 2006.

Little, Wilfred. "Our Family from the Inside: Growing Up with Malcolm X." *Contributions in Black Studies* 13, no. 2 (1995). https://scholarworks.umass.edu/cibs/vol13/iss1/2.

Lorde, Audre. "Age, Race, Class, and Sex: Women Redefining Difference." In *Sister Outsider: Essays and Speeches.* Trumansburg, NY: Crossing Press, 1984. Originally delivered as a paper at the Copeland Colloquium, Amherst College (Amherst, MA), 1980.

MacKethan, Lucinda H. "Mother Wit: Humor in Afro-American Women's Autobiography." *Studies in American Humor* 4, nos. 1–2 (1985): 51–61. https://jstor.org/stable/pdf/42573211.pdf?seq=1.

Malcolm X. *The Autobiography of Malcolm X.* In collaboration with Alex Haley. New York: Ballantine Books, 1992.

Malcolm X. "The Ballot or the Bullet." Speech delivered at Cory Methodist Church in Cleveland, Ohio, April 3, 1964.

Marable, Manning. *Malcolm X: A Life of Reinvention.* London: Penguin Books, 2012.

"Martin Luther King, Jr., Birth Home Tour." Martin Luther King, Jr., National Historical Park. National Park Service. Washington, D.C.: U.S. Department of the Interior. Last updated April 24, 2015. www.nps.gov/malu/planyourvisit/birth_home_tours.htm.

Martin Luther King, Jr., Research and Education Institute. "King, Alberta Williams: Biography." Stanford, CA: Martin Luther King, Jr., Research and

Education Institute, Stanford University. https://kinginstitute.stanford.edu /encyclopedia/king-alberta-williams.

Martin, Tony. *Amy Ashwood Garvey: Pan-Africanist, Feminist, and Wife No. 1.* Dover, MA: Majority Press, 1997.

"Mary Church Terrell." *Biography*, A&E Television Networks. Updated July 9, 2019. https://biography.com/activist/mary-church-terrell.

"Maryland Facts." Visit Maryland. Baltimore: Maryland Office of Tourism Development, 2020. https://visitmaryland.org/info/maryland-facts.

Maynard, Robyn. *Policing Black Lives: State Violence in Canada from Slavery to the Present.* Halifax: Fernwood Publishing, 2017.

McCauley, Mary Carole. "Paula Whaley's Poetry Flows from Her Hands." *Baltimore Sun*, September 5, 2014. www.baltimoresun.com/entertainment /bs-xpm-2014-09-05-bs-ae-whaley-profile-20140905-story.html.

———. "World War I Forever Changed the State of Maryland." *Baltimore Sun*, April 5, 2017. www.baltimoresun.com/maryland/bs-md-world-war-i -maryland-centennial-20170405-story.html.

McClain, Dani. *We Live for the We: The Political Power of Black Motherhood.* New York: Bold Type Books, 2019.

McDuffie, Erik S. "The Diasporic Journeys of Louise Little: Grassroots Garveyism, the Midwest, and Community Feminism." *Women, Gender, and Families of Color* 4, no. 2 (2016): 146–70. https://jstor.org/stable/10.5406 /womgenfamcol.4.2.0146.

McFarlane, Nichia. "U.S. Maternal Mortality Points to Institutional Racism: Is Philanthropy Listening to Black Women?" Washington, D.C.: National Committee for Responsive Philanthropy, April 23, 2019.

McWhirter, Cameron. *Red Summer: The Summer of 1919 and the Awakening of Black America.* New York: Henry Holt & Co., 2011.

Mechoulan, Stéphane. "The External Effects of Black Male Incarceration on Black Females." *Journal of Labor Economics* 29, no. 1 (January 2011): 1–35. https://doi.org/10.1086/656370.

Menard, Orville. "Lest We Forget: The Lynching of Will Brown, Omaha's 1919 Race Riot." *Nebraska History* 91 (2010): 152–65. Updated March 1, 2019. https://history.nebraska.gov/sites/history.nebraska.gov/files/doc /publications/NH2010Lynching.pdf.

Mikkelsen, Vincent. "Coming from Battle to Face a War: The Lynching of Black Soldiers in the World War I Era." Ph.D. dissertation. Tallahassee: Florida State University College of Arts and Sciences, 2007. https:// pdfs.semanticscholar.org/dc00/c316c4dfc74a4b2806b59e52d3a1615c13 2f.pdf.

Miller, James A. *Remembering Scottsboro: The Legacy of an Infamous Trial.* Princeton, NJ: Princeton University Press, 2009.

Mississippi Women Suffrage Association. "Senator Belle Kearney: Lecturer, Writer, Stateswoman (1927)." University: eGrove, University of Mississippi. https://egrove.olemiss.edu/cgi/viewcontent.cgi?article=1004&context =suffrage.

Moseley, Clement Charlton. "The Political Influence of the Ku Klux Klan in Georgia, 1915–1925." *Georgia Historical Quarterly* 57, no. 2 (1973): 235–55. https://jstor.org/stable/40579519.

Moynihan, Daniel P. *The Negro Family: The Case for National Action.* Washington, D.C.: U.S. Department of Labor, Office of Policy Planning and Research, 1965.

Myrdal, Gunnar. "The Negro Protest." In *An American Dilemma: The Negro Problem and Modern Democracy*, vol. 2. Abingdon, UK: Routledge, 2017, 747.

Nadasen, Premilla, and Tiffany Williams. "Valuing Domestic Work." New Feminist Solution series. New York: Barnard Center for Research on Women, 2007. http://bcrw.barnard.edu/wp-content/nfs/reports/NFS5 -Valuing-Domestic-Work.pdf.

Nash, Jennifer C. "The Political Life of Black Motherhood." *Feminist Studies* 44, no. 3 (2018): 699–712. https://doi.org/10.15767/feministstudies.44.3 .0699.

Nation of Islam official website, 2020. https://noi.org/.

National Association for the Advancement of Colored People. "Criminal Justice Fact Sheet." Baltimore: NAACP, 2020. https://naacp.org/criminal -justice-fact-sheet/.

———. "History of Lynchings." Baltimore: NAACP, 2020. https://naacp.org /history-of-lynchings/.

"The *Negro World* Newspaper." Cleveland: Universal Negro Improvement Association and African Communities League, 2020. https://theunia-acl.com /index.php/history/negro-world-newspaper.

New York Public Library Digital Collections. "*Negro World*: A Newspaper Devoted Solely to the Interests of the Negro Race." New York: New York Public Library Digital Collections, 1917.

*New York Times.* "Paid Notice: Deaths, Baldwin, Berdis Emma Jones." March 4, 1999. www.nytimes.com/1999/03/04/classified/paid-notice-deaths -baldwin-berdis-emma-jones.html.

*New York Times.* "Paid Notice: Deaths, Baldwin, David." March 13, 1997. www .nytimes.com/1997/03/13/classified/paid-notice-deaths-baldwin-david .html.

*NGE* staff, eds. "Georgia in 1860." *New Georgia Encyclopedia*, 2017. https:// georgiaencyclopedia.org/articles/history-archaeology/georgia-1860.

———. "Great Depression." *New Georgia Encyclopedia*, 2018. https:// georgiaencyclopedia.org/articles/history-archaeology/great-depression.

"(1905) Theodore Roosevelt, 'Lincoln and the Race Problem.'" BlackPast, June 7, 2010. https://blackpast.org/african-american-history/1905-theodore -roosevelt-lincoln-and-race-problem-3.

1961 Debate Between Malcolm X and James Baldwin. Transcript, *Democracy Now!* Berkeley, CA: Pacifica Network, February 1, 2001. https:// democracynow.org/2001/2/1/james_baldwin_and_malcolm_x_debate.

Norris, Keenan. "Justice and Time: Before and After Oscar Grant." *Boom: A Journal of California* 1, no. 2 (2012): 100–04. https://doi.org/10.1525/boom .2012.2.2.100.

"NYC Commission on Human Rights Legal Enforcement Guidance on Race Discrimination on the Basis of Hair." New York: NYC Commission on Human Rights, February 2019. www1.nyc.gov/assets/cchr/downloads/pdf/Hair-Guidance.pdf.

Office of the Surgeon General; Center for Mental Health Services; National Institute of Mental Health. "Mental Health Care for African Americans." In "Mental Health: Culture, Race, and Ethnicity: A Supplement to Mental Health: A Report of the Surgeon General." Rockville, MD: U.S. Department of Health and Human Services, Substance Abuse and Mental Health Services Administration, August 2001. www.ncbi.nlm.nih.gov/books/NBK44251.

Oparah, Julia Chinyere and Alicia D. Bonaparte, eds. *Birthing Justice: Black Women, Pregnancy, and Childbirth*. New York: Routledge, 2016.

Peatfield, Lisa. "How the West Indies Helped the War Effort in the First World War." London: Imperial War Museums, June 8, 2018. https://iwm.org.uk/history/how-the-west-indies-helped-the-war-effort-in-the-first-world-war.

Peck, Raoul. "Journeying with James Baldwin: A Personal Note from the Director of *I Am Not Your Negro*." *Guernica*, February 1, 2017. www.guernicamag.com/on-a-personal-note.

Peterson, Larry. "Black Workers Played Role on the Home Front." Letter to the editor. *New York Times*, November 25, 1992, section A, 20. www.nytimes.com/1992/11/25/opinion/l-black-workers-played-role-on-the-home-front-796992.html.

Phillip Payne. "Mixed Memories: The Warren G. Harding Memorial Association and the President's Hometown Legacy." *Historian* 64, no. 2 (2001): 257–74. https://doi.org/10.1111/j.1540-6563.2002.tb01482.x.

Phillips, Patrick. *Blood at the Root: A Racial Cleansing in America*. New York: W. W. Norton & Co., 2016.

Phone call between researcher and representative for the Edward H. Nabb Research Center for Delmarva History and Culture, Salisbury, MD, January 2019.

Phone interviews between researcher and three of Berdis Baldwin's living family members, October 2018–December 2018.

Pitts, Jonathan. "Lynchings in Maryland." *Baltimore Sun*. https://news.baltimoresun.com/maryland-lynchings.

Rabinowitz, Paula. "Street/Crime: From Rodney King's Beating to Michael Brown's Shooting." *Cultural Critique* 90 (2015): 143–47. https://muse.jhu.edu/article/586905.

Rasche, Christine E. "Minority Women and Domestic Violence: The Unique Dilemmas of Battered Women of Color." *Journal of Contemporary Criminal Justice* 4, no. 3 (1988): 150–71. https://doi.org/10.1177/104398628800400304.

Relman, Eliza. "The 25 Women Who Have Accused Trump of Sexual Misconduct." *Business Insider*, May 1, 2020. www.businessinsider.com/women-accused-trump-sexual-misconduct-list-2017-12.

Researcher's phone interview with a living relative of Louise Little, August 2018.

Researcher's phone interview with local Deal Island historian, February 2019.

Rickford, Russell J. *Betty Shabazz: A Remarkable Story of Survival and Faith Before and After Malcolm X*. Naperville, IL: Sourcebooks, 2003.

Roberts, Dorothy E. "Racism and Patriarchy in the Meaning of Motherhood." *Faculty Scholarship at Penn Law*. Paper 595. Philadelphia: University of Pennsylvania Carey Law School, 1993. https://scholarship.law.upenn.edu/cgi/viewcontent.cgi?article=1594&context=faculty_scholarship.

Rodriguez-Trias, Helen. "Sterilization Abuse." *Women & Health* 3, no. 3 (1978):10–15. www.tandfonline.com/doi/abs/10.1300/J013v03n03_02.

Roosevelt, Theodore. "On American Motherhood." In *The World's Famous Orations*, vol. 10, edited by William Jennings Bryan. New York: Funk & Wagnalls, 1906.

Ross, Loretta J. "African-American Women and Abortion: 1800–1970." In *Theorizing Black Feminisms: The Visionary Pragmatism of Black Women*, edited by Stanlie M. James and Abena P. A. Busia. London: Routledge, 1993.

Roth, Rachel, and Sara L. Ainsworth. "'If They Hand You a Paper, You Sign It': A Call to End the Sterilization of Women in Prison." *Hastings Women's Law Journal* 26, no. 1 (2015). www.prisonpolicy.org/scans/Roth_If_They_Hand_You_1_15_2015.pdf.

Rothman, Lily. "Read MLK's Moving Words Upon Receiving the Nobel Peace Prize." *Time* magazine, October 10, 2014. https://time.com/3479191/mlk-nobel-prize/.

"Ruffin, Josephine St. Pierre." Seneca Falls, NY: National Women's Hall of Fame, 2020. https://womenofthehall.org/inductee/josephine-st-pierre-ruffin.

Russell, J. "More Louise Little—Less Malcolm X." *On Wishes and Horses So Beggars Can Ride*, blog entry, June 13, 2011. http://onwishesandhorses.wordpress.com/2011/06/13/louise-little-malcolm-x.

Russell, Michele. "Slave Codes and Liner Notes." *Radical Teacher*, no. 4 (1977): 1–6. https://jstor.org/stable/20709056?seq=1.

Sanchez, James Chase. "Trump, the KKK, and the Versatility of White Supremacy Rhetoric." *Journal of Contemporary Rhetoric* 8, nos. 1–2 (2018): 44–56. http://contemporaryrhetoric.com/wp-content/uploads/2018/02/Sanchez8_1_2_4.pdf.

Sarrett, Jennifer. "To Stop Police Shootings of People with Mental Health Disabilities, I Asked Them What Cops—and Everyone—Could Do to Help." *Conversation*, November 12, 2019. https://theconversation.com/to-stop-police-shootings-of-people-with-mental-health-disabilities-i-asked-them-what-cops-and-everyone-could-do-to-help-126229.

Schaap, Jeremy. *Triumph: The Untold Story of Jesse Owens and Hitler's Olympics*. New York: Houghton Mifflin, 2008.

Schneider, Carl J., and Dorothy Schneider. "American Women in World War I." *Social Education* 58, no. 2 (1994): 83–85. www.socialstudies.org/sites/default/files/publications/se/5802/580206.html.

Schoen, Johanna. *Choice and Coercion: Birth Control, Sterilization, and Abortion in Public Health and Welfare*. Chapel Hill: University of North Carolina Press, 2005.

Scully, Pamela. "Rape, Race, and Colonial Culture: The Sexual Politics of Identity in the Nineteenth-Century Cape Colony, South Africa." *American Historical Review* 100, no. 2 (1995): 335–59. https://jstor.org/stable/2169002.

"The Second Great Migration." *In Motion: The African-American Migration Experience*. New York: Schomburg Center for Research in Black Culture. http://inmotionaame.org/print.cfm;jsessionid=f83044466145872931579 3?migration=9&bhcp=1.

Segrave, Kerry. *Lynchings of Women in the United States: The Recorded Cases, 1851–1946*. Jefferson, NC: McFarland, 2010.

"Separate Is Not Equal: *Brown v. Board of Education*." Washington, D.C.: National Museum of American History, Behring Center, 2004. https://americanhistory.si.edu/brown/history/1-segregated/detail/jim-crow-laws.html.

Seydi, Sarata. "Earl Little's Death: E. Michigan Ave and Detroit St." *Malcolm X in Lansing*, 2020. https://projects.leadr.msu.edu/malcolmxinlansing/items/show/17.

Shabazz, Ilyasah. *Growing Up X: A Memoir by the Daughter of Malcolm X*. With the assistance of Kim McLarin. New York: Ballantine Books, 2003.

Shetterly, Margot Lee. *Hidden Figures: The American Dream and the Untold Story of the Black Women Mathematicians Who Helped Win the Space Race*. New York: William Morrow, 2016.

Silver, Christopher, and John V. Moeser. *The Separate City: Black Communities in the Urban South, 1940–1968*. Lexington: University Press of Kentucky, 2015.

Silver, Michael G. "Eugenics and Compulsory Sterilization Laws: Providing Redress for Victims of a Shameful Era in United States History." *George Washington Law Review* 72, no. 4 (2004): 862–92. https://pubmed.ncbi.nlm.nih.gov/16211742.

Simon, Mallory, and Sara Sidner. "Trump Says He's Not a Racist. That's Not How White Nationalists See It." CNN, July 16, 2019. www.cnn.com/2018/11/12/politics/white-supremacists-cheer-midterms-trump/index.html.

Skloot, Rebecca. *The Immortal Life of Henrietta Lacks*. New York: Crown Publishing Group, 2010.

Slosson, Preston. "Warren G. Harding: A Revised Estimate." *Current History* 33, no. 2 (1930): 174.

Smith, Judith E. "The Rape of Recy Taylor." *Journal of American History* 105, no. 3 (2018): 782–85. https://doi.org/10.1093/jahist/jay440.

Smith, R. Drew, and Fredrick C. Harris, eds. *Black Churches and Local Politics: Clergy Influence, Organizational Partnerships, and Civic Empowerment*. Lanham, MD: Rowman & Littlefield Publishers, 2005, 7.

Smithers, Gregory D. *Slave Breeding: Sex, Violence, and Memory in African American History*. Gainesville: University Press of Florida, 2012.

Snowden, Lonnie R. "Barriers to Effective Mental Health Services for African Americans." *Mental Health Services Research* 3 (2001): 181–87. https://doi.org/10.1023/A:1013172913880.

Snyder, Thomas D., ed. "120 Years of American Education: A Statistical Portrait." National Center for Education Statistics. Washington, D.C.: U.S. Department of Education, Office of Educational Research and Improvement, January 1993. https://nces.ed.gov/pubs93/93442.pdf.

Staples, Brent. "When the Suffrage Movement Sold Out to White Supremacy." *New York Times*, February 2, 2019.

Starks, Glenn L., and F. Erik Brooks. *Thurgood Marshall: A Biography*. Santa Barbara, CA: Greenwood, 2012.

State of Michigan Petition for Reimbursement in the Matter of Louise Little, sent to Reginald Little on April 30, 1997. In author's possession.

Steele, Beverley A. "Grenada, an Island State, Its History and Its People." *Caribbean Quarterly* 20, no. 1 (1974): 5–43. https://doi.org/10.1080/00086495.1974.11829213.

Stern, Alexandra Minna. "Sterilized in the Name of Public Health." *American Journal of Public Health* 95, no. 7: (2005): 1128–38.

Stern, Stephen. "Reviewed Work: *Mother Wit from the Laughing Barrel: Readings in the Interpretation of Afro-American Folklore* by Alan Dundes." *Western Folklore* 32, no. 4 (1973): 287. https://jstor.org/stable/1498315?seq=1.

Stewart, Dianne M. "2019 Marked 400 Years of 'Forbidden Black Love' in America." *Washington Post*, December 26, 2019. www.washingtonpost.com/outlook/2019/12/26/marked-years-forbidden-black-love-america.

Suggs, Ernie. "Younger Brother Gets Lost in the Shadow of Martin Luther King." *Seattle Times*, January 19, 2014. www.seattletimes.com/nation-world/younger-brother-gets-lost-in-the-shadow-of-martin-luther-king.

Sullivan, Patricia. *Lift Every Voice: The NAACP and the Making of the Civil Rights Movement*. New York: New Press, 2010.

Swenson, Ben. "Deal Island, Maryland, and Better Days Gone By." Abandoned Country, February 25, 2013. https://abandonedcountry.com/2013/02/25/deal-island-maryland-and-better-days-gone-by.

Tate, Shirley A., and Katharina Fink. "Skin Colour Politics and the White Beauty Standard." In *Beauty and the Norm: Debating Standardization in Bodily Appearance*, edited by Claudia Liebelt, Sarah Böllinger, and Ulf Vierke. Basingstoke, UK: Palgrave Macmillan, 2018, 283–97. https://doi.org/10.1007/978-3-319-91174-8_12.

Taylor, Keeanga-Yamahtta. "Introduction." In *How We Get Free: Black Feminism and the Combahee River Collective*, edited by Keeanga-Yamahtta Taylor. Chicago: Haymarket Books, 2017.

Taylor, Michael. "Free People of Color in Louisiana: Revealing an Unknown Past." Baton Rouge, LA: LSU Libraries, 2015. https://lib.lsu.edu/sites/all/files/sc/fpoc/history.html.

Taylor, Sarah. *A Journey with Midwives: The Story of Birth and the Quest for Social Justice* (blog). "A Birth Story of Martin Luther King Jr.—Written with Love After Visiting His Birth Home," blog entry, January 20, 2014. sarahsojourner.blogspot.com/2014/01/a-birth-story-of-martin-luther-king-jr.html.

Taylor, Ula Yvette. *The Veiled Garvey: The Life and Times of Amy Jacques Garvey.* Chapel Hill: University of North Carolina Press, 2002.

Teicher, Martin H. "Childhood Trauma and the Enduring Consequences of Forcibly Separating Children from Parents at the United States Border." *BioMed Central Medicine* 16, no. 146 (2018). https://doi.org/10.1186/s12916-018-1147-y.

Terborg-Penn, Rosalyn. *African American Women in the Struggle for the Vote, 1850–1920.* Bloomington: Indiana University Press, 1999.

———. "Discontented Black Feminists: Prelude and Postscript to the Passage of the Nineteenth Amendment." In *The Black Studies Reader*, edited by Jacqueline Bobo, Cynthia Hudley, and Claudine Michel. New York: Taylor & Francis, 2007, 65–77.

Terrell, Mary Church. *A Colored Woman in a White World.* Amherst, NY: Humanity Books, 2005.

Thorsen, Karen, director. "James Baldwin: The Price of the Ticket." *American Masters.* New York: WNET/Public Broadcasting Service, 1989. https://pbs.org/wnet/americanmasters/james-baldwin-film-synopsis/2647.

Till-Mobley, Mamie, and Christopher Benson. *Death of Innocence: The Story of the Hate Crime That Changed America.* New York: Ballantine Books, 2005.

Trani, Eugene P., and David L. Wilson. "The Scandals." In *The Presidency of Warren G. Harding.* Lawrence: University Press of Kansas, 1989, 171–87.

Tredway, Kristi. "Serena Williams and (the Perception of) Violence: Intersectionality, the Performance of Blackness, and Women's Professional Tennis." *Ethnic and Racial Studies* 43, no. 9 (2020): 1563–80. https://doi.org/10.1080/01419870.2019.1648846.

Tribute to Alberta Williams King. *Spelman Messenger*, August 1974.

Trotter, Joe William, Jr., ed. *The Great Migration in Historical Perspective: New Dimensions of Race, Class, and Gender.* Bloomington: Indiana University Press, 1991, 73.

Trudeau, Suki. *The Biography of Sarah Breedlove: And the Story of the Madame C. J. Walker Manufacturing Company.* Scotts Valley, CA: CreateSpace, 2017.

Tucker, Susan. "A Complex Bond: Southern Black Domestic Workers and Their White Employers." *Frontiers: A Journal of Women Studies* 9, no. 3 (1987): 6–13. https://jstor.org/stable/3346254.

Umeh, Uchenna. "Mental Illness in Black Community, 1700–2019: A Short History." BlackPast, March 11, 2019. https://blackpast.org/african-american-history/mental-illness-in-black-community-1700-2019-a-short-history.

U.S. Department of Commerce. "We the Americans: Blacks." Washington, D.C.: Economics and Statistics Administration, Bureau of the Census, September 1993. www.census.gov/prod/cen1990/wepeople/we-1.pdf.

Vickrey, Robert. "Martin Luther King Jr., Man of the Year." *Time* magazine, January 3, 1964.

Vincent, Ted. "The Garveyite Parents of Malcolm X." *Black Scholar: Journal of Black Studies and Research* 20, no. 2 (1989): 10–13. https://doi.org/10.1080/00064246.1989.11412923.

Wacquant, Loic. "From Slavery to Mass Incarceration: Rethinking the 'Race Question' in the US." In *Race, Law and Society*, edited by Ian Haney López. Abingdon, UK: Routledge, 2017.

Walker, Alice. *In Search of Our Mothers' Gardens*. New York: Open Road Integrated Media, 1983.

Wall, Cheryl A. *Women of the Harlem Renaissance*. Boulder, CO: NetLibrary, 1999.

Wallace-Sanders, Kimberly. *Mammy: A Century of Race, Gender, and Southern Memory*. Ann Arbor: University of Michigan Press, 2009.

Walsh, Froma, and Monica McGoldrick, eds. *Living Beyond Loss: Death in the Family*. New York: W. W. Norton & Co., 2004, 167.

Weisbord, Robert G. "Birth Control and the Black American: A Matter of Genocide?" *Demography* 10, no. 4 (1973): 571–90. https://jstor.org/stable/2060884?seq=1.

Wellman, Judith. *The Road to Seneca Falls: Elizabeth Cady Stanton and the First Woman's Rights Convention*. Urbana: University of Illinois Press, 2004.

West, Emily, and R. J. Knight. "Mothers' Milk: Slavery, Wet-Nursing, and Black and White Women in the Antebellum South." *Journal of Southern History* 83 no. 1 (2017): 37–68. https://doi.org/10.1353/soh.2017.0001.

Wheeler, Timothy B. "Study: Will Restoration of Deal Island's Lost Dunes Halt Flooding?" *Chesapeake Bay Magazine*, October 29, 2018. https://chesapeakebaymagazine.com/study-will-restoration-of-deal-islands-lost-dunes-halt-flooding.

White, Eugene N. "The Stock Market Boom and Crash of 1929 Revisited." *Journal of Economic Perspectives* 4, no. 2 (1990): 67–83. https://jstor.org/stable/1942891?seq=1.

White, Thomas. "The Challenge of U.S. Racism and the Nazi Race Law in the Age of Trump." *Keene State College Journal*. Keene, NH: Keene State College. https://keene.edu/academics/ah/cchgs/resources/educational-handouts/contemporary-hate-rooted-in-the-american-experience/download.

Whitfield, Stephen J. *A Death in the Delta: The Story of Emmett Till*. Baltimore, MD: Johns Hopkins University Press, 1988.

Whitman, James Q. *Hitler's American Model: The United States and the Making of Nazi Race Law*. Princeton, NJ: Princeton University Press, 2018.

Wilkerson, Isabel. *The Warmth of Other Suns: The Epic Story of America's Great Migration*. New York: Random House, 2010.

Williams, Chad. "African-American Veterans Hoped Their Service in World War I Would Secure Their Rights at Home. It Didn't." *Time* magazine, November 12, 2018. https://time.com/5450336/african-american-veterans-wwi.

Williams, Oscar R. "Reviewed Works: *The Atlanta Riot: Race, Class, and Violence in a New South City* by Gregory Mixon; *Veiled Visions: The 1906*

*Atlanta Race Riot and the Reshaping of American Race Relations* by David Fort Godshalk." *Journal of African American History* 91, no. 4 (2006): 478–80. https://jstor.org/stable/20064135.

Williams, Rhonda Y. *The Politics of Public Housing: Black Women's Struggles Against Urban Inequality*. New York: Oxford University Press, 2004.

Williams, Vanessa. "Black Women—Hillary Clinton's Most Reliable Voting Bloc—Look Beyond Defeat." *Washington Post*, November 12, 2016.

Wohlstetter, Roberta. *Pearl Harbor: Warning and Decision*. Stanford, CA: Stanford University Press, 2005.

"Women in World War I." Kansas City, MO: National WWI Museum and Memorial, January 3, 2020. https://theworldwar.org/learn/women.

Wonham, Henry B. *Playing the Races: Ethnic Caricature and American Literary Realism*. New York: Oxford University Press, 2004.

"World War II." American History USA. https://americanhistoryusa.com/topic/world-war-ii.

Wurth, Julie. "Activist's Mom 'Stood Her Ground.'" (Champaign, IL) *News-Gazette*, April 7, 2016.

Wyatt, Jean. "Patricia Hill Collins's *Black Sexual Politics* and the Genealogy of the Strong Black Woman." *Studies in Gender and Sexuality* 9, no. 1 (2008): 52–67. https://doi.org/10.1080/15240650701759516.

Yancy, George, and Janine Jones, eds. *Pursuing Trayvon Martin: Historical Contexts and Contemporary Manifestations of Racial Dynamics*. Lanham, MD: Lexington Books, 2014.

Young, Jasmin A. "Detroit's Red: Black Radical Detroit and the Political Development of Malcolm X." *Souls* 12, no. 1 (2010): 14–31. https://doi.org/10.1080/10999940903571296.

# Index

Abrams, Stacey, 207
Abyssinian Baptist Church, 195
"Age, Race, Class, and Sex:
    Women Redefining
    Difference" (Lorde), 10–11
Allen, Bethany, 29
*All the Women Are White, All the
    Blacks Are Men, But Some of
    Us Are Brave* (Hull, Scott,
    and Smith, eds.), 5, 9, 214
American Nazi Party, 158
Anderson, Harold, 32
Angelou, Maya, 62, 174, 193
Asantewaa, Yaa, 21–22
Atlanta, Ga., 24, 48–50, 98
    as Black Mecca of the South, 28
    Ebenezer Baptist Church in, 25,
        27, 49, 50, 68, 71, 96, 98, 101,
        108, 111, 142, 158, 169, 170,
        182–86
    race riot of 1906 in, 27–28,
        108
    Sweet Auburn Historic District
        in, 27
*Atlanta Daily World*, 155, 183
*At the Dark End of the Street*
    (McGuire), 23
Aunt Jemima, 57
*Autobiography of Malcolm X, The*
    (Malcolm X and Haley),
    164–65
Ayer, Gertrude, 137

Baker, Ella, 39
Baker, Josephine, 63
Baldwin, Barbara, 91
Baldwin, Berdis (born Emma
    Berdis Jones), 4–15, 31–32,
    34, 35, 38, 41, 62–66, 79,
    89–94, 101–4, 107, 111–15,
    121–23, 125, 135–37, 139–41,
    152–55, 175–77, 192–200,
    203–7, 214–21
    birth of, 14, 31, 34
    death of, 195
    early life of, 53–58
    funeral for, 195–96
    grave of, 197
    marriage of, 15, 66, 72, 89, 112,
        114, 115
    meets David Baldwin, 64–66
    James's death and, 173, 174, 194
    parents of, 32–34, 38, 53
Baldwin, David, 15, 64–66, 77–79,
    89–94, 102, 103, 112–15
    death of, 114, 115
    mental illness of, 112–14
Baldwin, David, Jr., 91, 173–74, 195
Baldwin, Elizabeth, 91
Baldwin, George, 91
Baldwin, Gloria, 91, 195, 196
Baldwin, James, 5–7, 12, 13, 32,
    135–41, 152–55, 171–74,
    176–77, 179, 193–94, 196–98,
    200

Baldwin, James *(continued)*
　birth of, 64, 89, 154, 195–96
　*Blues for Mister Charlie*, 152,
　　155
　cancer of, 172–73
　childhood and teen years of,
　　89–94, 135–36
　civil rights movement and,
　　140–41, 152, 154, 155, 172
　death of, 8, 173–74, 187, 194,
　　197
　*The Fire Next Time*, 154–55
　"The Giver," 153
　*Go Tell It on the Mountain*, 65
　grave of, 197
　jobs of, 137–38
　King and, 141–42
　mental breakdowns of, 138
　*Nobody Knows My Name*, 154
　*Notes of a Native Son*, 154
　in Paris, 139–40, 142, 155
　police officers and, 136
　queer identity of, 140
　segregation and, 138–39
　in school, 137
　stepfather and, 90–92, 112,
　　114–15
　*The Welcome Table*, 173
Baldwin, Paula Maria, 91, 93, 115,
　　196
Baldwin, Ruth, 91
Baldwin, Wilmer, 91
Baraka, Amiri, 174
Baril, Lawrence G., 116
Bethune, Mary McLeod, 122
Beyoncé, 208, 213
Biles, Simone, 207
birth control, 94–95
*Birth of a Nation, The*, 50, 56
birth rates, 37–38, 94–95
Black Jacks, 32–33
Black Legion, 76, 115–17, 188
"Black Men, Blue Waters"
　　(Anderson), 32
Black Panther Party, 187

Bland, Sandra, 213
Blige, Mary J., 208
*Blues for Mister Charlie* (Baldwin),
　　152, 155
Booker, Muhlaysia,
　　212
Booyson, David, 23
Boston, Mass., 145–46
Braddock, James J., 122
Brando, Marlon, 193
Britain, 41–42
Brown, Michael, 214
Bryant, Carolyn, 151
Butts, Calvin O., III, 196


Campbell, James, 136–37
Canada, 44, 73
Carew, Jan, 14, 43, 75
Carr, Gwen, 213
Carroll, Charles, 36
Caribbean, 44
　Carib Indians, 19–21, 129
　Grenada, 19–22, 41–42, 44, 129,
　　192
　Leapers Hill, 20, 86
　World War I and, 42
*Chicago Defender*, 55–56
childbirth, deaths associated with,
　　211–12
Chisholm, Shirley, 207
churches, 24–25, 96, 113
　Abyssinian Baptist Church,
　　195
　Dexter Avenue Baptist Church,
　　143
　Ebenezer Baptist, 25, 27, 49, 50,
　　68, 71, 96, 98, 101, 108, 111,
　　142, 158, 169, 170, 182–86
　John Wesley Methodist
　　Episcopal Church, 53
　Olivet Baptist Church, 57
"Civil Disobedience" (Thoreau),
　　142
Civil Rights Act, 70

civil rights movement, 8, 28, 45, 46, 110, 123, 144, 171, 172, 174, 181, 183
    Baldwin and, 140–41, 152, 154, 155, 172
    King and, 142–44, 155–61, 167–69
    Malcolm and, 161
    March on Washington, 155
    Montgomery bus boycott, 143, 144
    Selma to Montgomery march, 168
Civil War, 24, 35, 100
Clark, Kenneth, 171
Clinton, Hillary, 217
CNN, 210
Collins, Patricia Hill, 208
Congress of Racial Equality, 152
Connor, Bull, 127
Cooper, Brittney, 12, 208
Counts, Dorothy, 141
Crenshaw, Kimberlé Williams, 208
crime, 210
    incarceration, 26, 210–11, 216
"crooked room," 12–13
Crow, Mae, 47–48
Crozer Theological Seminary, 142
C-sections, 7
Cullors, Patrisse, 208
Curry, Izola Ware, 158
Cyril, Malkia A., 201

Daniel, Oscar, 47
Deal Island, Md., 31–34, 53, 65
dehumanization, 5, 7, 10–13, 54
    pickaninny caricature, 54, 56
Depression, Great, 67, 90, 94, 96, 98, 146
Dexter Avenue Baptist Church, 143
Dior, Iyanna, 212
domestic violence, 209–10
Douglass, Anna Murray, 32

Douglass, Frederick, 31, 32
doulas, 211–12

Ebenezer Baptist Church, 25, 27, 49, 50, 68, 71, 96, 98, 101, 108, 111, 142, 158, 169, 170, 182–86
Edelman, Marian Wright, 200
education, 50
Edmund Pettus Bridge, 168
Edwards, Rob, 47–48
Ella Baker Center for Human Rights, 211
*Eloquent Rage* (Cooper), 12, 214
Equal Justice Initiative, 55
Essie Justice Group, 211
eugenicists, 94–95, 122
Evers, Medgar, 173
"Experiences of the Race Problem" (anonymous), 17, 34–35

Fauset, Jessie Redmon, 59, 77
FBI, 162, 164, 188
Fedon, Julien, 20–21
*Fire Next Time, The* (Baldwin), 154–55
First Annual Convention of the National Federation of Afro-American Women, 29
Fourteenth Amendment, 109
Frazier, Edward Franklin, 105, 124
Frederick Douglass 200 Awards Gala, 3–4
Fulton, Sybrina, 213

Gaines, Korryn, 213
Garner, Eric, 213–14
Garvey, Marcus, 43–46, 73, 75, 76, 83, 84, 88, 89, 161–63, 187, 188
Garza, Alicia, 208

*Georgian*, 48–49
"Giver, The" (Baldwin), 153
*Gone With the Wind*, 122, 183
*Go Tell It on the Mountain*
    (Baldwin), 65
Grant, Oscar, III, 214
Great Depression, 67, 90, 94, 96,
    98, 146
Great Migration, 41, 51–52, 54–55,
    62, 72, 79, 112
Green, Nancy, 57
Grenada, 19–22, 41–42, 44, 129,
    192
Gumbs, Alexis Pauline, 175
guns, 216
gynecology, 7

Haley, Alex, 164–65
Hamer, Fannie Lou, 127, 176,
    207
Harding, Warren G., 79–80
Harlem, 89, 91, 136
Harlem Renaissance, 62–64, 66,
    67, 77
Harper, Frances E. W., 29, 31
*Harper's Magazine*, 141
Harris, Kamala, 207
Harris-Perry, Melissa V., 12–13,
    29, 214
*Hate That Hate Produced, The*,
    163
health care, 211–12
Hinton, Johnson, 147, 162
Hitler, Adolf, 121–22
Hoffman, E. F., 119–20
homophobia, 152
Hull, Akasha (Gloria T.), 5
Hurston, Zora Neale, 63, 207

incarceration, 26, 210–11, 216
*Independent*, 34
*In Search of Our Mothers' Gardens*
    (Walker), 15

Institute for Women's Policy
    Research, 209
Institute on Domestic Violence
    in the African American
    Community, 209

Jacks, John W., 29–30
Jackson, Maynard, 186
James, Roy, 158–59
jezebel trope, 30, 63, 124
Jim Crow, *see* segregation and Jim
    Crow laws
Johnson, Wanda, 213, 214
John Wesley Methodist Episcopal
    Church, 53
Jones, Alfred, 32–34, 53
    death of, 111–12
Jones, Alfred, Jr., 53
Jones, Deborah, 192
Jones, Leah Esther, 32–34, 38, 53
Jones, Mary, 53

Kalamazoo State Hospital, 120–21,
    144, 161, 165, 187, 189–90
Kearney, Belle, 39
Kennedy, John F., 164
Kennedy, Robert F., 155
Khan-Cullors, Patrisse, 114
*Killing the Black Body* (Roberts),
    95, 214
King, Alberta (born Alberta
    Christine Williams), 4–15,
    27–28, 31, 35, 38, 41, 67–71,
    79, 96–104, 107–11, 121–23,
    125, 132–35, 142–44, 155–50,
    168–71, 175–77, 181–87, 192,
    195, 197–99, 203–7, 214–21
    assassination of, 185–86, 216
    birth of, 24–25, 27
    early life of, 48–50, 54, 56–58
    funerals for, 186–87
    legacy of, 182–83
    marriage of, 70, 72

Martin Jr.'s assassination and,
169–71
meets Michael King, 68, 69
parents of, 25, 27, 38
King, Alfred Daniel (A.D.), 97, 98,
156, 168, 170–71, 182
King, Christine, 96–98, 101, 156,
159, 160, 185, 186
King, Coretta Scott, 143, 144, 157,
158, 168
King, Martin Luther, Jr. (born
Michael Jr.), 5–7, 12, 13, 24,
141–44, 162, 167–71, 173,
176–77, 179, 181–82, 198
arrests of, 144, 158
assassination of, 8, 169–72, 216
assault on, 158
Baldwin and, 141–42
becomes co-pastor of Ebenezer
Baptist Church, 158
birth of, 97
bombing of house of, 157, 158
childhood of, 98–100, 132–34
as civil rights activist, 142–44,
155–61, 167–69
at Crozer Theological
Seminary, 142
grandmother's death and,
110–11
Malcolm and, 161, 163, 167
in Montgomery bus boycott,
143, 144
at Morehouse College, 134–35,
142
name changed by father, 101
Nobel Peace Prize awarded to,
160–61, 168, 181
in school, 134
on Selma to Montgomery
march, 168
speeches of, 157, 159, 169
stabbing attack on, 158
*Stride Toward Freedom*, 157
King, Martin Luther, Sr. (born
Michael King), 68–71, 77–79,

96–102, 103, 108, 110, 111,
132, 142–44, 156–59, 169–71,
181, 184
Alberta's assassination and,
185–86
becomes leader of Ebenezer
Baptist Church, 101, 111
changes name and son's name to
Martin Luther, 101
Martin Jr.'s assassination and,
169–71
police officer and, 100
segregation and, 99–100, 132
shoe store incident and, 99–100
King, Yolanda, 157
Knox, Ernest, 47
Ku Klux Klan (KKK), 35, 50–51,
76, 84, 164

La Digue, 22, 42–44
La Guardia, Fiorello, 154
Langdon, Edgerton, 44–45
Langdon, Edith, 22, 23, 38, 43
Langdon, Jupiter, 21–24, 42, 74,
117
Langdon, Mary Jane, 21–24,
42–43, 117
Leapers Hill, 20, 86
Lee, Spike, 187
Leeming, David, 152, 172
Little, Earl, 73–79, 84–89, 102, 103,
161, 190
death of, 15, 116–17, 119, 124,
131, 144, 206
house burned, 87–88
Little, Hilda, 84, 85, 89, 117
Little, Louise (born Louise
Langdon), 4–15, 19–20,
23–24, 35, 38, 41, 73–77, 79,
84–89, 101–4, 107, 116–23,
125, 129–32, 145–47, 161–67,
175–77, 187–93, 197–99,
203–7, 214–21
birth of, 14, 19–20, 22, 23

Little, Louise (*continued*)
  death of, 187, 192–93
  Earl's death and, 15, 116–17,
    119, 124, 131, 206
  early life of, 42–45, 54, 56–58
  grandparents of, 21–24, 42–43,
    117
  house burned, 87–88
  institutionalization of, 119–21,
    124, 125, 132, 144, 145, 161,
    165, 187, 189–91
  Malcolm's assassination and,
    166–67, 189, 192
  marriage of, 72, 75–77
  meets Earl Little, 73–74
  mother of, 22, 23, 38, 43
  religious beliefs of, 130
Little, Philbert, 84, 85, 89, 146, 190
Little, Reginald, 87, 89, 190
Little, Robert, 118, 191
Little, Wesley, 87, 89
Little, Wilfred, 84, 85, 89, 117,
  129–32, 147, 188, 190
Little, Yvonne, 87, 89, 191, 192
Lorde, Audre, 10–11, 81
Louis, Joe, 122
Louisiana, 64
lynchings, 26, 51, 52, 56, 69, 83


Malcolm X, 5–7, 12, 13, 20, 89,
  129, 144–47, 161–67, 171,
  173, 176–77, 179, 189, 198
  assassination of, 8, 166–67,
    171–72, 189, 192, 216
  *The Autobiography of Malcolm
    X*, 164–65
  birth of, 86
  in Boston, 145–46
  childhood of, 88, 115–19,
    130–32, 144–45
  civil rights movement and, 161
  Hinton beating and, 147, 162
  house bombed, 166
  imprisonment of, 146–47

  King and, 161, 163, 167
  marriage to Betty, 163
  Nation of Islam and, 146–47,
    162–64, 190
  in school, 145
mammy trope, 57, 63, 124
March on Washington, 155
marriage, 71–73, 83
Marryshow, Theophilus Albert, 88
Marshall, Thurgood, 31
Martin, Trayvon, 213
Maryland, 31, 52–53
  Deal Island, 31–34, 53, 65
maternal health crisis, 211–12
matriarchs, 124, 175
McDaniel, Hattie, 122
McDuffie, Erik S., 14, 188
McGuire, Danielle, 23
McSpadden, Lezley, 213, 214
medical care, 211–12
mental illness, 113, 114
midwives, 211–12
Milwaukee, Wisc., 87
Missouri Press Association, 29
Montgomery bus boycott, 143, 144
Morehouse College, 98, 134–35,
  142
Morrison, Toni, 174, 193
motherhood, 83, 85–86
Moynihan, Daniel Patrick, 149,
  174–75
Muhammad, Elijah, 51, 74, 146,
  147, 164
*Muhammad Speaks*, 163
Muslim Mosque Incorporated,
  164
"My Girl" (Allen), 29


National Association for the
  Advancement of Colored
  People (NAACP), 46, 48, 53,
  83, 108, 110, 144, 163, 183
National Association of Colored
  Women (NACW), 29–31, 83

National Center for Education Statistics, 50

National Committee for Responsive Philanthropy, 211

National Council of Negro Women (NCNW), 122

National Federation of Afro-American Women, 29

National Institute of Arts and Letters, 153

National Urban League, 91

Nation of Islam (NOI), 45, 146–47, 161–64, 187, 190

Nazi Germany, 95, 121–22

Nazi Party, American, 158

*"Negro a Beast, The," or "In the Image of God, "* (Carroll), 36

*Negro Family, The* (Moynihan), 174–75

*Negro Family in the United States, The* (Frazier), 105, 124

Negro History Week, 83

*Negro World*, 73, 88, 163

Nelson, Alice Dunbar, 47

*New York Times*, 158

Nineteenth Amendment, 61, 63, 79

Nobel Peace Prize, 160–61, 168, 181

*Nobody Knows My Name* (Baldwin), 154

*Notes of a Native Son* (Baldwin), 154

Obama, Michelle, 209

Ocasio-Cortez, Alexandria, 216

Olivet Baptist Church, 57

Olympic Games, 122

Omar, Ilhan, 216

*"On American Motherhood"* (Roosevelt), 37, 94

*Oprah Winfrey Show, The*, 187

Organization of Afro-American Unity (OAAU), 164, 166

Osaka, Naomi, 208

Owens, Betty Jean, 23

Owens, Jesse, 122

Pan-Africanism, 41, 45, 164, 188

Parks, Rosa, 143

pickaninny caricature, 54, 56

*Plessy v. Ferguson*, 25, 29

*Powell v. Alabama*, 109

pregnancy and childbirth, deaths associated with, 211–12

Pressley, Ayanna, 216

Prevost, François Marie, 7

prisons, 26, 210–11, 215

Quaker Oats Company, 57

race riots, 27–28, 55–56, 107

rape, 22–23, 26, 56, 85

"Rape, Race, and Colonial Culture" (Scully), 22–23

Reagan, Ronald, 187

Reconstruction, 36

Red Summer, 55–56

resistance, 11–12, 73

Roberts, Dorothy, 95

Roosevelt, Theodore, 36–37, 94

Ross, Tracee Ellis, 208

sailors, 32

St. Pierre Ruffin, Josephine, 30

Sanger, Margaret, 81

Scott, Bernice, 143

Scott, Patricia Bell, 5

Scottsboro boys, 109–10

Scully, Pamela, 22–23

segregation and Jim Crow laws, 25–27, 41, 51, 52, 55, 56, 62, 64, 83, 100

Baldwin and, 138–39

Hitler and, 122

King Sr. and, 99–100, 132

segregation *(continued)*
  Montgomery bus boycott
    against, 143, 144
  Till and, 152
Selma to Montgomery march, 168
Seneca Falls Convention, 61
Shabazz, Attallah, 192
Shabazz, Betty, 163, 166, 167, 192
Shabazz, Ilyasah, 44
*She's Gotta Have It*, 187
Simpson, Anna, 22–23
Sims, J. Marion, 7
*Sister Citizen* (Harris-Perry),
  12–13, 29, 214
slaves, slavery, 11, 19, 21, 26, 32,
  33, 50, 64, 85, 100
  gynecological experiments and,
    7
  marriage and, 71–72
  motherhood and, 85–86
  rape and, 22–23, 85
Smith, Barbara, 5
Smith, Bessie, 63
Southern Christian Leadership
  Conference (SCLC), 141,
  144, 158
Southgate, Martha, 201
Stanton, Elizabeth Cady, 59, 77
sterilization, forced, 95
stock market, 66–67
*Stride Toward Freedom* (King), 157
Supreme Court, U.S., 109–10
  *Plessy v. Ferguson*, 25, 29
  *Powell v. Alabama*, 109
syphilis studies, 113–14

Taylor, Recy, 23
Terrell, Mary Church, 29
Thoreau, Henry David, 142
Till, Emmett, 151–52
Till-Mobley, Mamie, 149, 151–52,
  213
*Time*, 160, 161
Tlaib, Rashida, 216

Tometi, Opal, 208
trans women, 212
Trump, Donald, 216–17
Tubman, Harriet, 17, 29, 33, 41
Turner, Hazel, 26
Turner, Mary, 26, 27
Tuskegee Institute, 113–14

Universal Negro Improvement
  Association (UNIA), 45, 46,
  73, 83, 88, 89, 103, 130, 188
University of Cambridge, 4

veterans, 55, 123
Vietnam War, 152, 181, 187
violence, 209–10, 212, 213
  domestic, 209–10
  gun, 216
  lynching, 26, 51, 52, 56, 69, 83
  rape, 22–23, 26, 56, 85
voting rights, 61–63, 79, 159,
  168

Walker, Alice, 15
*Warmth of Other Suns, The*
  (Wilkerson), 90–91
Washington, Fredi, 105, 124–25
Waters, Maxine, 207
*Welcome Table, The* (Baldwin),
  173
welfare, 117–18, 191
welfare queen trope, 95, 124
Wells-Barnett, Ida B., 29
*West Indian*, 88
*When They Call You a Terrorist*
  (Khan-Cullors), 114, 214
white supremacy, white
  supremacists, 26, 45, 55, 65,
  66, 76, 77, 116–17, 122, 159,
  216
  American Nazi Party, 158
  birth rates and, 37–38

Black Legion, 76, 115–17, 188
black marriage and, 71–72
Ku Klux Klan, 35, 50–51, 76, 84, 164
suffragists and, 61
Wilkerson, Isabel, 90–91
Williams, Adam Daniel, 25, 27, 48–49, 52, 71, 107–8, 110
death of, 101, 109, 111
Williams, Jennie Celeste, 25, 27, 38, 48–49, 52, 71, 101, 108, 109
death of, 110–11
Williams, Serena, 207, 208
Wilson, Woodrow, 41

Women's International League for Peace and Freedom, 110
women's rights, 61
suffrage movement, 61, 63
Woodward, Yvonne Little, 87, 89, 191, 192
World War I, 41, 42, 46–47, 50–52, 55
World War II, 91, 107
Pearl Harbor attack and U.S. entry into, 122–23

YMCA, 47
YWCA, 110, 183

*About the Author*

———

ANNA MALAIKA TUBBS is a Cambridge Ph.D.
candidate in sociology and a Bill and Melinda
Gates Cambridge Scholar. After graduating
Phi Beta Kappa from Stanford University with
a bachelor's degree in anthropology, Anna received a master's degree from the University of
Cambridge in multidisciplinary gender studies.
Outside of the academy she is an educator and
a diversity, equity, and inclusion consultant. She
lives with her husband, Michael Tubbs, and their
son, Michael Malakai.